Other Books by Julie Peakman

The Pleasure's All Mine: A History of Perverse Sex (Reaktion, 2013)

*Mighty Lewd Books, The Development of Pornography in
Eighteenth-Century England* (Palgrave Press, 2003;
reissued in paperback 2012)

Emma Hamilton, a Biography (Haus, 2005)

Lascivious Bodies: A Sexual History of the Eighteenth Century
(Atlantic, 2004)

(ed.) *A Culture of the History of Sexuality* (Berg, 2011) 6 volumes

(ed.) *Sexual Perversions, 1650–1890* (Palgrave, 2009)

(ed.) *Whore Biographies, 1700–1825*
(Pickering & Chatto, 2007) 8 volumes

PEG PLUNKETT

PEG PLUNKETT

Memoirs of a Whore

Julie Peakman

Quercus

First published in Great Britain in 2015 by

Quercus Publishing Ltd
Carmelite House
50 Victoria Embankment
London EC4Y 0DZ

An Hachette UK company

HB ISBN 978 1 78206 773 3
TPB ISBN 978 1 78206 774 0
EBOOK ISBN 978 1 78429 103 7

Every effort has been made to contact copyright holders. However, the publishers will be glad to rectify in future editions any inadvertent omissions brought to their attention.

10 9 8 7 6 5 4 3 2 1

Text and plates designed and typeset by Hewer Text UK Ltd, Edinburgh

Printed and bound in Great Britain by Clays Ltd, St Ives Plc

For Jad

Thus crafty Females practise arts
To lie in wait for human Hearts,
Put on severe, grave, sober Airs
Curse the male Sex, and say their Prayers
Richard Walsh, Miscellanies in
Verse and Prose (Dublin, 1761)

Contents

Acknowledgements

My first thanks go to the Scouloudi Foundation, who funded a trip to Ireland. Without them I would not have gained the insight that I did into Peg's eighteenth-century Irish life. Thanks to the staff at Trinity College Dublin Manuscripts Room, students at the time who helped me find some of Peg's former clients; to the staff at the National Library of Ireland for help accessing genealogy records; and to the curators at the National Gallery of Ireland, in particular Adrian Le Harivel for the information he provided on images of Peg. Thanks also to the tour guides at Dublin Castle, and the staff at Collins Barracks, Dublin.

I am especially grateful to many individuals who took time out to look after me and show me around the buildings in their care: to Alan Ruane, who took us on a two-hour, private guided tour of Leinster House (now the Irish Parliament building); to Leo Lawlor, a porter at the Royal Exchange, 16 Castle Street, Dublin (previously the Newcomen Bank, now the rates office), who supplied some quirky information about the Royal Exchange and 'ladies of the night'.

At Russborough House, I was graciously looked after by Clodagh Gale, who gave me a very detailed tour, Matty Brown the security man, who gave me a typewritten handbook on the history of the Milltowns, and Anne Marie O'Grady, sales and marketing manager – all the staff were incredibly helpful. And thanks to the tour guides at Castletown House, and Helen Rogers who showed us round Carton House, now a hotel. All these houses are in Kildare.

Thanks to the staff of Cork Tourist Information Centre; and to Mary Clifford at Cove Tourist Information Centre, who gave us lots of maps and certificates.

Thanks to the man in the church hall next to St James's Church, St James's Street, Dublin, who directed me to Peg's grave; and to the barman in the pub next to St James's graveyard for opening the padlock to let me into the graveyard.

Thanks to all the lovely people of Ireland who I bumped into during my trip: the men labouring in Bracklyn who directed me to the Bracklyn estate; the various friendly hotel staff who looked after me on my travels, and all the people I met who were kind enough to offer information.

Last, but most of all, to the ever-patient Jad Adams, with whom I have been enjoying the delights of our own elastic bed for many a year, and who accompanied me on this journey both at home and in Ireland.

Preface: The Memoirs of Mrs Leeson

The Prudish were fearful that my memoirs would be totally *unfit to be read* by any female of delicacy.

The cream of Dublin society awaited *The Memoirs of Mrs Leeson*, alias Peg Plunkett, with some trepidation. Peg had had countless affairs with titled men, at least two of the lord lieutenants (or viceroys) of Ireland, barristers, lawyers and various captains and colonels in the army. Her exposé threatened to ruin the reputation of those dishonourable men who had been foolish enough not to honour their debts to her or had treated her badly. Of them she said, 'Some actually robbed me, others have borrowed my money, and to this hour have never paid me. *But I shall in my next volumes, lay before the public a list of all who are in debt to me, with the sum, and how long owing.*' Her memoirs were published in successive volumes and therefore her list was a method of extracting money from these men before the next volume came out; if they paid up, their names would be withdrawn. So in some sense the final published versions were manipulated, or at least amended to protect those who had sent her money.

Although Peg was destined to become the first brothel-keeper to publish her memoirs, she was not the first scorned woman to put pen to paper to expose her maltreatment by past lovers, nor would she be the last. Peg had no doubt been influenced by the best-selling memoirs of fellow Irish woman poet Laetitia Pilkington, who had already published her memoirs in three volumes earlier in the century (the first two published in 1748, a third posthumously in 1754) after being ill-treated, then abandoned by her husband Matthew Pilkington. A clergyman and mediocre poet, she showed him 'in his proper colours':[1] while having an affair of his own with a Drury Lane actress, he schemed her ruin. First he encouraged a young poet by name of William Hammond to make advances towards her, in order to snare her into adultery, but she was unwilling. After various contrivances, he finally caught her with Robert Adair, having burst in on them reading, but unchaperoned after midnight, having taken twelve witnesses with him. This was to ruin her reputation. Although she had been a close friend of Jonathan Swift in the 1730s (he had coached and encouraged her as one of his favourites), he now called her 'the most profligate whore in the kingdom'. Once in London she became a friend of both novelist Samuel Richardson and actor, play-wright and poet Colley Cibber, the latter suggesting she write her memoirs after she was arrested for debt and incarcerated in debtors' prison.[2] In the same year as Laetitia's memoirs, *An Apology for the Conduct of Mrs. Teresia Constantia Phillips, more particularly that part of it which relates to her Marriage with an eminent Dutch Merchant* were printed for the author, again in three volumes. This not only detailed her rape by an infamous 'Mr Grimes' but exposed the legal wrangling with her husband (*Oxford Dictionary of National Biography* suggests her rapist to be Lord Chesterfield, but her biographer Lydia M. Thompson suggests this was Thomas Lumley, 3rd Earl of Scarborough; her husband was a Mr Henry Muilman).[3] These memoirs fit in a genre of 'whores' biographies' which were to depict eighteenth-century women as both victims and people of independence and vitality. Such admired courtesans as Harriette Wilson and Julia Johnstone would continue the tradition and expound on the vices and virtues of various lovers in their memoirs, which were published in 1825.[4]

Peg's memoirs were published in three volumes, with the first two in 1795 earning her £500. The third volume was published post-humously in 1797, and sold for the princely sum of ten guineas. The 1798 edition is prefaced with an advertisement:

The demand for the third volume in particular (which takes in the last twelve years, being the most remarkable and interesting period of this celebrated IMPURE'S memoirs) has been so great, that is was found necessary in order to satisfy public curiosity at as low a price as possible, to give a new edition, with the addition of all the singular adventures, and every pleasing anecdote and scene that appeared in

the two first volumes, with the omission merely of those long unin-
teresting love epistles that were written to her by some of her *Buckish*
and *unlettered* GALLANTS.

One of the problems in interpreting her memoirs and setting them in
context is that Peg rarely gives dates, and timelines become increasingly blurred. This confusion is exacerbated by the fact that she talks
about people at a time when she may have not yet met them, and
allots titles to men who have not yet assumed them. Also she has a
tendency to simply skip over the events she finds boring, racing ahead
to the most interesting parts of her life. This is a common occurrence
in courtesans' memoirs, where their recollections have become hazy
and the focus is on supplying the reader with the most titillating reve-
lations. Even when Peg recounts her life story chronologically, it is
hard to establish the dates unless there is some external evidence to
point to when events occurred. As with other such memoirs, the pages
are littered with accounts of rivalries, petty jealousies, retributions,
accusations of infidelity and broken promises – but then this all
contributes to an entertaining read. This biography is, to some extent,
built on Peg's own words.

Violence and Family Affairs

A period was soon put to those Halcyon Days.[1]

Settling down in her armchair, a glass of porter at her side, Peg Plunkett opened her copy of the *Freeman's Journal* to see who had married or died. The year was 1779. She made it her business to keep up with events so she could hold her own with society gossip. The candlelight flickered, illuminating the salon with its high ceilings and panelled walls. The full-length velvet curtains had been pulled to by the maid only a few hours before. Earlier in the evening, normally at around seven, the maid changed her old woollen dress for a clean, more presentable one, and tied a fresh linen apron around her waist, her hair scraped back under a neat-looking bob cap. As she walked back and forth from kitchen to dining room, she would carry an array of trays with fresh oysters and steamed asparagus, known aphrodisiacs to stimulate the passions of the gentlemen clientele. All Peg's gentlemen callers had to be catered for with plentiful food and champagne. Despite being pregnant, Peg felt the business had been no slower than usual, and she had spent a busy evening entertaining some of Dublin society's gentlemen.

The men would normally start rolling in after having finished their business at Dublin Castle or the Royal Barracks and not leave until the early hours of the morning, some not at all. The men came from all walks of life, from titled landowners, lawyers and bankers to soldiers, students and shopkeepers. Tonight had been no exception, and the men were more than keen to enjoy themselves with Peg and her girls. After an evening full of pleasure, all the men had left satisfied, and the evening's work was finished. The maid had undertaken her duty with her usual care and attention to detail, and had been told her services would no longer be required and she could retire for the night.

Now left alone, Peg wanted nothing more than a bit of relaxation before going to her bed. As she settled back into the comfort of her armchair, the fire crackled in the hearth, its flames lighting up the mantelpiece, above which hung a tapestry brought back by one of her beaux from his stint with the East India Company in Bombay. Half dozing, her head hanging on her chest, Peg was abruptly awoken as she heard a loud shout outside. At first she thought nothing of it, and settled back down into her armchair, but the voice was joined by two, then three more. The shouting grew louder, coming towards the house from the end of the road. On a Tuesday mid-week in upmarket Drogheda Street, it was usually quiet at this late hour, but she soon realised a throng of ruffians had gathered outside. Dropping her newspaper to the floor, Peg stood up expectantly and listened. Suddenly, behind her, she heard the shattering of glass and turned around to see her curtain shaking and glass on the floor. Sensing trouble ahead, Peg picked up the poker from the hearth and prepared herself for a fight. She already knew about various gangs of unruly men who thronged the streets attacking innocent people just of the fun of it. The Pinking Dandies (Peg called them 'Pinking Dindies') were one particular set of violent blackguards who ran drunk though the streets most nights, knocking down whoever they met. They came from an aristocratic background and had no fear of the law. They attacked and beat up watchmen, broke into the homes of unfortunate women, and treated their victims with brutality. Although most of them were from noble families, they disgraced them with their behaviour, romping through town, wrecking taverns and brothels.

Grasping the poker tighter as she heard rapping at the door, she wondered how far away the midnight watchmen might be, and how long it would take them to get to her house. But the watch would come only if they had been alerted, and she was unsure if any neighbours or passing strangers had yet seen the gathering of men outside. Surely someone must have heard the commotion. Another knock came, this time louder and more assertive. Peg stood there upright, bristling, waiting. She had no intention of answering it. Finding the door locked, the person behind it began to rattle it for all it was worth. 'Let us in, you whore, or we shall break every window in your house,' the voice shouted. Another sound of shattering glass came from behind her, accompanied by a dull thud as the stone hit the curtain and fell to the floor. The curtains were the only thing protecting her.

No stranger to danger, Peg thought hard how she might best defend herself. Adrenalin coursed through her veins as her mind raced through all the possibilities. The banging at the door intensified until the wood shattered and the figure of a youth burst through. Peg recognised him immediately. He was the leader of the Pinking Dandies, none other than 'Mr Balloon' (as Peg called him), soon to be better known to the public as Richard Crosbie, Ireland's first aeronaut. His brother, Sir Edward Crosbie, had succeeded his father as 5th Baronet of Crosbie Park in 1773, six years earlier, leaving Richard now second in line. As the young Crosbie lurched forward, Peg saw that he was completely inebriated, but not to the point that he could not stand. He was just drunk enough to still have fire in his belly and strength in his loins. He caught Peg by the waist but she wrestled free and ran into the living room. As she did so, the rest of the gang swarmed into the house, each taking a separate part of the living room to wreck. In her bid to escape, Peg tripped and fell to the floor. As the gang leader fell onto her and started hitting her, she screamed and fell into a fit.

For several more minutes, the ruthless gang continued to destroy the sumptuously fitted house, smashing ornaments, ripping down curtains and reducing the furniture to matchwood. Hearing the commotion, neighbours started to gather in the streets, a couple of them bravely advancing into the hall armed with shovels. Another raced off to find the watch, by which time Peg lay unconscious on the floor, and the gang sensed that time was running out for them. Shouting all the way down the street, three watchmen finally burst into the house and assailed the gang. Backed by the law, the previously cautious neighbours now waded in with abandon. Fists were waved and punches thrown, causing cuts and bruises on both sides, by which time most of the people on the street had moved in to see what was happening. Such was the seriousness of the incident that the sheriffs arrived with a party of the military. Wanting to avoid prison, the dandies had dispersed as soon as they heard the magistrates were on their way.

At this time, the two sheriffs holding office were Messrs Moncrieff and Worthing, both vigilant magistrates who did their utmost to keep the peace. When they arrived, they quickly assessed the situation and left the house surrounded with soldiers for Peg's protection. Three weeks later, Peg was delivered of a dead baby. Two weeks after that, she was back on her feet and seeking revenge. Armed with a list of all her previous customers, men with connections in high society and the law, Peg was now ready for battle. Few of her antagonists would escape her wrath unscathed.

The beginning of Peg's life had been less dramatic, at least in its early stages. As the daughter of an Irish landowner, Matthew Plunkett, and his wife, the former Miss A. O'Reilly, Peg could claim some connection with aristocracy, the Earl of Cavan being a distant relation of her mother. Peg was born in Killough, Delvin, County Westmeath in the province of Leinster, 'where my father Matthew Plunket, Esq possessed a very handsome property near Corbetstown'.[2] Now known as Killagh, if the original Plunkett estate remains, no one has yet been able definitely to identify it.[3]

Her mother and father were first cousins; such unions were discouraged in the eighteenth century. The Pope had deemed these close marriages only permissible with a dispensation, but wealthy families often thought this was a small price to pay for keeping family money together. They were, however, often thought not to be made without consequences, as Peg pointed out: 'I never knew much happiness to derive from the marriages of Cousin Germans [*cousins germains*], or such near relations with each other.' Whether this was believed to be divine retribution or simply connected to fear of hereditary traits, she does not say. It meant that Peg's paternal grandfather was brother to her maternal grandmother, both being Plunketts. Her grandmother married into the O'Reilly family.

Peg was brought up in the Catholic faith, which would have had implications for her family. The Popery Act of 1704 prohibited Catholics from buying land or for leasing it for more than thirty-one years. In an attempt to weaken Catholic families and their wealth, the law deemed that on the death of the landowner, his estate would be divided up between his sons rather than being inherited by the eldest. A Catholic father with a Protestant heir would be reduced to the status of a tenant-for-life. It may well be that the Plunkett family decided officially to become Protestants, while continuing to practise as Catholics within the home.

Peg's date of birth has proved elusive. The third volume of her memoirs was published after her death, and the publishers have included an 'Impromptu' verse at the end of the book which states she was 'in the 70th Year of her Age' at the time of her death, making her birth date 1727, but this makes her far too old to have been at the height of her fame in 1780s.[4] If we are to believe this, then she would have been bearing children in her fifties. It would mean that when she and the young 'spark' Purcell went on the trip to Killarney in 1789, she was in her sixties. It would also mean that she was having constant affairs with men in their twenties when she was in her sixties, which again, while possible, is unlikely, given there were plenty of younger, equally good-looking prostitutes to choose from. Peg may well have aged badly during her final years, having been incarcerated in debtors' prison, existing close to poverty, and having been raped and contracted venereal disease. Francis Leeson, who edited her memoirs in the form of an unpublished typescript in the 1960s, also points out the unlikelihood of young blades choosing a woman so much older than themselves:

> It is hard to credit that if Peg was indeed this old at her death, she would have been receiving letters only fourteen years previously, when she was 56, from a young man in such terms as, 'I wear your picture the whole day; and when I go to bed I have it under my head, lest the heat of my hand should disfigure your lovely face.'

Francis Leeson also points to Walter Strickland's comments in the *Dictionary of Irish Artists,* where he makes a reference to Peg being only sixty-one at the time of her death. Leeson concurs, 'I prefer to accept this age as more probable. This would give her birth year as 1736 and eliminate an otherwise unaccounted-for decade in her life story.'[5] I would place her birth even later than this, from the evidence Peg herself provides.

Although she rarely mentions her age, she does state she was fifteen when she went to Dublin for the first time after her mother died, and she was gaining suitors. She appears to have met Dardis, her first lover, a couple of years later. She mentions being at the arrival of the French army at Carrickfergus in 1760 with Dardis. During the Seven Years War, in February 1760, the whole town was briefly captured and held to ransom by French troops who had landed there after the defenders had run out of ammunition. She could therefore only have been about seventeen or eighteen years old, as she met Dardis a few years after she had been to Dublin for the first time, and stayed with him for only about a year. Furthermore, later in her memoirs, she also refers to herself after one and half years of retirement, 'I, who had been in the habit of every vice for the space of thirty years and upwards'. This would put her in her fifties. This fits much better with what we know about the ages of her various lovers, the dates she met them, and accounts for the years she describes, with no decades missing. From internal evidence, it would seem that Peg was born around 1742.

Ireland at the time of Peg's birth was ruled by the British, and the country was subjected to the command of the British monarch. Poynings's Law (named after the man responsible, Sir Edward Poynings, Lord Deputy of Ireland) had been passed in 1495, in Drogheda, in effect placing the Irish Parliament under the authority of the Parliament of England. Only a century before Peg's birth, the Cromwellian conquest of Ireland (1649–53) saw further defeats for the country, with brutal atrocities and the confiscation of vast tracts of Catholic-owned land, resulting in great famine for Ireland's poorest inhabitants. Many different classes of people lived off the land, among them among them bound labours, casual labourers, farm servants, renters of land on the conacre system (renting small patches of land for strip farming for tillage) and cottiers (peasant farmers who rented a cabin and a small plot of land of about an acre). Most grew potatoes, oats and flax. The renters were usually on an insecure yearly contract, the labourers, whether indentured or not, reliant on the famers for their living. No one except the landowning farmer was secure.[6] Five thousand or so Protestant families were in possession of about ninety-five per cent of the land, with Irish Catholic tenants paying for their rents in services or in kind.[7] An elite Protestant Ascendancy (a class of people linked to Anglicanism, the Normans and Cromwellians) ruled Ireland. They usually held peerages from Britain as well as Ireland, and often intermarried with the English nobility and acquired English estates.[8] Catholics and Presbyterians – who together made up a large majority of the Irish population – were completely excluded from public life at this time under the Penal Laws in force in Ireland from 1691 until the early 1780s, as a result of the defeat of the Catholic Jacobites in the Williamite War in Ireland. Of a population of about three and a half million in 1767, at least three million Catholics were excluded by law from politics.[9] The penal code banned Catholics from inter-religious marriages, practising law, holding public office, or positions in the army or government. Various statutes limited property and inheritance rights, outlawed Catholic clergy, and restricted the practice of Catholicism. After a century under the penal code, by 1778 they still owned only five per cent of the total land in Ireland. Only with the passing of the Constitution Act in 1782 would Catholic Ireland be able to legislate independently and economic and political freedom be obtained, although it took the Act of Union to formally annex Ireland to the United Kingdom in 1801 and for rights to become more equal.

Because of the unfair legislation, the Irish (the majority of them Catholics) were left at a distinct disadvantage by being ruled over by the minority Protestant Ascendancy. The extreme poverty suffered by the majority of the population led Jonathan Swift to write one of his most memorable satires in 1729, *A Modest Proposal for preventing the children of poor people in Ireland, from being a burden on their parents or country, and for making them beneficial to the publick*, a pamphlet of which Peg would become aware. In it, Swift exposes the poverty of Ireland:

> It is a melancholy object to those, who walk through this great town, or travel in the country, when they see the streets, the roads and cabbin-doors crowded with beggars of the female sex, followed by three, four, or six children, all in rags, and importuning every

passenger for an alms. These mothers, instead of being able to work for their honest livelihood, are forced to employ all their time in strolling to beg sustenance for their helpless infants who, as they grow up, either turn thieves for want of work, or leave their dear native country, to fight for the Pretender in Spain, or sell themselves to the Barbadoes.

Appalled by the state in which people were left to starve, Swift's satire suggested babies of 'Popish paupers' be fed to the starving. He wrote, 'I have been assured by a very knowing American of my acquaintance in London, that a young healthy child well nursed, is, at a year old, a most delicious nourishing and wholesome food, whether stewed, roasted, baked, or boiled; and I make no doubt that it will equally serve in a fricasie, or a ragoust.'[10]

At around the time of Peg's birth, poverty and destitution were endemic. A wet summer and autumn had been followed by a severe frost between December 1739 and September 1741. Hedges had been stripped bare and trees felled at an alarming rate as people tried in vain to keep warm. As cattle died of cold, animals also starved along with their owners. The severe frost meant that the corn could not be ground and potatoes were inedible: since these were the staple diet of the poor, thousands starved to death. Dead and dying people were everywhere, with bodies found in ditches and fields. The poor who survived were existing on leaves and nettles. On 19 January 1740, in an unprecedented move, William Cavendish, the 3rd Duke of Devonshire, then the Lord Lieutenant of Ireland, prohibited the export of grain out of Ireland to any destination except Britain. Nonetheless, of a total population of three million, at least 400,000 people died. The Bishop of Cloyne reported that complete villages had been wiped out in County Limerick, declaring, 'the nation will probably not recover this loss in a century'.[11] As a result, thousands of people emigrated to Britain and North America. Peg's family, for the most part, had escaped the direst of situations themselves, but nonetheless the family witnessed widespread death and starvation.

To most travellers in Leinster, the countryside looked drab. Chief Baron Wilkes, an assize judge, was to describe the landscape in 1759: 'Round the whole circuit of Leinster I did not see one grown timber tree (as we see in every hedgerow in England) till I came to Luttrellstown within five miles of Dublin. For though there is a premium for plant-ing timber trees, yet one sees none but small plantations for pleasure about gentlemen's houses.'[12] The Irish Parliament and gentlemen's societies such as the Royal Dublin Society were encouraging land-lords and tenants to dig ditches and plant hedgerows and new trees. Although remnants of the ancient forests could still be seen, they were in the more remote parts of the countryside.

Peg was born into this Irish countryside. Giving birth to children on a yearly basis was an unavoidable plight for a woman born in the eighteenth century. Of the twenty-two children Peg's mother bore, only eight survived, the death of an infant being an all too common event. Many fatal diseases were circulating, most notably smallpox, which carried off children before they reached adulthood. With little in the way of contraception available, and coitus interruptus frowned upon by the Catholic Church, women were left to a constant round of childbearing with the ever-present possibility of death in childbirth. All too often a woman's health was drained with each successive child-birth. It was a hard life for many in Killough, but at least Peg's family had some money. For the most part, Peg was protected from the harsh realities of life outside the country estate.

Her father's property in Corbetstown afforded the family an income and indicated his status as a gentleman. Peg grew up with more than sufficient for her needs, and knowing affection from both her parents. They provided a good education for all their children, but the music and dancing to which Peg had been introduced would stand her in good stead for her future career as a courtesan. As yet, this was a distant fate. For now she could enjoy herself in gentrified country life with its pleasant rural distractions. As Peg herself said, 'life glided on in the paths of innocence and content'. The two sons and daughter of their close neighbour, Mrs Darcy, who lived in nearby Corbetstown, provided agreeable companions and threw concerts and soirées to which Peg was invited. Peg's world was safe and secure, and Peg was content.

This life of pleasure came to an abrupt end with the fatal illness of her beloved mother. Left exhausted by constant childbearing, Mrs Plunkett no longer had the strength to ward off disease and quickly succumbed to 'spotted fever'. Measles and smallpox were usually mentioned separately in medical records, so this appears to be a different disease. It could have been either typhus, a louse-borne disease, or meningitis, both of which produced a dark spotted rash known as purpura, a bleeding under the skin. One doctor from Dublin commented some years later:

> That certain classes of disease arise suddenly among a people previously healthy, and having increased for a series of months or years, then gradually decline or altogether disappear, is well known to every observer. The causes which render sickness at certain times thus epidemical, are also in some instances sufficiently obvious . . . But why fever, which is at all times present in countries where many or most of the inhabitants must be susceptible of its attacks, should at particular times become epidemical, does not so easily admit of explanation.[13]

Mr Plunkett, fearing for the lives of his children, hastily packed them off to relatives – two of Peg's younger sisters went to the older married ones. Her eldest sister had married Mr Smith of Kinnegad, who ran a malt house and brewery at Tullamore in the King's County (now County Offaly); the second eldest sister had married Mr Beatty, who ran a china shop in Arran Street in Dublin. Peg went to her uncle in Cavan, and the two younger brothers were farmed out to neighbours. Only the eldest boy remained loyally tending to his sick mother, but to no avail. Mrs Plunkett died, leaving her family bereft, the boy following soon after. It was these deaths which were to alter Peg's life irredeemably. She realised that it was the death of her mother which led to the destruction of her world and ultimately to her own downfall: 'Ah fatal death! the dire cause of all my wanderings, and the source of all my misfortune.'

The children all returned home but her father was left desolate and also afflicted with rheumatism. As time went by, it became increasingly evident he was unable, or unwilling in his grief, to continue to manage the household affairs. He had simply lost heart. Instead he handed over the running of the family estate to his eldest remaining son, Christopher, on condition that he would look after his siblings. The result was disastrous. Peg could only watch as her brother began to dominate her and her siblings and became a bully in the household. He became increasingly demanding and aggressive. He was not only squandering the family's wealth, but according to the now fifteen-year-old Peg, he had become 'a harsh, unfeeling cruel tyrant', begrudging every shilling he spent on his siblings. He was failing miserably to provide for them, while spending a fortune on his own entertainments. The remaining members of family household did their best to escape.

One of the younger unmarried sisters had managed to gain her father's permission to go and live in Dublin with her older sister, who had married a Mr Beatty. While there, several youths flocked round her, asking to court her, and one of her admirers, an affluent tradesman, Mr Brady, asked for her hand in marriage. The couple planned to visit Peg's father to seek his consent, but while Mr Plunkett seemed agreeable to the match, Christopher had other plans. Peg recalled, 'He therefore artfully resolved to set his face against any proposal of that kind; and with a malignant cunning redouble his ill-treatment, in hopes it might drive them to a desper-ation, which might bring them to take steps, that might warrant him his refusal of their property.' With a promised settlement due to the sister on her marriage, Christopher was doing his utmost to avoid parting with any of the family money now under his control. He therefore argued that it was not a good match, all the while seething with anger at his sister's good fortune. Meanwhile Mr Brady suspected Christopher's real reason for disapproving of the marriage and showed his worth by politely refusing any dowry, declaring he would be happy to take the eldest unmarried Miss Plunkett for his wife whatever her financial situation.

Having gone so far with his plan, to have given in at this stage would have exposed Christopher's motive – that of his miserliness. He there-fore continued to protest that he was against the match and ignored all pleadings from other quarters. Nonetheless, unwilling to miss her one opportunity to escape her brother's domineering behaviour, Peg's sister obtained her father's blessing and married her Mr Brady as soon as she could. Before she left the family house for ever, she derided her brother bitterly, denouncing his shabby treatment of them all, but her words fell on deaf ears. As Peg looked on, she knew this would not be enough to change her brother's behaviour, later admitting, 'I knew my brother too well to entertain even a distant hope, that he would be the least amended by the spirited rebuke my sister had given him.'

Despite having promised his father that he would look after his sisters, Christopher had refused to make settlements for the older ones and failed to look after the younger ones. Luckily for Peg, her sister's marriage gave her the opportunity to escape from the treatment she endured at home and spend the next three months in Dublin, the newly wedded happy couple being only too willing to take Peg with them in order to give her some respite. At fifteen years old, the unmarried Peg landed in Dublin with the world at her feet.

At this time, Dublin was an up-and-coming city with new buildings being erected in place of old, ramshackle ones. The banker Luke Gardiner had developed the area between Henrietta Street and Gardiner Street in the 1720s, the first truly fashionable quarter for the new elite. Georgian town houses were built in Molesworth Street in 1727, the street becoming one of the most prestigious addresses in the capital after the completion of Leinster House in 1747. Prominent persons associated with the street would include the rebel leaders Robert Emmet and Lord Edward Fitzgerald (1763–98), the latter a famous Irish nationalist who died of wounds received while resisting a charge of treason. He was the twelfth of nineteen children born to James Fitzgerald, 1st Duke of Leinster (1722–73) and his wife Emily Mary (1731–1814), daughter of Charles Lennox, 2nd Duke of Richmond and Sarah Cadogan. Fitzgerald would be elected MP for County Kildare in 1790 and would become involved with a group of radicals, including Tom Paine. He had an affair with Elizabeth Linley, wife of playwright Richard Brinsley Sheridan, and she bore his daughter Mary, who later died of consumption in 1792 while in Sheridan's care. His brother, William Robert Fitzgerald, would become the 2nd Duke of Leinster (1749–1804), and was such a regular client of Peg that she kept a spare bedroom ever at the ready for him.[14]

Peg was delighted to land in Dublin; she declared, 'My time passed in pleasing scenes of delight; a constant round of company and amusement occupied the three months I staid there, which appeared to me but as many days.' During her stay, she attracted the attention of plenty of young gentlemen. Her happiness ended with a summons from her brother to come home. While she was reluctant, she was not without hope, for while she was in Dublin she had collected a couple of suitors. One was Mr O'Reilly, a friend of Mr Brady, her brother-in-law, and her sexual feelings were awakened; she admitted, 'I began to feel emotions in my youthful breast, to which I had been hitherto a total stranger.' Another, whom she merely refers to as Mr L____y, also fanned the flames of passion, but neither of them was successful in winning over her brother.

The situation at Killaugh grew worse on her return, as Christopher refused to let Peg or her younger sister take up invitations to stay with their close neighbours, the Darcys and Fetherstons of Dardistown.[15] This was circumvented by the neighbours applying directly to their father to allow them the pleasure of the young women's company. But although they managed to escape for the occasional evening, their brother's disapproval awaited them on their return home. Now his meanness turned to physical violence. He seemed intent on keeping his siblings at home so he could inflict brutality upon them, and they became increasingly subject to his intolerable whims and anger. Peg and her sister were 'frequently horse-whipped and [he] beat us in most savage manner, so that our bodies were often covered with wheals (sic) and bruises.'

With nowhere to go, and no one to turn to, Peg contemplated her options. As with most women in her position, she owned little of her own except her clothes and was dependent on her male relatives. Men were the heads of the household, and women had to look to fathers, brothers, uncles or a husband to provide them with food, pin money and protection. When male family members failed to provide, women were left to fend for themselves as best they could. Women seeking employment might find work in domestic service, sewing, or as mantua-makers, but it was barely enough to live on. With even fewer work opportunities for 'respectable' women, the only way to survive was to look for a husband. In Peg's case, she held no share in the family estate and her brother was in total control of the finances. Unable (and unwilling) to endure the beatings, Peg went to stay with her elder married sister, now Mrs Smith, in Tullamore.

But Peg was about to get herself into her first bit of trouble . . .

The First Indiscretion

If a smallest breach is made in the mounds of Chastity, vice rushes in like a torrent.

Desperate to escape from her brother's tyranny, Peg was only too happy to accept her sister's invitation to stay with her and her husband in Tullamore. The town lay in the middle of Ireland, its undulating hill sitting snugly in the plain of Magh Lena with the Esker Ridge to the north and the Shannon river to the west marking the boundaries of the territory. The area took its name from the hill ('Tullamore' meaning 'great mound') and had been part of the first English plantation in Offaly in the 1570s. By 1622 it was a small but expanding town, since new settlers had been arriving from England, Scotland and Wales from the beginning of the century. It possessed a ruined castle, two water mills and various cottages, but gradually new houses were being built. At the end of the road sat the large house of John Moore, the first Lord Tullamore. His family had erected a church in the 1720s in the Shambles area.

Having fled her brother's clutches, Peg landed in Tullamore with the light heart of a girl having escaped her jailor. Relieved at her new-found freedom, she started to take pleasure in walking out with her sister and brother-in-law on promenades. She took in the fresh air on her daily walks, being particularly pleased to note the large number of soldiers in the area. The nearby garrison was a strong British presence in the small town, having been built in 1716. The army's initial intention was to house one hundred foot soldiers, but this was to increase, and another barracks had to be built in 1756.[1] She remarked,

'The change of scene, and variety of company, speedily restored me from the languor into which I had fallen. Our frequent walking parties were delightful and some of the military in the garrison constantly mixed with us.' The attraction to soldiers was one that would stay with her for the rest of her life.

For Peg, this was a time of gay abandonment. She flirted with the young soldiers as they politely enquired as to her state of health and generally made small talk. While she greatly enjoyed these diversions, at the back of her mind was the imminent fear of returning home. She knew she had to think about how she could permanently avoid her brother and his violent behaviour.

Few prospects existed in Ireland for a young woman of Peg's circumstances. Now fifteen, she was of marriageable age, but with no dowry because of her brother's unwillingness to provide for her, her prospects seemed slim. She had turned away all previous suitors, and they had been too afraid to continue their pursuit. While women of a lesser social status might find some sort of employment opportunities as domestic servants or governesses, this was not something a woman of Peg's standing might consider. There was little doubt in her mind – she knew she had to find a husband.

The first proposal of marriage during her stay in Tullamore came from a rich grocer whom she described as 'ill-made, hard-featured, with the countenance of a baboon, shabbily dressed' and, worst of all, he wore a full wig. While long, powdered and curled wigs had been popular with older gentlemen, more to Peg's liking were the shorter, pony-tailed toupees of the younger officers. Not thinking of her-long term interests, Peg was quick to reject him. His money held no charm for her when compared to his other deficiencies. She admitted, 'It was in vain that my friends constantly extolled his goodness of heart, his great humanity, and his mild gentle disposition. All this was true, but he was a grocer, he was ugly and – he wore a wig – insuperable objections.' Nonetheless her brother-in-law duly despatched the offer from the grocer to her father, as was his duty. Meanwhile, as the days passed, Peg was cultivating a dalliance of her own.

A certain young man had seen her and introduced himself. He began making advances, telling Peg how pretty she was and how delightful her conversation. In fact, this handsome 'man of business' showed her so much attention that Peg was happy to ignore the fact that he already had a lover, a Mrs Shannon, who lived close to where Peg was staying. Peg thought, 'He was really of a most engaging person and winning address, and from my first coming to town, had shewed me every possible mark of attention and respect.' While Peg was fairly smitten, she was committing some of the biggest *faux pas* in the eyes of respectable society. Firstly, her admirer had not been formally introduced to Peg in a proper social setting. Secondly, she was meeting him unchaperoned and in secret. Finally, he was in a relationship with someone else. By flouting such codes of conduct, she was already pushing the boundaries of respectability. It would seem that even at this young age, Peg's moral compass was way off.

On hearing of her father's agreement to the grocer's proposal, a wedding to the old 'baboon' looked possible, the alternative being her imminent return to her brother's maltreatment. With the situation growing more desperate by the day, when her new lover proposed they elope together, unsurprisingly, she jumped at the chance. The couple hatched a plan to escape to Mullingar, about twenty-six miles away, and marry there. They hastily loaded up their immediate essentials and took off for Kilbeggan, where they hired a room for the night at the local inn. However, other plans were being made by the rest of her family and their plan was quickly quashed by the speedy actions of Peg's brother-in-law, Mr Smith. As soon as he heard about Peg's disappearance, he hastened to the inn accompanied by two of his friends. With pistols in hand, he broke into their room and dragged Peg off while her paramour made a hasty exit out of the back window. The escapade brought forward the event Peg had been dreading for so long; her stay at Tullamore was curtailed and she was unceremoniously dispatched home into her brother's hands. She could only be grateful that her brother-in-law had been generous enough not to mention the elopement.

On resuming her life at Killough, the brooding darkness of violence hung over her once again and Peg sank into despondency. Under the oppression of her brother Christopher, her younger sister had grown greatly emaciated and her father's health had deteriorated. The whole house echoed with despair. Garret, her younger brother, was the only hardy companion left in the household. As her sister's health continued to decline, Peg watched helplessly: 'Her gentle spirit was entirely broken, a settled gloom hung upon her, she had become quite emaciated, and she soon after took to her bed and died.' Peg was bereft. The girl with whom she had grown up and shared her life was gone, and there was little left on the horizon to promise Peg a better life. Instead she continued to suffer at the hands of her brother for the smallest of causes. One day, after she had gone to church, taking a horse from the stable without permission, she endured such a ferocious attack by her brother that she was left severely injured. Peg said, 'He beat me with his horse-whip so vehemently that the sleeve of my riding-habit could not be got off my swelled arms till they were slit open.' The injuries kept her in bed for ten days. Peg knew she had to escape her brother permanently or suffer the fate of her young sister. She entreated her father to obtain money enough to send her to Dublin. Her sister, Mrs Smith, previously in Tullamore, had now moved there to share the running of the china shop with her sister Beatty, and they would take her in.

However, Peg's second trip to Dublin was brief. She received a letter from Garrett telling her how he had been in a fight with their elder brother, but for the first time had won. This victory meant that Christopher was now subdued and that it was safe for Peg to come home. She had sorely missed her father, who had now taken to his bed, his health considerably worse. Convinced the situation had changed, Peg hastened home and, for a period of three months, tranquillity reigned. The peace was soon shattered, however, as Christopher fell back into his old, tyrannical ways. Their neighbours in Dardistown did what they could to help, inviting her to their house and visiting when Christopher was away from home. The crux came after a ball thrown by her friend Mrs Fetherston, when she insisted that Peg stay over at her house for the night. A message was sent to Peg's father to inform him of the fact and that she would be coming home the following day. As soon as she walked through the door the next morning, Christopher fell on her and beat her so badly she vomited blood. Peg recounted, 'My shrieks and cries reached the ears of my poor father who, as soon as a servant could help him on with his cloaths, came down to my assistance.' Although he managed to stop the horsewhipping, she lay in bed for three months covered in bruises, according to Peg, 'being several times at the point of death'. As soon as she could stand, she hired a carriage and left. Her father had procured enough money from his tenants to enable Peg to make her way back to her sisters. Peg set out for Dublin for the third time, vowing never to return.

Dublin was still developing rapidly. At the beginning of the century more than 70,000 inhabitants had made their life there, growing to 90,000 by 1750. By the time Peg arrived the population had risen substantially – estimated at 140,000 by 1760, and rising again to 154,000 in 1778.[2] For centuries, the River Liffey had been used as a rubbish dump, the houses facing with their backs to the pungent smell. Now the river was cleared and houses built to face out onto it. Improvements had been made to the flow of traffic throughout the city, with the markets and slaughter houses moved to the outskirts to make way for carriages going through the centre of town. Regulations were introduced to prevent dumping and improve hygiene. Major rebuilding had begun, and the narrow medieval alleyways had been pulled down to make way for airy Georgian streets and houses with elegant facades.

Peg would become familiar with the sight of the new buildings which became central features in the city. Political power was centred in Dame Street and College Green, while military and medical institutions were strategically moved out to the western periphery. A new parliament building designed by Edward Lovett Pierce erected in 1728 became a proud symbol of the political confidence of the governing classes of Ireland. Its grand forecourt and piazza rivalled the west front of Trinity College, with its new library built in 1732 and its printing house and dining hall in the 1740s. At the same time, a number of charitable institutions were being established. The workhouse designed by Thomas Burgh had been founded in Mount Brown in 1705 to house beggars who were made to work mainly in linen-making. Philanthropic ventures were also made in the establishment of free schools and hospitals, such as the Bluecoat School founded in 1669 and Jonathan Swift's St Patrick's Hospital for Imbeciles established in 1745. Swift, the Dean of St Patrick's Cathedral and author of *Gulliver's Travels*, bequeathed his entire estate to the founding of a hospital for the 'fools and mad'. He himself had been declared of unsound mind by the Commission of Lunacy in 1742.

Despite these civic improvements, when Peg arrived the slums in the north and south-west of the city remained, and she could not have helped but notice the growing number of hungry people moving in from the countryside to eke out a living. Various ruffian gangs had emerged from the poverty-stricken districts, some of them related to different trades. Two of the most notorious were the Liberty Boys and the Ormond Boys; the former were mainly Protestant weavers from the area known as the Liberties, and the latter were Catholic butchers from Ormond Market on the north side. Bloody street battles broke out between the two factions, the butchers' signature punishment being the houghing (or hamstringing) of their victims. Both sides were often heavily armed, which resulted in numerous fatalities. When Peg arrived, such battles were a fixture of Dublin life. There were regular hostilities between the two factions during 1750–51, and further incidents would peak between 1765–69, sometimes involving the army. One traveller in 1775 remarked, 'The soldiers and the butchers in Dublin are always at enmity, and from time to time inhumanly hough, or hamstring each Other. Many of these barbarians have been executed, which nevertheless has not yet put a stop to that savage practice.'[3] Other violence erupted from disgruntled crowds who frequently stood outside the Irish Parliament to demonstrate about various grievances – they complained about everything from the cost of corn to unemployment, to the unfair and unpopular laws being passed.[4]

Peg was overjoyed to see her two sisters and their families, and they welcomed her with genuine warmth and affection. Her earlier, aborted elopement had been forgiven, if not entirely forgotten. While her family thought they had successfully rescued her, Peg felt she had failed miserably, and her disastrous earlier return to Killough had caused a setback to her health. She came back to Dublin depressed, her spirits sunk so low that she took a while to recover. Once her depression lifted, she resolved to enjoy herself with a greater abandonment and recklessness than ever before. She was not one for suppressing her emotions, so this new freedom spelt trouble. This time it came in the form of an introduction by her brother-in-law to his friend Mr Dardis.

Initially, her suitor was careful to maintain propriety, and kept his courting behaviour in line with the moral expectations of her family. They were, after all, respectable traders, and had a reputation to maintain. Hence, Dardis was circumspect, showing Peg only the utmost respect, and, to all appearances, was an upright and trustworthy gentleman. Unbeknown to Peg's sisters and brothers-in-laws, however, he had been secretly courting Peg at night, a state of affairs that would have horrified them all. After a few weeks, he asked Peg to marry him.

Since he had little money, he knew he would be regarded by her family as an unsuitable husband. She, however, was comforted by his assurances of marriage: 'This indeed, Mr Dardis continued to promise as soon as circumstances would permit; and these assurances reconciled my mind to repetitions of our guilty joys, and lulled both conscience and remorse asleep.' But his proposals of marriage were simply a ruse to weaken Peg's resolve and allow him to consummate their relationship. In England, before Hardwicke's Marriage Act of 1753, secret marriages were recognised as being legal and binding, and even marriages contracted without parental consent were recognised by the Church.[5] In Ireland, elopements which led to clandestine marriage were covered by criminal law (embodied in a series of acts passed by the Irish Parliament between 1707 and 1749).[6] But such betrothals – of which there were many – which had not been made in front of witnesses, counted for nothing. The enamoured Peg was happy to believe anything she was told, and that Dardis would marry her and look after her, but the reality of the situation was something quite different. Many an unwed mother had started off in exactly these circumstances – a well-turned out young man had wooed a young woman who accepted all her paramour's promises of a wedding. On such a vow, chastity was easily breached. Witnesses to this were the many orphans deposited in the Foundling Hospital, the unwanted results of such unions. Although a poorhouse had been established in 1703 next to Swift's Deanery, it would only take in children over five years old. From this, in 1729, had emerged the Foundling Hospital, which took in babies, its aim being to prevent 'exposure, death and actual murder of illegitimate children' and to bring them up in the Protestant faith, with a policy that no enquiry was made about the parents, and no money received. To preserve anonymity, unwanted children could be placed in a revolving basket placed at the gate of the hospital. The porter would revolve the basket inwards when a bell was

rung, thereby avoiding any contact with the person who had abandoned the child. Between one and half to two thousand children were
deposited each year. Sadly, the orphanage did not live up to expectations, and one out of every three children in its care died. Of the 1,468
children admitted between 1749 and 1750, 420 died within the year
from 'measles, small pox, chinkcough [sic] and other diseases'. It has
been estimated that at least 10,000 children died out of the 14,311
admitted between 1756 and 1771. As a result of its failure, the institution was closed in 1835 by the Irish Secretary of State, Lord Glenelg.[7]

Hearing the daily gossip about the experiences of other young
women, Peg must have been forewarned. Their seduction and
abduction was a topic on everyone's lips. The main concern of most
families was to keep their unmarried daughters from harm's reach
until they could find suitable beaux for them. Books decrying the
plight of seduced women were legion, and would have been widely
available from booksellers. Peg would probably have read and digested
Daniel Defoe's novel *The Fortunes and Misfortunes of the Famous Moll
Flanders* as soon as she was old enough, as it was first published in
1722. The story tells of the precarious nature of a woman's lot – how
Moll had been raised by a goodly foster mother, but upon her employment as a household servant becomes the centre of the attention for
two of the employer's sons. The elder son seduces her, first by convin-
cing her to 'act like they were married' in bed, but is then unwilling to
marry her. Defoe stuck to much the same theme in *Roxana*, published
two years later, revealing the unequal status of women and how easy it
was for a woman to fall from virtue.

If these warnings were not enough, Peg and her sisters would surely
have pored over Samuel Richardson's *Pamela: Or, Virtue Rewarded*,
more recently published in 1740. Again, the plot acted as a warning to
young girls about the unscrupulous character of some young men
who would stop at nothing to gain the trust of a young woman.
However, Peg may have been more enamoured with Henry Fielding's
parody of *Pamela* in his *An Apology of Mrs. Shamela Andrews*,
published in 1741, which made the protagonist appear much less
virtuous and much more scheming. The whole narrative was more
comical and fun, and less moralistic than Richardson's, and would
have been much more to Peg's liking.

Unfortunately, having promised to marry her, Mr Dardis saw this commitment as his entitlement to all that a husband might ask from a wife, with Peg only too willing to comply. She admitted that she gave up her chastity easily, and felt she was just as much to blame: 'How can I call him seducer, when I met the seduction halfway?' She was far too enamoured with Dardis to refuse him. Yet at a time when a woman's honour was based around her virginity, by her actions she also gave up her prospects of a respectable marriage. She was acutely aware of the calamitous situation in which she had placed herself. How could her lover possibly value her when she had given away her most prized possession? Peg knew she could hardly rely on Mr Dardis to marry her when she had allowed herself to be seduced so easily. Concerned about the shaky ground on which she now stood, Peg clung on to Dardis's promise and counted on his honour, although even she lamented: 'Yet what reliance could I justly have on his honour, when I had weakly given up my own.'

The couple managed to arrange their clandestine encounters at night, but since she was still living with her sister and brother-in-law, there was every chance they would be discovered. Peg's family would certainly have forbidden such dalliances under their own roof. She wrote to her father in the hope he might be able to send her some money, but Christopher had already told all the tenants not to give money to his father, thereby leaving him without means. Her father did, however, manage to send Peg forty pounds via her uncle, who was in town picking up his daughter, who boarded in the nearby nunnery in Channel Row.

Although Peg does not mention much more about this cousin of hers, other relatives had become nuns and can be traced through the convent records. The nunnery in Channel Row in Dublin had been set up in 1717 to house a group of eight Dominican nuns. Two of them, Mary and Catherine Plunkett, were nieces of 'Blessed' Oliver Plunkett and were distantly connected to Peg through their forefathers. The convent was protected by the Duchess of Tyrconnell and became a lodging for young women. It attracted a superior type of young female boarder, as the records for 1725 show that Viscount Netterville and Lady Craven had daughters at the convent's school as 'parlour boarders' where they were taught music, dancing and 'fiddle strings'.[8] Any boarder would, of course, have to be chaste and have money, so Peg would have been ineligible. Her profligate nature made her reckless and prone to gratifying her immediate desires. The £40 her father gave her might have kept her quite comfortably for a while at a time when the income of a female domestic servant was around £2 per annum, and that of a skilled housekeeper between £6 and £8, but Peg's natural inclination was never thrift.

Peg's fears mounted as she realised she was pregnant and thus had lost all her bargaining power. Her lover's previous promises began to drop off. Dardis argued that he could not marry her in public as he might lose his reputation, and his inheritance along with it. No father would countenance his son's marriage to a woman who had so lightly given up her virginity, particularly one who came with no inheritance or dowry. Instead Dardis thought the best method of avoiding detection was to remove Peg from her sister's house and place her in lodgings. To this end, under the cover of night and leaving all her belongings behind her, Peg removed herself from the protection of her family. From now on, she had only her lover to rely on.

The Crossroads

Neither look back without remorse, nor forward without apprehension.

With her belly growing daily, Peg found her options quickly dwindling. While she was cheerful in that she could see more of Dardis, she was also wracked with guilt. A marriage in secret would hardly avert the gossip, so now it seemed pointless. The only comfort was that Dardis had found her apparently genteel lodgings on Clarendon Street and had promised to support her. Unfortunately, as yet unbeknown to Peg, the place was owned by a whore called Mrs Butler. Despite the outward appearance of both the house and its owner, the residence was known as a disreputable resort of prostitutes. Peg recalled, 'She was one of the impure ones, and therefore, not a fit habitation for the recovery of character; but this I did not know till after I had left her.'[1]

While Dardis continued to visit Peg when he could, she was lonely and missed her family. She confessed, 'I was oppressed with anxiety, and could neither look back with remorse, nor forward without apprehension of what might follow.' Her biggest concern was what her sisters and father might be making of her disappearance. She had fled her sister's house telling no one where she was going and had left behind all her clothes. Anxious about the distress she was causing her family, she pleaded with Dardis to try and find out what they knew of her situation.

At first her family had thought she might have committed suicide, and they were anxious to try and track her down. In despair, her sister and brother-in-law went down to the North Wall to see if she had drowned and her body been washed up. The North Wall had been built to improve the port of Dublin in 1714, and this was the most likely place for Peg to have thrown herself into the sea. However suicide was seen as a mortal sin, condemned by both Catholics and Protestants, as well as a crime, and was extremely rare. Anyone who committed suicide could not be buried in consecrated ground. The fear of going to hell was too much for many, hence the low suicide rate in Ireland.[2] Certainly, such a fear was prevalent in Peg's mind.[3]

None of Peg's family had heard anything about her whereabouts. The last time they had seen her she had told them she was going on a visit. Only when her brother-in-law Smith had the intelligence to track down the coachman did they have some success. Having remembered the driver was left-handed, Smith had gone round every coach station until he found the driver, who told him where he had set Peg down. Following his directions, Smith and Peg's other brother-in-law, Brady, found their way to Clarendon Street and enquired after Peg, only to be told she was living in a disreputable house next door. It was at this stage they aborted their mission, believing she had fallen too far to save. She recalled, 'They gave me up as an abandoned woman, and went away without condescending, or indeed wishing to see me.' In a panic she wrote to her sister, Mrs Brady,[4] and asked her if she could visit her at the Brady family home the following day. Peg, now nearing her time of delivery, swathed herself in her cloak to hide her bulky figure. Unaware of her true predicament, her sister pleaded with her to return home, only parting on Peg's promise to dine with her the following evening. Dardis was frightened her now bulging stomach would expose them, and tried to put Peg off visiting. He even suggested he take Peg to England, but the idea of travelling by sea filled her with horror. Her fear was not of being seasick but of drowning. It was after this visit from her sister that Peg knew she had to remove herself from society and find a secluded place where she could have the baby.

It was not unusual for single pregnant women to escape to the country to give birth undetected, although the poor women of Dublin tended to use the hospital which had been built specifically for them. The Dublin Lying-in Hospital had been founded by Bartholomew Mosse in 1745, and situated initially in George's Lane. He had built it after finding women 'in cold garrets open to every wind, in damp cellars, subject to floods from excessive rains, destitute of attendance, medicines, and often of proper food, by which hundreds perished with their little infants'.[5] He later raised enough money to establish the Rotunda Lying-in Hospital, which opened in 1757. Next to the main building, he had the foresight to lay out pleasure gardens in the style of Vauxhall Gardens in London, complete with a coffee-stall and concert hall in order to raise enough money to build and run the new establishment. It is highly unlikely Peg ever used these hospital facilities, as her first child was to be born outside of Dublin, and for her subsequent births she had enough money to hire a private accoucheur or male midwife.

In any case, the hospital was intended more for poor *married* women, and its rules of admission based on this moral consideration, so Peg would not have been allowed entrance, although her friends might well have been. They would have had to submit to the demands of the hospital, which placed the women on display at charitable events given at the hospital and its gardens, 'all decently clothed in uniform at the expense of the hospital, each in a blue calamanco gown and petticoat, shift, handkerchief, cap and apron and thus appeared before his Grace as President of the Hospital, the Duchess and the rest of the Governors and Guardians, with many of the nobility and gentry, who all expressed the highest satisfaction'.[6] Nobody thought to ask what these poor women thought about being used as such a spectacle for the benefit of the benefactors. No doubt some of them were grateful they had a comfortable place to give birth and be cared for, but at what a price of enforced humility and gratitude. Women also had to be free from sexually transmitted diseases, the rules deeming that 'no Woman great with Child is to be received into the Hospital if she hath any contagious Distemper, or the Venereal Disease'. While Peg might still have been pox free at this stage, plenty of her future friends would have been excluded on these grounds alone. Records indicate that success in preserving life was not all it should be. One report made in 1781 indicated that 'when the hospital was imperfectly ventilated, every sixth child died within nine days after birth, of convulsive disease; and that after means of thorough ventilation had been adopted, the mortality of infants, within the same, in five succeeding years, was reduced to one in twenty'.[7]

The only possible way of hanging on to the threads of respectability was to hide away in the country and give birth discreetly. To this end, Peg planned to go to Drogheda, find comfortable lodgings and stay quietly away from society. The drive down to Drogheda from Dublin was horrendous. Peg was filled with anxiety: about Dardis, her family and the imminent birth, and the coach ride was uncomfortable and tiring, particularly for someone at her late stage of pregnancy. Although the roads were becoming better, they were still extremely uneven. Little more than tracks, they were subject to the extremes of weather – in the dry summers, they were hot and dusty, and in the winter they were prone to floods and potholes.[8]

Peg took one of the twice-weekly stagecoach services from Dublin to Drogheda, handing over the costly fare of 5s. 5d. It was reported that the coach 'goes and comes constantly, passenger or no passenger'. It carried ten people inside and more on top, with luggage limited to 20 pounds unless a passenger was prepared to pay a surcharge.[9] Six horses drew the coach, and passengers felt as if they were flying through the air they were jolted so much. But their discomfort was aggravated by the problems with some of the fellow passengers. One contemporary commentator complained, 'I go in the coach – its odours were many, varied and unpleasantly mingled with the passengers, a half drunken sailor and an old woman, did not impress me with the prospect of a very pleasant journey.'[10]

Apart from the discomfort of the journey, the other problem for Peg was that she had found herself sitting next to a close relative in the stagecoach, Mrs Drumgoold of Drogheda, who was returning from business in Dublin. An amiable lady, she recognised Peg immediately and started up a convivial conversation. Peg was mortified she would be found out, and kept her cloak tightly around her, her mind busy with excuses. The only reason she could come up with for her travelling was that she was on business for her brother-in-law Smith, going to Drogheda to collect some money on his behalf. Mrs Drumgoold, swallowing Peg's falsehood, invited her to stay with her. Caught in a bind, Peg relented and promised to go with her. Sitting back in the carriage, she quickly executed a plan of evasion. Once the coach stopped, she informed her relative that she had to call in at the inn to enquire after the person she was supposed to be doing business with.

Instead, she hastily procured a man and horse and swept off to the nearest town of Dunleer, seven miles away.

Dunleer was a small village located on the White River, close to where the Battle of the Boyne had been fought in 1690. Peg took lodgings for the night in an inn which hopefully would have been rather better than the lodgings Richard Twiss described on his tour of Dunleer in 1775: 'the inclosures are mostly of loose stones piled on each other; over the door or chimney, the same opening serving for both, of many of the cabbins, I observed a board, with the words "good dry lodgings"; however as I was sure that hogs could not read I avoided mistaking them for styes.'[11]

Peg was alone and exhausted: 'I was totally a stranger in the town.' Although she went to bed she had little sleep and cried all night. She recalled, 'I had leisure to consider the horrors of my situation. I became prey to reflection, and lay condemned without alleviation of a single excuse for my conduct.' The next morning Peg felt no more refreshed than when she had gone to bed. Her clothes were crumpled, she had little money and was a complete stranger in town. Seeing a kindly chambermaid, she enquired as to the type of place she was in and whether she should remain in the town. Getting a positive response, Peg found a place to stay with a farmer and his agreeable wife for half a guinea a week. It is unlikely at this stage that Peg would have informed the farmer's wife of her pregnant condition, although it would soon have become obvious. She was still morose and missing her family, but she took solace in praying in the chapel nearby, all the while tormenting herself with the terrible deed she had done.

Her situation brought home to her all that she had lost through her elopement. No sisters to care for her, her mother long dead, and her father incapable, the thoughts of her family preyed on Peg's mind. There was plenty of time for contemplation and remorse, although not all was lost. The man Peg loved had not abandoned her and he was providing for her in her confinement.

The anguish she felt at the separation from her family was compounded by the trepidation she felt as she gave birth. Fear of death in childbirth was ever present for women in the eighteenth century, and Peg would have been no exception. Labours were difficult, there were no effective painkillers and there was no guarantee that her child would be born safely. An obstructed delivery could lead to the death of both mother and child, since Caesarean sections were not successfully performed until the nineteenth century. Most women had some sort of birth attendant, either a male or female midwife, partly due to a statute of 1647 which forbade the concealment of a birth. Although she makes no mention of it, Peg was probably attended to by a local midwife and afterwards looked after by the farmer's wife. Most married women would have known how to assist at a birth, and it was common to attend female relatives' births to offer both moral support and physical assistance. It is unlikely Peg brought in a male midwife as it was costly, too many questions would have been asked and she needed to keep the birth discreet. In the event she gave birth to a baby girl in the tiny rented room in a cottage in Dunleer.

As soon as she had recuperated, Peg packed her belongings and set off back to Dublin, accompanied by a nurse whom she had hired to look after the baby. As the coach arrived at the inn in the city, she was overjoyed to see Dardis standing eagerly awaiting her return. He was pleased to see Peg and his new daughter, both looking in good health. Dardis paid off the nurse (presumably she wanted to return to her own village, or maybe Dardis thought it better to release her so gossip did not spread), hired a new one and took his small family to new lodgings. There they continued to live as man and wife, but now with the added responsibility of a tiny infant.

Although Peg obtained a nurse, she may well have suckled her first-born herself. However, it is likely that her future children would have been palmed off to a wet nurse, a woman who suckled other women's babies. Mothers of higher social standing tended to use a wet nurse, but this was a more frequent occurrence in France than in England or Ireland. Wet nurses had often recently given birth themselves. This meant the infant death rate was horrifically high, the mother invariably favouring her own child over her charges, added to the fact that diseases spread easily between infants at the breast. Many physicians disagreed with the idea of handing over a baby to another woman, and thought it harmful for the child. William Cadogan, who was to become physician to the Foundling Hospital in London, mused:

how it comes to pass that people of good sense and easy circumstances will not give themselves the pains to watch over the health and welfare of their children: but are so careless as to give them up to the common methods, without considering how near it is to an equal chance that they are destroyed by them. The ancient custom of exposing them to wild beasts or drowning them would certainly be a much quicker and more humane way of dispatching them.[12]

Lower-class mothers in any case tended to breastfeed their own babies, but wet nurses were used at the foundling hospitals for want of a mother's breast.

Despite her happiness at the birth of her daughter and at being reunited with Dardis, Peg continued to miss her family and thought about them constantly. Such was her distress that Dardis urged Peg towards a reconciliation with her sisters. The couple agreed it would be best to approach her sister, Mrs Smith, to tell a tale which did not involve too much detail, yet provided a believable excuse for Peg's absence. Having bumped into her relative Mrs Drumgoold on the way to Drogheda, Peg had the idea of saying she had been to visit her. It would, of course, have been easy for her sister, if she suspected a falsehood, to have simply written to her cousin to verify Peg's tale. Unfortunately, there was no need for this, as Mrs Drumgoold, slighted by her rude behaviour, had already written to Peg. The letter had lain on the mantle of Peg's sister's house for weeks awaiting Peg's return, but her concerned sister, unable to hold off any longer, had opened the missive and discovered the truth about Peg's whereabouts – or at least about where she wasn't.

Peg stood on the doorstep, unaware that her sister knew of her deception, so was taken aback to see her in a vitriolic mood and unwilling to let her in. Mrs Smith shouted at Peg, 'You vile wretch,' and promptly pushed Peg back through the door and slammed it in her face. Resilient as ever, Peg decided to approach her other sister, Mrs Brady. However, the reaction was much the same – if anything, even more virulent. Rebuffed but desperate, Peg dashed off to see a more distant relative in the High Street,[13] but her luck was out and she met with the same disapproval. This time the rebuke was so robust that her male relative threatened to beat her if she ever showed her face at his door again.

Whether the family knew about Peg's pregnancy and baby at this stage is not known, but it would have been difficult to keep it quiet following her return. At the very least, they knew that she had gone away in secret without a chaperone and had been seen travelling across the country in a stagecoach unescorted. Since they knew of her prior involvement with Dardis, they probably assumed she was now living with him, even though it is unlikely Peg would have admitted it. What they did know was that she had sullied both her own and, by association, the family's reputation in leaving the care of their home.

In response to the round of rebukes, Peg solemnly resolved never to see Dardis again. This was a somewhat unwise decision, given that he was the one person who was willing to look after her. So far, there had been no suggestion that he might abandon her. They were living together as a family and he had even hired a nurse to help her. Why she chose to abandon him at this stage can only be surmised. No doubt her mind was in a whirl of fear, her family's fresh rejections hurting her feelings. But to leave Dardis as well was pointless, and reflects the flighty and often unpredictable nature of Peg's thinking. Maybe she believed that if she abandoned Dardis, her family would take her back. Given their previous actions, this was highly improbable.

The last chance for Peg lay in a letter she penned to her father, and here her real fear is revealed. It is unsure whether she told him about the baby, but he would at least have been informed by her sisters about her elopement She confessed to him that she had 'sinned against Heaven and before him, and was no more worthy to be called his child', quoting the Bible. In other words, if she stopped 'sinning', she might be able to recover her soul, if not her reputation. Peg's turning to God at every crisis was to become a typical reaction reflex through-out her life. She had prayed in the chapel before her daughter's birth, and she would turn to God at the end of her life. But there were other reasons she reached out to her father. Her filial affection demanded that she seek her father's forgiveness – and it was a daughter's reliance on her father's constant and unconditional love which drew Peg back to her father. Denied the comfort of her sisters, she turned to him once more. Touched by her words, her father beckoned Peg home. Without hesitation, she flew back to the stagecoach station, and before she had time to gather her breath was on her way home to Killough. It is unsure what Peg did with the baby, whether she took her with her or not, but most likely she left her with her nurse in Dublin. For Peg to have even contemplated going home after all the abuse she had suffered at the hands of her brother shows how upset and confused she must have been. Rejection from her family in Dublin had so distressed her that Peg was no longer thinking straight. Her natural instinct was to go back to the first man who had loved her.

4

The Downward Spiral

The real cause of the multitude of unhappy women, is the harshness of their own sex.

Though her father had welcomed the idea of Peg's return with an open heart, the door of her old family home remained firmly shut. To her horror, nothing had changed. Her brother Christopher refused to admit her to the house despite Peg dissolving into tears on the doorstep. His only reaction to her plight was to give her a guinea and book a carriage to take her as far as Kinnegad. With only a handful of trinkets and a few clothes, she was forced to remove herself from the family house and move on. Peg landed at her next destination in a state of shock.

Only sixty miles from Dublin, Kinnegad might as well have been a thousand miles away. On the borders of County Westmeath and County Offaly, for Peg it was a crossroads in more ways than one. The village had a long tradition of providing hospitality for the travelling public as it lay at the junction of two major routes in Ireland, where the roads from Dublin to Galway and Sligo meet. But there was little solace on offer for Peg in a small town with no one she knew. Rejected by her family, desolate and lonely, she knew she had to at least find a bed for the night. The next morning, she took the stagecoach back to Dublin, where she began to look for new lodgings. She took a small lodging for five shillings a week and decided to withdraw from the world to lick her wounds.

Peg was now in a more precarious position than ever before. Having sold her clothes off bit by bit to support herself and her baby, she had no alternative but to again apply to her two sisters in Dublin for help. By now, her sister Smith had young children of her own but remained unwilling to listen to Peg when she returned to visit their household. Peg even offered to make clothes for them in a bid to placate her and to try and earn a living, but she was met with the same obstinate refusal. Her other sister, Mrs Brady, was no more compassionate, and declared, 'If a morsel of bread would save me from death and destruction, I would refuse it to you.' It is difficult to understand such a lack of compassion when Peg was in such a desperate predicament.

Chastity was revered above all other virtues, particularly for women. While many men of all classes sowed their wild oats as youngsters and often continued to visit brothels after marriage, eighteenth-century morals dictated that a woman should remain chaste before marriage. The double standard of morality for men and women – so very well established in England – to a great extent also held in Ireland.

Now Peg was reduced to surviving on a few ounces of watered-down beef broth and some potatoes. Unable to come up with any other solution, she decided that she might prevail upon her father's labourers to shelter and feed her. She surmised, 'Whilst I had lived at my father's house, I had been frequently serviceable to the tenants and their wives; I had no doubt, if I could get down amongst them, their gratitude and hospitality would afford me shelter in one of their cabins, and give me at least potatoes and butter-milk.' After all, this was the staple diet of most poor people in the countryside, and she could manage with a little assistance where she was known in Killough. With this in mind, she borrowed a cloak from her landlady and set off towards the stagecoach station to make a trip to her old estate. Her clothes were now 'mean and much worn', and Peg must have looked down on her luck. As she walked up Strand Street towards Smithfield, two gentlemen, a Mr Strange and a Mr Droope, approached her and invited her to drink tea with them and go on to a play. She quickly made her excuses and escaped into a jeweller's shop on the Inns Quay where she came face to face with the owner, a Mrs Moore whom she had known long ago. Thankful to see a friendly face, she was grateful when her old acquaintance pressed her to stay for tea. By now, Peg was ravenously hungry and devoured everything put before her. After a hearty meal and as much conversation as she could muster, she thought it time to take her leave of the genial hostess before it was dark. Peg thanked her, wrapped her cloak around herself, and made her way to Smithfield, from where the coach was due to leave. To her great annoyance, all the places were already taken and she had no alternative but to return to her lodgings for another night.

It is unclear at this stage what she had done with the baby, but it is unlikely that she had taken her along with her. On her way home, she again bumped into the same men, and this time, having no idea how she was going to manage to keep body and soul together, agreed to go into the tea house with them. Although still in its infancy, tea drinking was already established in Ireland in the 1740s and tearooms had sprung up to cater for the habit. Although it was not considered appropriate for a respectable woman to go into a tearoom with men she hardly knew, this was exactly what Peg decided to do. The trio were joined by a Mr Thomas Caulfeild, who immediately drew Peg into conversation, asking her a multitude of questions. He then asked to walk Peg home, dropping two guineas into her bosom en route, leaving her in no doubt as to what his intentions were. Although he made no physical advances that evening, he promised that, if she would allow him, he would become her protector and she would want for nothing.

As she closed the door behind her, Peg felt reassured that her immediate predicament had been resolved: 'I entered my room in a very different disposition from that with which I had quitted it a few hours before. Then, all was distress, doubt and uncertainty. Now my mind was tranquil and I looked forward with hope.' This rapid shift in thinking was typical of Peg, and would see her jump from one bad decision to another. At no time did she think what a fool she had been to abandon Mr Dardis in the first place. For now, she was simply relieved that she had been rescued from complete destitution and found another keeper.

Thomas Caulfeild wasted no time in finding Peg an apartment in Dublin. Having settled her in new lodgings, Peg was content to let him shower her with attention and gifts. He was well connected, with a pedigree to his name, a fact to which Peg was not immune. James Caulfeild (1728–99), who was to become 1st Earl of Charlemont in 1763, was his cousin's son.[1] The Earl was a well-known lover of classical art and culture, and had spent nine years on the grand tour in Italy,

Greece, Turkey and Egypt. On his return to Dublin he had employed the Scottish architect Sir William Chambers to remodel his main residence at Marion House and to design a town house which was to become known as Charlemont House. He also built the Casino at Marino outside Dublin. Somewhat surprisingly, Thomas Caulfeild's ancestors were connected with Peg's two hundred years previously, as one commentator has described: 'The first Viscount Charlemont is credited with having shown some kindness to the Catholic Primate Oliver Plunkett. He is said to have told him "when you want to administer Confirmation, don't go any more to the mountains, but come to the courtyard of my Palace".'[2]

Thomas Caulfeild had money of his own from a successful wine business.[3] His shop was located on Abbey Street, one of the principal shopping streets of Dublin, running from the Customs House and Store Street in the east to Capel Street in the west. There had been a huge surge in demand for wine in the early eighteenth century.[4] Indeed, Bordeaux had become so popular with the Irish gentry and nobility that, in a letter to a friend, Jonathan Swift referred to 'Irish wine' as a synonym for claret. The hospitality of the elite depended on good quality wine – and plenty of it. Indeed it was consumed in such vast quantities that often men in high political office were rendered incapable of making solid decisions. During his term as Lord Lieutenant in Ireland in 1745, the Earl of Chesterfield famously despaired that 'nine gentlemen out of ten are impoverished by the great quantity of claret . . . drunk in their houses' and believed that the Irish gentry were ruining themselves through excessive expenditure on claret.[5] However, he knew that 'no one in any position in Dublin would have thought himself truly hospitable unless he provided large quantities of claret for his guests'. Drinking, gambling and womanising were all part of the social glue which bound the *bon ton* together. One of Peg's future lovers, Charles Manners, the 4th Duke of Rutland (1784–87), in his capacity as viceroy despatched a member of his military staff, George Kendall, to France in order to secure only the best of wines for Dublin Castle.[6]

While with Caulfeild, Peg admitted 'I lived in a genteel stile [sic], unnoticed and unsuspected.' His attention to her increased daily, he visited her at the apartment he had taken for her, and entertained her at his house in Abbey Street. She was not in love with him, but he treated her well and her days with him represented for her 'protection, endearments and plenty'. Although Peg had enjoyed herself with Caulfeild, and bore him a son, their relationship did not last above a year. As with every young man of wealth, he could have his pleasures as he wished, but when it came to marriage, it would be to a rich heiress and on the advice of his family.[7] Peg recalled, 'He told me he never intended to marry, and he feared he should never have a child', but his relations began to pressurise him. A certain Miss Hawkesworth was deemed worthy, and in no time at all, he was betrothed. The only claim Peg had on him was that she had borne him a son. 'This event for a while gave me most poignant sorrow, and as my temper was become somewhat violent, I was greatly provoked at his abandoning me.' For a while, Caulfeild kept his promise to look after Peg and his child and gave her an annuity. It was common for a mistress not to give herself up to a man without some sort of commitment to pay her in lieu of marriage and to pay her off for the time they had spent together. Annuities were therefore sometimes drawn up in a legal document, like a promissory note to pay the bearer a given sum of money. All payments, for a mistress in Peg's position, were made after a verbal promise. In all cases, these were entirely dependent on the man's whim and could be stopped at any time. A woman and her dependents would be left to fend for themselves as best they could.

It is uncertain what had happened to Peg's first child, her daughter by Dardis. Few men would take on another man's child or even pay for its keep. Frequently, courtesans would put their children out to a family, paying them a weekly remittance to look after them. These children would often be kept secret from their new lovers. If a courtesan was lucky enough to find a generous man, he might pay for her previous child's maintenance.[8]

Peg's own annuity from Caulfeild was dependent on her quitting her 'impure' life and cutting herself off from her libertine friends. This, in itself, is an indication of what Peg had been up to on her days off from Caulfeild. She had established a set of friends with similarly tarnished reputations, and was spending all her spare time with them. Dublin was awash with merry-making and amiable company, with balls and masquerades held on a regular basis, as well as cosy dinners amongst the *demi-monde*. Taverns regularly put on musical entertainment for their clientele, such as at the Bull's Head in Fishamble Street, home to the Charitable Musical Society for the Relief of Imprisoned Debtors. Money raised helped build the New Musick Hall, where Handle's *Messiah* had been performed in 1742.

One particular female friend Peg took a liking to was an entertainer who performed in a tavern in Smock Alley. At this time, taverns operating in Smock Alley included the King's Arms, adjacent to the theatre, operated by Michael Duff since 1750; the Hoop Petticoat tavern which had been running since 1753; and the Globe, only opened in 1760.[9] Caulfeild admonished Peg for mixing with such disreputable friends. She later recalled, '[H]earing of my new acquaintance, [he] called on me to warn me against her. He told me he entirely disapproved of this lady, that she was a very improper companion for me. That there were as many women ruined by their female as their male connections, and ended with forbidding me to see her.' Caulfeild had been cruel enough to desert her, but was arrogant enough to still want control over her life. Unsurprisingly, Peg ignored him and continued to go out with her friend and went to see her performing in a concert. The taverns around Smock Alley were not of the highest quality and boorish behaviour was usual, with men jeering and brawling. If a performance was enjoyed, however, cheers and money would greet the fortunate performer.

Despite now being separated, Caulfeild continued to demand that Peg drop all her connections with the demireps (women of questionable reputation), threatening to cease her annuity. He thought his ex-mistress should have all the appearances of respectability, even if they were fake, but this was too much to ask of Peg. Consequently, she ignored him and he fulfilled his threat. This sudden dip in finances, rather than leading her to consider the consequence of her actions, pushed Peg into yet more extravagant behaviour in the pursuit of pleasure: 'My mind indeed, became again tortured with disappointment and anxiety, so that I could not find peace at home, and therefore fled to my old remedy of being constantly abroad.' Caulfeild did, however, continue to pay for their son until the child's sudden death of 'an inward complaint'. In truth, Caulfield probably wanted a way out of paying her a costly annuity and Peg's behaviour gave him the excuse he needed. It was not long before her funds were once again drying up, and Peg was plummeting into debt.

Oscillating between plentiful wealth and near destitution was a way of life for many women who had made courtesanship their career (prostitution was not a name they would use). More often than not, this was not a matter of choice but a path a woman fell upon having lost her virginity to a seducer. Although it was a precarious existence, the life of a courtesan brought certain freedoms for women, along with perils. A woman had to be careful in deciding who she could trust to protect her. Too many women made poor choices, and were led into a life of the lowest prostitution as a result of desertion. Love sometimes came into the equation, which clouded their decision-making. A protector should preferably be rich, or at least wealthy enough to keep a coach and four horses. A title also came in handy, as good connections went a long way in polite society. Even when these conditions were satisfied, there was no guarantee of comfort and security, and a courtesan might easily go broke. Extravagance and generosity were common traits among courtesans, and most of them were not natural savers. Their autobiographies are littered with descriptions of their excessive spending, as well as their charitable donations to those less fortunate. In any case, the cost of keeping up appearances was high – a well-kept courtesan had to have expensive jewellery, brocaded dresses, coiffured hair, elaborately furnished apartments and her own carriage. Many of these women were extremely generous, and had no hesitation in spending money on their friends, as well as the beggars they found in the street.

Peg did, at least, have the perspicacity to realise her financial predicament, remarking, 'But a life of dissipation cannot be maintained without some funds.' A way out had to be found.

An Honourable Man

Every comfort, convenience, and even luxury of life, I was to enjoy.

Now in her early twenties, Peg had already been a mother twice by two different lovers.[1] One of the peculiarities about Peg was that she often left herself in precarious positions, leaving one keeper only to end up in exactly the same position with another of whom she was no more fond. She left her first lover after having his baby because of guilt over her sexual downfall, but then ended up being mistress to another man and having his baby. Cast off through her own refusal to bow to the dictates of her previous protector on the company she could keep, Peg was now about to go to another who would tell her exactly the same thing.

While she was not destitute, past experience told Peg that she had to find another keeper, as this was her only means of survival. She also knew she had to find a man with money, one who was at least rich or well connected. If she were to find a well-bred gentleman, the best move for a woman in Peg's current position would be to be have him properly presented to her – it was a matter of protocol. It was through such a formal introduction by a female friend that Peg met her next two lovers, a Mr Jackson and his friend Mr Lawless. Unfortunately, though both were lively company and well connected, neither of them had enough money to keep her and were therefore unsuitable for Peg as long-term lovers – although she was perfectly willing to accept their advances on a casual basis.

Casting her net further afield, Peg came across Mr Leeson, a 'wealthy English gentleman' who met all her immediate requirements and became her next keeper. He was 'a very opulent man', who was able to provide for her and quite happy to give Peg her own line of credit. It was from him she would take her working name, Mrs Leeson. There were, however, still drawbacks, only to be presumed in such a life. Like Caulfeild, Mr Leeson demanded she give up all her friends, both male and female, and give herself to him alone. Having little option, Peg consented to see only him, although in truth she was no longer willing to remain faithful to, or pander to, one lover. She had already started on a course which would involve juggling several men. She had been privately entertaining both Mr Jackson and Mr Lawless when Mr Leeson began to pay her attention. She was determined to continue her liaison with them, but for the moment was willing to pretend to acquiesce to Mr Leeson's demands for fidelity so that he would keep her as his long-term mistress and allow her to enjoy the luxurious lifestyle he offered her.

Though Peg never gives his full name, referring to him only as 'Mr Leeson', she says her new keeper was related to Joseph Leeson II (1701–83), the 1st Earl of Milltown.[2] The Leeson family's forefather was Hugh Leeson of Culworth in Northamptonshire, who first came to Ireland in about 1680 as an army officer, and later made a fortune as a brewer, acquiring much property in the area around what is now Dawson Street; Suesey Street in Dublin was renamed Leeson Street after the family in 1728.

Peg's lover had property in Kildare, the seat of the Leeson family, and it is most probable he was Joseph Leeson III (1730–1801), the son of the 1st Earl by Cecilia, daughter of Francis Leigh, of Rathangan. He had been educated at Eton from the age of twelve and later did a grand tour with his father, having his portrait painted by Pompeo Batoni while in Italy in 1751, and continuing to travel a great deal over the next twenty years. He was elected to the Irish Parliament for Thomastown in County Kilkenny in 1757, a seat he held until 1761. It is likely that Peg met him through her connections with Caulfeild since his family knew the Leeson family.[3] Caulfeild's uncle, the 1st Earl of Charlemont, was on amicable terms with the 1st Earl of Milltown while on tour in Italy. He had taken a house in the English quarter around the Piazza di Spagna, where he was joined by his son. On the creation of his father's earldom, Leeson styled himself Viscount

Russborough, until he was made 2nd Earl of Milltown in 1783 upon his father's death.[4] He never married, which meant he could live with Peg for a year in the same household some time in the early 1760s (he would die without issue). Leeson was listed in *Fair Game for the Ladies* among a list of unmarried peers in the *Hibernian Magazine for 1785*. He was also a known womaniser, though Joshua Reynolds depicted him as a dunce in his painting *Parody of the School of Athens*.

At first, the newly established couple lived in Dublin and Peg enjoyed her new life. She admitted, 'Mr Leeson was certainly very kind and good natured, and fully demonstrative of his regard.' It is unlikely, however, that Peg saw much of a social life under the watchful eye of Leeson, as her new beau kept her sequestered. No doubt the concerts and plays attracted her, and she may well have attended some of these with him, but while he was enamoured with her, he was also wary of her potential encounters with other men. He had set her up in salubrious lodgings, and he visited her regularly. On a couple of occasions, he saw Jackson and Lawless passing Peg's door and became increasingly suspicious. She was indeed dallying with both, but at this stage Leeson was willing to believe her denials. As a precaution, he dismissed Peg's mantua-maker. These seamstresses had a reputation for dabbling in sexual matters and encouraging illicit relationships between young women and their beaux; they were also known for carrying messages between lovers, keeping secrets and generally helping their clients to make cuckolds of their protectors. But sacking Peg's dressmaker did not ease Mr Leeson's anxieties about her possible infidelities, and eventually he could no longer bear for her to stay in Dublin. He resolved to move her to his country estate and place her away from temptation.

Kildare was an exception to most small rural Irish towns, which had shown few signs of improvement over the centuries. Instead, it possessed attractive hunting lodges built for the elite. A pack of twenty-four hounds, a couple of good horses and a huntsman cost around £40 a year, making it expensive enough to be a preserve of the aristocracy.[5] Lying between the natural boundaries of the Wicklow mountains in the east and the River Barrow to the west, much of the Kildare countryside was given over to farming. For generations up until the eighteenth century, farming had been undertaken in strips, with tenant farmers planting different crops next to each other as they wanted. Cattle and sheep were grazed on common land. By the mid-century, enclosures were taking place, and strip-farming declined as land was fenced in. Common land was also incorporated into the enclosures, leaving many poor tenant farmers without their former strips of land or free pasture for their animals.[6] Kildare farmers were managing better than most, and were comparatively wealthier than most 'common tenants' elsewhere. Many farmers had managed to build two-storey houses and accumulate up to 250 acres of land through the enclosures – some arable, some grass in irregular patterns – and landlords were planting on a much large scale.[7]

Leeson kept 'an excellent house, and beautiful demesne' in the county of Kildare and, for the time being, Peg was content to leave Dublin for a life of leisurely pursuits and to assume the lifestyle of her wealthy protector. His father had commissioned Russborough House in Kildare, which was to become the family estate. The house is a particularly fine example of Palladian architecture designed by Richard Cassels and built between 1741 and 1755, an estate which Peg would certainly have been familiar with, and one which her lover would eventually inherit.

On his own property in Kildare, Leeson at least seemed placated, and the couple settled into the gentle sway of country life. Away from the various distractions of life in the *demi-monde*, Peg did her utmost to satisfy her new keeper, and together they spent many a tranquil day together. Although deprived of the entertainments of Dublin, there was enough to keep them occupied. The couple would have gone out hunting, as it was a common sport in Kildare. Home entertainments included singing and playing the piano or viola, dancing or playing cards. For now, Peg was enjoying her new-found prosperity with Leeson and was content to attend to his needs. She would not have to bother with domestic duties as servants would have been employed on the estate to undertake all chores.

Although Peg does not mention them, she would have known about the Lennox sisters who were living on neighbouring estates and were friends of Leeson. When Peg was still young, Emily Lennox Fitzgerald had come to live in Ireland after marrying the 1st Duke of Leinster in 1747 when she was only fifteen. She lived first at Leinster

House in Dublin and then at Carton House, just up the road from where Peg was now living. Louisa and Sarah Lennox had been brought up by their sister Emily after the death of their parents.[8] Leeson was an old beau of Louisa's sister, Sarah, two years her junior. Louisa Lennox Conolly was nearly the same age as Peg and had recently become mistress to a similar estate in nearby Castletown on her marriage to Tom Conolly in 1759. She was not yet to know it, but in the years to come, Peg would keep a bed warm for Emily's son, William Robert Fitzgerald, 2nd Duke of Leinster.

Households in Kildare had a hierarchy of servants, as seen in the houses of Carton and Castletown. A steward would have been responsible for all the servants under him, from the head cook to the pantry boy. He would deal with tradesmen such as the chandler the brewer, as well as the grooms and general labourers, supervise the duties of the housekeeper, the butler and the clerk of the kitchen.[9] All Peg had to do was dress attractively, make sure her hair was properly coiffured, and entertain Leeson with romantic evenings and some witty chat.

Meals were usually taken at set times, and Peg might well have organised the menus, acting as the mistress of the house. Breakfast in rural Ireland was usually a simple affair such as bread and butter with tea, coffee or chocolate, although these beverages were considered luxuries to all but the rich; black tea from China was a favourite (Peg's preference was gunpowder), costing three shillings for half a pound in 1758 (about £20 in today's prices). For this reason, tea tended to be locked away in tea caddies, and the cook held the key. Dinner was usually taken between two and four o'clock in the afternoon – early for some, but considered suitable for fashionable society. It would consist of anything from fourteen to twenty-four dishes. One contemporary described the types of food on the table of a typical wealthy Irish household: 'First course – Turkeys endove [endive], boyled [boiled] neck of mutton, greens, soup, plum-pudding, roast loin of veal, venison pasty. Second course – partridge, sweetbreads, collared pig, creamed apple tart, crabs, fricassee of eggs, pigeons.'[10] A variety of puddings and tarts would be offered for dessert. Supper would be later in the evening, commonly consisting of cold meats such as brawn beef of ham, or leftovers from dinner, again served cold. While supper was a lighter meal than dinner, some physicians denounced it as a pernicious custom, sure to overload the digestive system. Salting, smoking or pickling were the only methods of food preservation available, so food tended to be seasonal.

Their life was to change when Mr Leeson was called back to Dublin on a matter 'of the greatest consequence'. Whether this was personal, political or business, Peg does not specify. Unwilling to leave Peg behind, he rented a furnished house in Ranelagh Road – on the outskirts of town rather than in the centre of Dublin – in the hope that this would be far enough away from her old friends. It was a pleasant, sophisticated area, as one newspaper described:

> The Circular Road, that leads from the Park Gate to Summer Hill, continued to be the daily exhibition of everything that is gay, beautiful and brilliant the capital can produce. The Duchess of Rutland, Countess of Antrim, Mrs Beresford, Mrs Phopoe,[sic] drive their ponies with spirit and much grace. Mr Fitzgibbon now takes the lead with his blacks; Lord Howth, Lord Sudley, are content with a single pair. Mr Westby gives four bays, well managed; several other phaetons sport in style. The ladies who take the air mounted are almost incredible, while the crowds of heroes in brown powder who follow are innumerable.[11]

Here they lived quietly for a year, yet unbeknown to him, and despite Leeson considering making her his wife, Peg was already up to her old ways. She was allowing both Mr Lawless and Mr Jackson into her house while Mr Leeson dined out, and acknowledged, 'Stolen pleasures are generally held to be very sweet, and in spite of his vigilance, I sometimes enjoyed them to compensate for the external constraint I was forced to assume.' She even took into her confidence Leeson's manservant, who kept watch for his master's homecoming through the parlour window while Peg entertained her suitors.

Peg was unwilling to remain faithful, particularly if bound to a man she did not love. She railed against the double standards of morality, declaring, 'Chastity I willingly acknowledge is *one* of the characteristic virtues of the female sex. But may I be allowed to ask – Is it the *only* one?' The injustices she saw around her, particularly the different morality applied to men and women, exasperated her.

How could a woman be a drunk, a scandalmonger and a cheat, but still be considered virtuous if she remained chaste? She would no doubt have been familiar with *A Modest Defence of Chastity*, published in 1726, which had gained great popularity when it summed up contemporary opinion:

> Separate a Woman from Modesty, she becomes quite another Creature than God made her. Her Strength lies in her Virtue, Purity, Chastity; without these, she is a Monster & Dunghill, not to be endured without Charity and Compassion, in Order to be reclaim'd ... A Plying Prostitute is an abandon'd Wretch, a walking Common Shore?, a Light-house to the Wife, an Ignis fatuus to Fools.[12]

Mr Leeson wanted to set Peg up in a brand-new house in Dublin which had just been built for her. She pronounced, 'Prior to his setting out for the country, he had taken a house for me in Park Street which was just built, and having had it fitted up in an elegant manner, he pressed me to go and reside in it before he departed.' By now Leeson was so smitten, and so convinced of Peg's reformed character, he even wanted to introduce her to his relatives. He had watched her over the past year and she had complied with his terms. She had given him her full attention while in the country and proved a challenging and witty companion. To prove his trust, he gave her a bill of credit on a merchant who was a friend of his, and allowed her whatever money she needed during his absences on business. He had even bought a field near their house in Dublin, in which he put two cows he had purchased simply to indulge Peg's fondness for fresh milk.

Peg was not so convinced of her affections for Leeson. While she enjoyed his company and was grateful for the pleasure and protection he had given her over the last year, she could not see herself as his bride. While she claimed in her memoirs that Mr Leeson had proposed, this was probably not true. For why would a man trouble himself with marriage when he had all the comforts he could gain from a wife already? Also, a reputable man would have had difficulty contemplating marrying a woman with such a sullied background as Peg's, although there were certainly occasions on which a known mistress had bagged herself a titled man for a husband.[13]

In any case, she was unwilling to sacrifice her freedom for security. The attraction of various young men was already proving far too strong, and her willingness to commit to a life of fidelity was non-existent. While Peg was aware she must live with a wealthy protector, she was always looking for love and excitement elsewhere. She easily grew bored and her natural inclination was for gaiety and self-indulgence rather than restraint and commitment. While Leeson was kind to her, he was hardly good-looking, and Peg was easily swayed by a handsome man. She also wanted independence. The idea of moving into a new house overseen by his relatives grated on her. She confessed, 'This did not suit the mode of living I intended to follow in his absence.' She excused herself from moving into Park Street on the grounds that the house was still damp, it would give her a cold and that she preferred to remain in her current home in Ranelagh Road while he was away.

Once back in Kildare, Leeson's suspicions redoubled. He instructed his friend the merchant to find other lodgings for Peg, but unbeknown to him, the merchant was already infatuated with her, and it is possible that she was providing him with sexual favours to buy her freedom. At that moment, the merchant had only Peg's interests at heart, and she was allowed to embark on whatever pleasures she fancied. Fortunately for Peg, but unluckily for Leeson, the lodgings he had chosen belonged to friends of hers who would do all they could to keep Peg's extracurricular activities secret. When Mr Leeson returned to Dublin earlier than expected, with Peg not at home to greet him, they attempted to cover up her absence. Peg was, in fact, with Mr Lawless in his private apartment. As Leeson banged on the door of Peg's lodgings, the owners called down to him that they knew nobody of that name and told him to go away. Enraged, and feeling duped, he ran to the merchant to demand knowledge of Peg's whereabouts. His friend said, quick-wittedly, that the people of the house had informed him that Peg did not live there so as to keep away unwanted visitors, just as Leeson had instructed. He issued discreet instructions to Peg for her to go home post-haste and pretend she had been there all along, while retaining Leeson at his place for as long as possible.

Peg admitted she had problems with fidelity: 'My conduct, with respect to Mr Leeson, will fully shew, that neither pleasure, content, affluence nor gratitude, can bind a woman of a loose turn of mind, and changeable disposition.' Her views on sexual life she likened to an acceptance of polygamy. 'Polygamy was not wrong in its own nature, but merely as it was a great difference between what was *evil in itself* and what was *evil by human prohibition*.' While the law forbade a multitude of husbands, since Peg was not married, the crime could not apply to her. Her ideas on marriage certainly sound remarkably progressive to a modern-day reader. 'I looked upon marriage merely as a human institution, calculated chiefly to fix the legitimization of children, and oblige parents to bring them up and provide for them; to ascertain the descent of property; and also to bind two persons together, even after they might be disgusted with, and heartily tired of one another.'

Meanwhile her undoing approached. At the behest of Leeson, a friend of his, an 'Englishman' named John Van Nost the Younger, had started to watch her movements carefully. Van Nost was becoming a respected sculptor, having settled in Dublin around 1749. He joined the Royal Dublin Society, which had been founded in 1731, to encourage collaboration on scientific pursuits and experiments. Members discussed everything from mathematics, physics and medicine to literature, philosophy and history, and the RDS would establish a museum, laboratory and botanic garden.[14] Van Nost made busts of the society's founding members, and he was to become the foremost sculptor in Ireland.[15]

Now engaged as Leeson's personal spy, he followed Peg, and saw Jackson and Lawless proceeding to Peg's lodgings accompanied by a band of musicians. As Peg later confirmed, 'He heard the concert, saw the entertainment go in, and did not see them depart.' He drew the obvious conclusion. Reporting back to his friend in Kildare, Van Nost sent Leeson a full account of Peg's philanderings. Leeson lost no time in dispatching a letter to his merchant friend, telling him to cut off Peg's credit, followed by a longer letter to Peg upbraiding her for her lax morals and loose living, not to mention her faithlessness and 'abandoned conduct'. He cut her off without further contact, although that hardly bothered Peg. She admitted, 'I was more distressed with the loss of his purse than his person.' She was ready to move on.

Some years later, at the height of her success as a courtesan around 1783, Peg would declare 'a noble Lord of my own name . . . expressed a great regard for me, and was one of my constant visitors. He often urged me to name what I particularly wanted, that he might make me a present of it.' She claimed he showed her great favour. Rich and generous, he showered presents of diamonds on her, but the best gift he bought for her was a French-styled palliasse. The large, thick, padded mattress filled with straw and sawdust incorporated coiled springs and provided 'the best sleep a person might have'. On such luscious piling Peg confessed to having slept admirably. Now rid of Leeson, she could turn her thoughts to love.

Love of a Lifetime

The Man I So Sincerely Loved.

Despite her sobs and tears, Peg overcame the initial shock of aban-donment indecently quickly. She really had no love of Mr Leeson, although she admitted he had been 'fond, amiable, and generous'. As with other courtesans in her position, her real concerns were of avoid-ing the 'misery, sorrow, poverty and distress' which she had suffered by living without a protector.

The horizon was perhaps not so bleak after all. Buck Lawless had been enjoying her company, and had recently found himself better off financially.[1] The recent death of his eldest brother meant that Lawless was the recipient of all his personal property. Unfortunately, this did not include a huge inheritance, but at least now he had enough to take Peg under his protection. Like many of the other well-connected men in Peg's life, Lawless was related to nobility, a 'near relation' of the Countess of Clonmel, Margaret Lawless, daughter of a Dublin banker, Patrick Lawless. Peg could not have known her as the Countess of Clonmel when she first met Lawless but was writing in retrospect. Margaret Lawless was born in 1763, and only became countess after she married the barrister and judge John Scott, 1st Earl of Clonmel, on 23 June 1779. Lawless was a generation above Scott, possibly her uncle.[2]

Peg moved in with Lawless to a modest house in Wood Street in central Dublin. This was possibly a house he had bought for them, as she would later rent it out. Her time with Lawless over the next few years was to be the happiest and most stable period of her life. The move meant she could now live with a man of her choice, the man she

loved. She admitted, 'I inwardly rejoiced that I should have an opportunity of quitting that kind of life, to which I had submitted during Mr
Leeson's reign.' Peg was no longer content to give up her body purely
for money – she wanted to enjoy love.

During the early 1760s, Dublin was replete with a wealthy resident
aristocracy who lived much of their lives in public. Everyone knew
everyone else, and the city was the hub of Ireland's social life. Mornings
for the wealthy were taken up with riding out on horseback or driving
out in a carriage, depending on the weather. This gave everyone a
chance to meet and greet and wave to passers by. It was also a chance
to show themselves off dressed in fine clothes. Gentlemen would go
visiting, but never in the afternoon, as it was presumed dinner engage-
ments had already been made. Dinner was usually between 4 and 5
p.m., with supper a few hours later, polite company usually leaving
before 10 p.m. Although there was a well-delineated class system,
people mingled at leisure time, the Dublin shopkeeper mixing with
the nobleman at a public assembly, while the fashionable beau shared
a joke with the builder.

The couple rarely went out without each other, and both of them
enjoyed Dublin's fashionable social life. They spent time at the
theatres in Smock Alley, Crow Street, Fishamble Street and Aungier
Street, watching acclaimed actors such as Charles Macklin, taking in
concerts and dining with friends.[3] The Theatre Royal in Smock Alley
was one of the most popular places for entertainment, and one of
the main theatres in Dublin. Years before, actor-manager Thomas
Sheridan had introduced the running of different plays most nights of
the week and the tradition had continued. Command performances
were often given in honour of the most recent Lord Lieutenant, and
benefit performances were given for a variety of good causes, among
them the Hospital for Incurables, the Infirmary of the Inns Quay
Lying-in Hospital, the Charitable Music Society 'for the decay'd and
indigent musicians and their families' and 'for the Relief and
Enlargement of poor Prisoners confined for debt in the several City
Marshalseas, and for the Release of Prisoners'. Performances were also
sometimes given for the benefit of the performers.

Theatres catered for everyone, from labourers to businessmen and
courtesans, from the lower orders in the upper gallery to the upper

crust in the boxes. Prices ranged from 2d. in the upper gallery, 2s. 2d. in the gallery, 3s. 3d. for the pit and 5s. 5d. for a box.[4] At a time when a skilled craftsman could earn 1s 10d. a day, they might save up to go there, but might not attend weekly. Unique to Dublin were the 'lattices' built into the proscenium arch, a premium 'showing off' space for courtesans,[5] Peg's favourite seats, from where she could watch the plays. The theatre was a noisy place and order was often hard to maintain in an audience. People would chat to each other throughout the performance, chomp on oranges and nuts they had bought from the strolling sellers with their baskets, and even throw things at the actors. In 1761, notices in a Dublin newspaper requested that gentlemen refrain from pirouetting on the benches in the pit during the performances. One young, overdressed fop even took to reclining full length on the rail on the top of his box with his back to the stage in an attempt to be admired, his quest failing when he fell off into the pit, much to the hilarity of the audience.[6]

Peg and Lawless would have attended at least some of the performances at Fishamble Street running through winter and spring during the 1760s, when a series of twenty-two weekly subscription oratorios and concerts were given in aid of the widows of the Vicars Choral, the men who were employed to sing in the choir of St Patrick's Cathedral. Morning concerts were held in the New Gardens in Great Britain Street from April onwards, every Monday, Wednesday and Friday between twelve and three o'clock, running up until 1 June, when thirty-two evenings of summer concerts began. At Smock Alley, the season began in October and closed around June the following year. Passerni presented oratorios at Crow Street and Fishamble Street Music Hall, and actresses Mrs Barry, Kitty Clive and Nancy Dawson had their Dublin debuts. Among the most successful Irish playwrights, Peg would have known of Samuel Foote as his popular satire *The Orators* had run in the autumn of 1762, with him acting in it. The main pieces performed during the 1760s were *All for Love*, *The Beaux Stratagem*, *The Beggar's Opera*, *The Fair Penitent*, *Love A-la-Mode*, *The Jealous Wife*, *The Female Officer*, *The Constant Couple* and *The Old Bachelor*. Shakespeare was still very much admired, with such plays as *The Merchant of Venice*, *As You Like it*, *King Lear*, *Macbeth* and *Romeo and Juliet* firm favourites.

Over the next five and a half years, Peg bore five more children. She says nothing in her memoirs about what happened to her daughter by Dardis, but possibly Peg was paying for her keep with another family, or had taken her into their household. However, her relationship with Lawless grew increasingly tempestuous. At the beginning of their fourth year together, signs of distrust surfaced between the lovers. On Peg's part, she had been faithful and done her utmost to please him; for his part, he had provided for her and their children. She remarked, 'If at a play, I even accepted an orange, or returned a salute from any gentleman, he immediately insisted on our return home.' Like all the men before him, Lawless started to become uneasy when Peg was approached by other men in public and was annoyed when she spoke to her old friends, female as well as male. She started to suspect him of keeping the company of other women as he began to go out more and more without her. Both were quick to anger, and arguments grew increasingly violent. On occasions when he stayed out late, Peg would don her dowdiest clothes, pounding the streets looking for him in the pouring rain, mud splattered all over her dress. Accompanied by her maid and a watchman, she searched every tavern, gaming house and place of public amusement. She listened at the keyholes of parlour windows to see if she could hear his voice. Peg knew how bitter she was becoming and the effect it was having on their relationship: 'O jealousy!' she declared, 'wild and insatiate fiend! Let every female guard against its first approaches, for she knows not to what horrid lengths it may carry her.'

Lawless was coming in at six o'clock in the morning, while Peg was thinking about attacking him with razors. Lawless was often to be found propping up the gaming tables with Buck English and Buck Whaley at Daly's Club at nos. 2–3 Dame Street, where 'nearly half of Ireland is said to have changed hands'.[7] The place was described as 'the only society, in the nature of [a] club, then existing in the Irish metropolis'.[8]

During this acrimonious phase, Captain Benjamin Matthews came back into Peg's life, a man she had known before she knew Leeson or Lawless, but to whom she had paid little attention. He had been sent with his regiment to fight the French in America in what would become known as the Seven Years War, recently ended in 1763. Young and agreeable, he had 'a pretty fortune' as a result of his post in the army (he would later fight in the American Revolution of 1775–83 in South Carolina in 1779, leading the Colleton County Regiment) and would go on to own a sponging house in Angel Court.[9] These houses were originally taverns or victualling-houses where arrested debtors were detained by a bailiff for twenty-four hours in order to give the debtors a chance to find friends who might assist them and pay off their debt. They were usually the homes of the bailiffs, and derived their name from the extortionate charges made for the accommodation provided.[10]

Matthews had seen Peg ride by in her coach while he sat in Daly's Coffee House. In an attempt to rekindle their relationship, he sent her a diamond ring. She immediately returned it, but he misinterpreted her action. Fearing he had not offered her enough, he quickly sent it back, along with another one of equal brilliance. When Peg returned both rings, he sent them back again, this time along with a wad of banknotes. He eventually proposed marriage, but by this time Peg was too involved with Lawless and had eyes for no one else. Although Peg liked Matthews, she was in love with Lawless, despite their fierce arguments. Of Matthews she remarked, 'His whole estate would have appeared insufficient to induce me to infidelity, to the man I so sincerely loved.' However, one incident she described reveals the extent to which her relationship with Lawless had deteriorated. By this time, Peg was four months pregnant.

A friend of hers had decided to throw a dinner party for the couple, but the evening did not go well. Another woman at the table flirted with Lawless all evening – harmless enough in itself, but Peg could hardly contain her displeasure. As soon as they were out of the house and installed in the carriage, she unleashed a verbal tirade. She shouted at Lawless about his behaviour and upbraided him for all his shortcomings. She then threw his gloves and hat out of the carriage window, along with her muff. Their recriminations grew louder and more violent once inside their house. Still in a sulk, she refused to retire, so Lawless threw her down on the bed, cut the strings of her clothes and beat her up. In a manner typical of some women subjected to male violence, Peg blamed herself and treats it in her memoirs as a warning to other hot-tempered women: 'Reflect on this, ye Females of turbulent tempers. See what ye gain by being, what is too frequently your boast, *women of spirit*.' Yet her injuries were so bad that Lawless had to send for two doctors, and she ended up losing the child she was carrying.

Since Peg and Lawless were not even married, she had little recourse to any sort of justice, even if she had wanted to prosecute him. Mistresses, prostitutes, women who had children by men they had long-term relationships with – all of them were lumped in the same category of debauched women. In a period where women had few laws to protect them, even rape victims who were virgins had a hard time prosecuting their attackers. Few cases came to court, since to admit rape was to publically admit loss of virginity and thereby forfeit marriageability. Rape carried a capital punishment, and few witnesses or judges were prepared to send a man to his death for a woman who was already 'soiled', or had previously had sex outside of marriage. A single woman's parents might sue, and they would be the recipients of any financial restitution (not their daughter). Similarly, if married, a woman's husband might prosecute another man accused of raping his wife and, if successful, a payment would be paid to him (not his wife). However, a woman had no recourse to the law if raped by her husband. Peg was therefore in a poor position to take legal action even if she had thought about it, which she did not.

Another matter to put a serious strain on the couple's lives was the dwindling of Lawless's finances. His small inheritance from his brother had long since dried up. With only a few watches, rings and ornaments between them, they began to sell off or pawn what they had. Their clothes went first, followed by their household furniture. The worst was yet to come. Over the following months each of the children died one by one, from unexplained causes. While Peg does not give details in her memoirs, it was probably one of the many childhood diseases which affected them in turn, passed on between them. The last to survive was a little boy who seemed to have escaped death as he had been looked after by a nurse at the upper end of Bride Street. Peg called to see him twice a day and he was attended to by Dr Cleghorn. However, he was to suffer the same fate as his siblings and eventually followed them to an early grave. Peg believed the deaths to be a result of divine retribution, declaring, 'These illegitimate children gave me pleasure, and were taken from me to punish me.' Now nothing held her and Lawless together, although by now she was once again pregnant.

Just before their relationship was totally derailed, they decided to take an excursion together. Lawless suggested they go to the country-side to enjoy themselves – Peg was to go ahead with friends and he would come and join her. A popular Irish outing was whipping down in a coach and four to County Kildare to watch the horse races. The Curragh was one of the oldest racecourses in Ireland, and had been established well before the eighteenth century, but its rules were only formalised in 1717. One traveller through Ireland wrote in 1780 that the racecourse was 'where all great matches are run. It is the Newmarket of Ireland, and the sportsmen say that the turf is equal to any in England . . . it is a fine sod for the diversions, and if it has any fault, it is evenness.'[11] The first recorded races was held in 1727, but were still going strong in the 1760s (and indeed, still are today) as an attraction for keen gamblers. The races were free, and attracted all classes from labourers to aristocrats, but attendance by the lower orders was increasingly condemned by the Irish Parliament for promoting debauchery and idleness 'to the great ruin and detriment of their families'. To encourage elite patronage, the government annually gave out 'two plates of one hundred pounds each to be run for'.[12] Extra amusements were put on for the benefit of racegoers. Fairs often coincided, dances were advertised and various other activities were laid on. Because of all the additional entertainments, a day at the races was popular with both men and women. Peg could not wait to take advantage of all that was on offer – gambling on thoroughbreds, dining on good food and drinking champagne.

As the coach rattled down to the Curragh, drawn by four beautiful bay geldings, Peg was accompanied by her friend and rival courtesan Katherine Netterville, whom Peg sarcastically referred to as 'Kitty-Cut-A-Dash'.[13] At the time, Netterville was under the protection of James Cavendish, son of Henry Cavendish, 1st Baronet of the Devonshire family. Later she would come under the protection of a plantation-owner Mr Stone of Jamaica, who would go insane and commit suicide in her high-class residence on Grafton Street.[14]

Kitty and Peg were accompanied by Cavendish on horseback, but

Lawless was notably absent. After the races, the trio took off to Burchell's inn at the Nineteen-mile House for something to eat and to find rooms for the night. The place was packed, and there was not even a room in which to dine, far less in which to sleep. Their hosts were kind enough to offer to put the women up by sharing their own bedroom divided by a cloth and pulling in another 'pallet' or bed for them. Kitty refused, as she wanted to sleep with Cavendish. While they were ruminating on what to do for the best, Cavendish came across two of his friends, Mr Trotter and Lord Boyne, Frederick Hamilton.[15] When Boyne was still a minor in 1737, he had, to the distress of his family, married a poor young woman called Elizabeth Hadley. In accordance with the law, if a boy was under age, technically his parents or guardian could void the marriage. Although Boyne's guardian attempted this in 1738, the case was decided against the guardian and Boyne remained legally married. Some years later, in 1746, he had 'married' another woman, Miss Mooney, without divorcing his first wife, and had several children by her.[16] Since he was living with a mistress himself, he was quite content to be seen out at entertainments with disreputable women such as Peg and Kitty.

Having dined at Burchell's together, the group then went off into the night to try and find a bed in Kildare town. The night was pitch black and the roads were bad, and they knew the journey was going to be difficult. Their accompanying groom swore he knew 'every foot of the road' but they had proceeded no further than a couple of miles when he mistakenly led them towards a ditch. In high spirits the horses leapt over the ditch, the rattling carriage flying through the air behind them. Peg recalled:

> Our horses being mettlesome and high fed, made no stop, but leapt and bought out coach clear over undamaged. We screeched and begged to be let out, but in vain, for the coachman, as self-conceited as our guide, said he would soon gain the road, and wheeled about, but in turning, ran the pole against the ditch, when it snapped in two.

With no means of covered transport, a discussion ensued on the best course of action to take. The gentlemen wanted to sleep in the carriage, but Peg resolutely refused. As she later explained to Kitty, she was concerned about attempts being made on her person by one of the gentlemen in their company as he had dropped hints about his intentions. The group resolved to move on to Kildare, making the three-hour journey on horseback. Peg took a seat in front of Lord Boyne while Kitty swung herself onto the horse behind Cavendish. Mr Trotter led the vanguard on his grey horse, while the servants were left behind to look after the coach. 'We travelled in this manner, backwards and forwards for above three hours; and never did I suffer more than I did that night, being almost perished with cold, and almost ready to drop from the horse.'

Despite improvements from the 1730s onwards, Ireland's roads remained perilous. Rarely was more than forty miles a day made even in the 1760s and 70s. The increasing demand from people needing refreshments, places to stay and stables for their horses meant that a series of inns had developed along the major routes, but once away from the main towns, it was a fair ride to the next stopping post.[17] By the time the group arrived in Kildare, it was three o'clock in the morning and they were exhausted and near frozen. Not only had Kitty fallen off her horse many times, but Mr Trotter and his horse had inadvertently ended up in a sand pit, and were unable to get out for quarter of an hour.

Once in Kildare, the men searched all over town for accommodation, but to no avail. Peg was furious with Lawless, who had failed to join them as promised, and she was in a foul mood. She turned her resentment on Kitty, whom she felt had ruined their day. However, Farrell, a piper from one of the taverns, was kind enough to let them have the keys to his 'wretched habitation' where they stayed fully clothed for the remainder of the night before repairing to the tavern for breakfast. They returned to the races, supposedly for another day's entertainment, but Lawless had still not turned up and Peg's suspicions grew. After only one race she decided to go home to find him, dragging a reluctant Kitty behind her.

Once back in Dublin, Peg dismounted at Dame Street and walked straight to a well-known brothel further down the street, obviously having an inkling where Lawless might be. With a single rap on the door, and without waiting for an answer, she marched into the parlour. There she beheld her beloved Mr Lawless sitting with the lady of the house, Mrs Johnston, 'tete-a-tete and drinking Champaigne'. Peg screamed and trembled as she snatched up a nearby decanter, ready to thrust it into the face of the astonished Mrs Johnston, a woman she had considered a friend. Quick as a flash, Lawless jumped up to grab her hands, thereby preventing serious assault. The intended victim sat motionless in her chair in a state of shock. Somehow, Lawless managed to drag Peg home.

Despite the incident, Peg remained with Lawless at their home, but she could not let the matter rest. In a move calculated to do her female rival most harm, Peg contacted Mrs Johnston's protector and informed on her, telling him how she had found his paramour with Mr Lawless, then adding a list of further transgressions, thereby breaking up their relationship for good. Meanwhile, Peg's own relationship with Lawless had somehow muddled through the bitter jealousies, rivalries and violent verbal and physical attacks. However, their financial situation was now so dire that a solution had to be found. Friends suggested that perhaps Lawless should quit the country and try his luck in America. Neither wanted this to happen, but if he did not make some money, soon both would be plunged into greater debt. They both wept together at the idea. 'Oh my dear Margaret,' Lawless cried, 'If I am to go abroad, will you still bear me in you remembrance? Will you cherish and love, for my sake, the babe you carry, if it comes to maturity, as it is the sole one that will be left of our all.' Peg, pregnant yet again, was senseless with grief at the thought of him leaving her.

While Lawless could easily emigrate to America and make a living, he was well aware of the life Peg would have to lead to survive when he left. Her only option would be to either try and obtain another keeper, or run a brothel. Yet his main concern was whether she would remember him and still love him. His selfishness was typical of many men of his standing who faced financial ruin. Even if his affections were true, which undoubtedly they were, his self-interest was stronger. He may well have intended to send her money for herself and his child, but in the event, he never did.

Lawless's father would give him no money while he remained in Ireland, but he consented to provide him with a draft on merchants he knew in New York, Messrs Smith and Ramage, to be paid over on his arrival.[18] His father knew of his involvement with Peg, and would give him nothing that would encourage him to stay with her. Lawless reserved his passage to America, but kept it a secret from Peg. He packed his bags and left the house, telling her he was to visit his uncle. Unable to confess his true intentions, he had instead left a letter with his friend, who brought it round to the house the following morning. As soon as Peg saw the letter, she knew what to expect. Upon reading the first lines, 'I sail this morning to America', she fell into a faint, and burst out crying. She eventually plucked up enough courage to read the rest of the letter. Lawless had written,

> I could not bring myself to tell you, my love! I was going to leave you. Do not be angry then with your dear Lawless, when real affection and a disposition not to give you pain, was the cause that made him thus abruptly break from those bonds, by which he would joyfully for ever be united to you. Yet rest in peace and be certain of hearing from me by every opportunity, and as you love me, my dear Peggy! take care of our baby – Adieu!

Unsurprisingly, she grew livid: 'I tore my hair, I beat my breast, rent my cloths, and became outrageously and raving mad.' Exhausted with these remonstrations, she made herself ill and felt 'the whole frame of my nerves were palsied'. Peg's friends were so worried about her that they called for her doctors. One of them was George Cleghorn, an eminent Scottish physician and an amiable man. He had taught anatomy at Trinity College and built up a highly lucrative practice where he had treated Peg on previous occasions.[19] He was state physician and was to become a member of the board at the Westmorland Lock Hospital. The Lock hospitals had been set up to treat people suffering from venereal disease, the first in the middle of the century at Donnybrook. Another Lock hospital was located in Clarendon Street, Dublin. Dr Cleghorn probably helped Peg and her girls on matters relating to any gynaecological problems and sexual diseases as well as their general health. On this occasion, her other doctor was William Collum from Moore Street, who also rushed to her side. He was master of the Lying-in Hospital between 1766 and 1773 and had sanctimoniously argued against teaching at the hospital lest it provoke a 'breach of modesty'.[20] Both of them instructed

Peg to leave Wood Street for the outskirts of the city, where the air was purer, which she did. However, little could be done for her health as she was in a serious state of nervous collapse. All her energies were dissipated and she could only sit for two hours a day in the garden propped up by pillows. Her spirits then at their lowest ebb, Peg gradually began to recover her health.

Some time later, Peg gave birth to a little girl. Her resemblance to Lawless only made their separation harder to bear. Peg, after a relatively stable family relationship, was once more alone.

A Young Clergyman

In short, I was to become a compleat *Coquet*.

Now in her early thirties, Peg had just given birth to her eighth child.[1] She found herself living alone once again in Ranelagh Road, while slowly trying to regain her strength. Taking stock of her situation, Peg compared her position to that of the infinitely better-off Lawless in America. She admitted,

> I imagined he would be more easily consoled than I should be, as he had many more new objects of consolation than I had. He had a comfortable subsistence; the means of mine were drained. He had incessantly a variety of new objects surrounding him to give him pleasures, and banish me from his mind; I was confined to constant sameness, and everything around me only presented what brought him momentarily to my recollection.

When she thought about the possibilities of him being with another woman, her heart contracted. She pined, her physical health was gone, and she felt 'sickly and emaciated'.

The loss of her financial security worried Peg, and, once again, she wondered how she was to make a living. She tended to stay with a man until she became bored, or someone more attractive came along, although she was not below having flings behind their backs. She also entertained a couple of dalliances between longer-term affairs. In one sense, it was obvious that she would have to find another protector. However, the variables included whether he would be someone she could live with, be attracted to, or even fall in love with. Obviously, he had to have money. Though she could hardly contemplate seeing another man at this stage, she knew she would have to go back to central Dublin to find another keeper.

In order to bolster her finances while living in Ranelagh Road, Peg had rented out the house in Wood Street which she had shared with Lawless to one of her acquaintances, Miss Fleetwood. At that time, Fleetwood was mistress to Lord Clanwilliam, Sir John Meade, an extremely wealthy man in possession of estates worth £10,000 a year, most of them located in the Golden Vale of County Tipperary, situated in the barony of Clanwilliam.[2] Of Lord Clanwilliam it was later reported in *Sketches of Irish Political Characters* (1799): 'This nobleman has dissipated a noble fortune. His attachment to the ladies and to the turf and certain anecdotes respecting him are too generally known to justify the relation of them here.' Horace Walpole (in a letter to Sir Horace Mann dated 20 December 1779) declared that Lord Clanwilliam had been responsible for the murder of 'a younger, handsomer, swain' favoured by one of Clanwilliam's mistresses.[3] Miss Fleetwood was obviously one of his earlier mistresses, as he would have been in his twenties at the time of keeping Miss Fleetwood, and for now she was handsomely kept in finery and great comfort. This was all to Peg's advantage, as she received enough rent to allow her to take lodgings in the country for her lying-in and recuperation from giving birth.

Peg had also become acquainted with Sally Hayes, a woman who was to become one of her closet and dearest friends. Hayes had rented out a room at Wood Street for half a guinea a week, and Miss Fleetwood was allowed to take the house on the condition Hayes retained a room. Still sick with grief from losing Lawless, Peg pulled herself together enough to pack up and return to Wood Street and join them. Her house was conveniently situated just behind Dublin Castle, a considerable advantage being its proximity to potential military beaux.

On her return to the centre of the city, Peg began to settle back into her life of freedom. On advice from her friends, she began to go out more and, although she was still tired and listless, new flirtations began to revive her. Although she had grieved for all these months, Peg had not yet given up hope of hearing from Lawless. She lamented, 'I conceived he must have been dead, or what was still more grievous to me that he was ungenerous, ungrateful, and had forgotten me.'

Despite his lack of consideration, she was determined to remain faithful to him, admitting, 'Faithless though he was to me, I still had so much affection for him, that I could not reconcile to myself the admitting any other person to my bed.' This was not for want of admirers. Since she had returned, swarms of old friends gathered round to pay suit to her. Her absence had made her a 'new face' about town, and men were asking her out and paying her attention. Her old swain Captain Benjamin Matthews temporarily re-emerged, but she continued to resist his advances, even though he had offered to take her to America to try and find Lawless on condition she marry him if their quest failed. Jilted once again, Matthews returned to England.

Lawless had left for America at a time when emigration from Ireland was becoming increasingly commonplace, with over 100,000 people leaving for America in the eighteenth century. As early as the 1720s, concerns were raised about the number of people leaving Ireland; Primate Boulter, Church of Ireland Bishop of Armagh rued it, 'The humour has spread like a contagious distemper, and the people will hardly hear anybody that tries to cure them of their madness. The worse is that it affects only Protestants, and reigns chiefly in the north, which is the seat of our linen manufacture.'[4] Many emigrants were of Scottish-Irish origin, mainly Presbyterian, or were first- or second-generation descendants of Scottish men who had settled in Ulster and then moved to North America. However Anglicans and Quakers of English stock also left, as well as Catholics, who made up around 75 per cent of the total emigrants.[5] Ships were leaving from ports such as Belfast, Derry, Cork and Newry. Greg, Cunningham and Company had four ships plying between New York and Dublin, Newry, Belfast and Derry. Irish imports were vital to New York, so much so that one merchant had written in 1762, the 'scarcity of provisions which are dear would be distressful only for Irish imports'. David Colden, interested in land colonization in America, would write in 1773, 'I find many settlers are coming in this year from Britain and Ireland.'[6] However, no official records of arriving immigrants exist for the United States prior to 1820. And so, once again, Peg was left to fend for herself as best she could.

* * *

Eighteen months after Lawless had left, Peg still had no news from him. One morning Mr C., the same friend who had previously carried Lawless's final letter to her when he was about to leave for New York, called at Peg's house. This time the news was even less welcome, and angered rather than upset Peg. Mr C. informed her that Lawless had written to both his uncle and his brother and, on his asking them if a letter had been sent via them to Peg, the answer was negative. Her response was predictable:

> Cruel, base, deceitful, ungenerous man! Have I for this lived in obscurity, and refused the ample and generous offers of several gentlemen, to be thus neglected? No, I will no longer entertain any affection for thee! From this moment I will tear thee from my heart! From this hour I hate, I loathe, I detest thee; and I swear I will yield myself to the first agreeable and profitable offer that is made to me.

From then on, Peg resolved to cut all ties with Lawless. Her first regret was to have rejected Matthews, but it was too late, as he had already left for England. Now she resolved to give way to all the flattery of her suitors while giving them no satisfaction. 'In short', she says, 'I was to become a compleat *Coquet*.' She confessed, she 'gave them all hope, yet yielded to none'. It was time to accept some of the gifts on offer.

Sometime in the mid 1770s, Peg had recovered enough to embark on another affair, this time with a clergyman, Revd Thomas Lambert. As Peg explained, he 'had been very sedulously after me, while taking his degree for the Church, in the College. He renewed his acquaintance with me, and I gave him more encouragement than before.' Trinity College Dublin was seen as the university of the Protestant Ascendancy and was full of students, often from rich families buying their sons a good education. The college was a central point in Dublin and acted as a hub of young social life. Parliament could be seen on the other side of College Green. Those who were poor but clever sometimes obtained a scholarship and were allowed a free education in exchange for menial tasks. Known as sizars, they were usually 'sons of poor parents, frequently the clergy'.[7]

Lambert's parents, William Lambert and Catherine Barton, appear on the peerage list,[8] but Thomas was intelligent (and presumably poor enough) to be awarded a scholarship. He had graduated in 1767 as a Bachelor of Arts, and was already a clergyman when he finally embarked on an affair with Peg.[9] Clergymen in the eighteenth century were less prone to follow propriety or remain chaste than today. It was said that Peg's establishments were even patronised by bishops.[10] Many were caught up in the various scandals of the day, and as long as they remained discreet during an affair, it was unlikely to attract any gossip. Each morning Lambert called to see her and, when she allowed him to, take supper and wine with her in the evenings. Peg was still an attractive-looking woman, with men swarming round her. She enjoyed the attention and was really only interested in Lambert as a protector, whom she admitted 'supported me in the most luxurious manner'. Peg was as fertile as ever, as she said, 'I soon proved with child of which he was not a little proud.'[11] The last one, fathered by Lawless, was sent out to a nurse.

Peg's children seem to have given her great enjoyment, even though she rarely mentions them. Of her children with Lawless she said, 'My care of them filled up every vacant hour of time. Happy period . . .' The constant round of childbearing was a major concern for women during the eighteenth century and any sexually active woman risked pregnancy. Apart from abstention and *coitus interruptus*, there was little available in the way of contraception for the Irish people in general as it was not something the Catholic religion allowed. Neither method was an option for courtesans. That which was in use was primitive to say the least. Sponges and douches, although popular in France, were not much used elsewhere. In England, condoms were available, but these tended to be used as a prophylactic against venereal disease rather than as a contraceptive. They were made of animal membrane such as catgut, with neat ribbons tied round the base of a man's penis, but were generally baggy and ill-fitting.

For those who contracted certain sexual diseases, infertility resulted, which at least allayed the fear of yet another pregnancy. In England, women had to resort to methods of early abortion using herbs or potions to dislodge the foetus, but there is little information to show how widespread this was in eighteenth-century Ireland. While the promulgation of a strict moral code was supposed to make the Irish more reticent to engage in sexual activity, it also had the effect of encouraging infanticide, the fear of stigmatisation contributing to its spread.[12]

Many men preferred to go without protection, and pick up prostitutes who were 'fresh in town' or had not been in prostitution for very long. Consequently, venereal disease was soaring. Most prostitutes came into contact with it at some time in their careers, and would suffer from vaginal sores, gleets and pubic lice. Syphilis and gonorrhoea were spreading rapidly all over Europe, and were still being treated as the same disease. Not until 1797 would they be suspected as being separate infections, a suspicion only confirmed in 1837. No effective cure was available, the main treatment being the use of mercury to induce salivation. Taken as a pill or smeared on as an ointment, it would poison the system and induce sweating to 'pull out the toxins'. No effective cure was available right through the following century. As late as 1868, surgeons such as Robert McDonnell told his medical students that there were 'few subjects at once so interesting and so perplexing'.[13]

Whether the health of women in Peg's position was any better than that of other women is impossible to say. No doubt Peg would have been better fed and sheltered than the street whores, so her body would have been physically stronger, but then venereal disease was an easy leveller. Men from the gentry such as James Boswell described their battle with venereal disease and doctors' complete failure to cure it. Boswell's dismay is palpable when he wrote in his diary that he had once again found himself afflicted with an eruption of the disease after beginning a fling with Anne Lewis, the actress whom he called Louisa. The entry for 18 January 1763 states, 'I this day began to feel an unaccountable alarm of unexpected evil: a little heat in the members of my body sacred to Cupid, very like a symptom of that distemper with which Venus, when cross, takes it into her head to plague her votaries.' Even when they kept long-term mistresses, men were often unfaithful and attended bagnios and brothels, seeking their pleasures elsewhere.

The affair between Peg and Lambert was short-lived. Despite Lambert supporting her 'in the most abundant manner', she was still restless. When Lambert left for the country, leaving her with enough money for her keep, she took up with a Mr Cashel, 'young, gay handsome, and an undoubted gentleman', but he had no money. The fact that she was 'very big with child' at this stage did not deter him. One night as she was entertaining him, he had to make a hasty retreat when Lambert unexpectedly returned from the country. Despite the fact that Lambert had sent in supper and wine, Peg refused to allow him to stay long, affecting an indisposition caused by her pregnancy. A considerate man, Lambert left her for the evening. The following night, she informed him that she would not be able to receive him again until after her lying-in because the pregnancy made her feel unwell. She suggested he take another mistress in the meantime, and introduced him to Kitty Netterville.

Such manoeuvrings were usual business for courtesans. Up until now, Peg had been a kept woman. She could have been any other woman cohabiting with a man who was not her husband but in a long-term relationship. She was, however, increasingly moving into the world of courtesanship. She obviously knew many of the women who were courtesans, like Kitty, who provided sex and companionship in exchange for luxurious accommodation, expensive gifts and an extravagant lifestyle. The difference between a kept woman (or a mistress) and a courtesan was slight but significant. A woman in Peg's position might well have lived with a man for protection, but she had not totally sold herself for purely material benefit. Now, she was on the cusp of turning professional. Courtesans often shared lovers, or passed on protectors. Harriette Wilson, Peg's literary successor in the world of courtesanship, related in her memoirs how she shared her lovers with her rival Julia Johnstone. In this sphere, these women often relied on each other for favours. The transition of Thomas Lambert from Peg to Kitty was therefore not unusual, and was swiftly undertaken one evening when the three of them dined together at Kitty's house on fashionable Grafton Street and Peg came home alone. A popular area among the elite, the street, named after Henry FitzRoy, the 1st Duke of Grafton, had regal connections. Kitty's elaborate house was a clear indication of her wealth, a necessary show if she were to acquire high-class clients. Although the trio had parted company amicably, with Peg strategically leaving Lambert behind in Kitty's care, Peg's fickleness was only too evident. She admitted, 'I had no sooner turned my back on the couple I had put together, but my old companion, jealousy, came to visit me. I resolved in my mind the agreeable hours I had passed with Mr Lambert, all his good and amiable qualities recurred to my remembrance. I saw they were all lost to me.'

Watching as the couple's affair progressed – despite having manipulated the switch herself – Peg soon began to see her mistake. As Kitty demanded various gifts of diamond jewellery, and expensive silks and satins for dresses from her new beau, she grew richer while Peg grew poorer. Peg complained, 'I could have cut my tongue for having desired him to visit Kitty', for now she 'made him bring her presents from every shop'. No longer attracted to Mr Cashel (who had been too poor to shower her with gifts), Peg saw her previous cash flow redirected towards her rival, although she had not had the foresight to fleece him quite so effectively as Kitty. Bitter with jealousy, Peg once again resorted to the same measure she had used before when Lawless had been caught in the house of Mrs Johnston, and told Kitty's protector about her dalliances with Lambert. Kitty's keeper, Alexander Kirkpatrick, an alderman and sheriff's peer of the City of Dublin known as the 'Nabob', had run up considerable bills for Kitty with Grogan the mercer, Tom Collins for silks and satins, and Moore the jeweller, so he was understandably vexed to find his mistress unfaithful.[14]

Given how serious it was for a mistress to lose her protector, Peg was showing a particularly malicious side to her personality. Taking vengeance when a woman had done her wrong was understandable, but Kitty had acted in good faith in this instance, even doing Peg a favour by taking the unwanted Lambert off her hands. Peg's excuse was that 'Kitty treacherously told him [Mr Kirkpatrick] all my secrets, and my attachment to Cashel.' What rankled with Peg was that Kitty had so ensnared Lambert that he would never return to her now. Gentleman that he was, Lambert paid for all Peg's lying-in expenses as she gave birth to his daughter. Kirkpatrick meanwhile ditched Kitty and found a suitable heiress to marry, a relation of the Earl of Belvedere. As revenge on Peg, Kitty hired a gang of uncouth ruffians to shout abuse in the upper gallery of the theatre whenever Peg attended.

Sometime in the mid-1770s, disillusioned with relying on men, Peg abandoned the life of a kept woman and turned to running her own brothel. Along with her friend Sally Hayes she opened a plush

establishment and commenced independent living. Sally was already a
fêted belle a decade earlier when a poem had appeared in the classified
ads in the *London Chronicle* for 20 September 1764, probably placed by
a past male admirer.

> Let me, unblest with native fire,
> A living subject praise;
> Who never struck the warb'ling lyre;
> And sing of Sally Hayes.
>
> Restless maid! Whose lovely face
> In every charm is dres'd;
> Whose mind possesses every grace
> That fills the human breast.
>
> The magic glance of such an eye
> Can nameless wishes raise,
> And bid the coldest bosom high
> For charming Sally Hayes.

With nothing and no one to hold her back now, Peg opened her first
house of entertainment on Drogheda Street. Although essentially a
place where men could go for companionship, sex and merriment, no
owner of such an elite establishment would have called it a brothel.
Those places were for common prostitutes, and Peg's women were
hand-picked, classically beautiful, charming and seductive. Each
would have their own particular allure.

The area was up and coming, and had been newly laid out only
twenty years before. The whole span from Drogheda Street running
down to Henry Street was developed to create an exclusive residential
square on an unprecedented scale. Full of bay-windowed houses, a
mall ran down the central section of the street, lined with low granite
walls and obelisks topped with oil-fuelled lamp globes. Newly planted
trees topped off the effect, to create a new, elite quarter intended for
richer merchants. A grand mansion, Drogheda House, which lay on
the eastern side, was rented by the 6th Earl of Drogheda. In 1777, the
Wide Streets Commission would obtain a financial grant from

Parliament and, over the next ten years, a myriad of dwellings and other buildings were demolished, and a new roadway and terraces laid out. Upon completion in 1790, one of the finest streets in Europe had been created.

Having settled into their new house, Peg and Sally were fast becoming the centre of attention in the city and set upon making Dublin their playground. They attended all the new plays, put themselves on show and invited all the men who displayed interest back to Peg's house for entertainment. While men were obviously expecting sex, operating a flash house entailed much more than simply providing it. Spectacular food had to be on offer and champagne flowing. Gentlemen might expect convivial conversation on all types of subjects from poetry and plays to current scandals. A courtesan had to be witty, pretty (or at least have an attractive personality) and be up to date with all the current gossip. Peg and Sally were all of these. Consequently, money was pouring in from clients, gifts were showered upon Peg and Sally, and they had plenty to live on. Nothing seemed about to dampen their spirits, and they had each other for companionship and support.

The city was opening up to offer new places of entertainment. Ranelagh Gardens had opened only a few years earlier in 1768, in imitation of its successful London version, a venture of William Hollister the organ builder. Mosse's Pleasure Gardens were still highly successful, and Peg and Sally would show themselves off to the *bon ton* as they paraded around the elegantly laid out shrubberies and paths. Open-air concerts provided music for the strolling visitors. Two or three nights a week, light music of the *divertimento* type such as arias from operas would fill the air. On specific celebrations, Handel's *Music for Royal Fireworks* would accompany the explosions which lit up the sky.[15] Arthur Young, who visited Dublin around this time, commented:

There is a very good society in Dublin in a Parliament winter: a great round of dinners and parties; and balls and suppers every night in the week, some of which are very elegant; but you almost everywhere meet a company much too numerous for the size of the apartments. They have two assemblies on the plan of those of London, in

Fishamble Street, and at the Rotunda; and two gentlemen's clubs, Anthry's and Daly's, very well regulated.[16]

The height of fashion was worn by all the city courtesans, and Peg and Sally were no exception. By necessity, they had to keep up with the latest style, although it was frequently they themselves who set the fashion. Their gowns were richly embroidered with brocades, silks and ribbons. They dressed their hair with ornaments – a few small ribbons, pearls, jewels, flowers, or decorative pins – but decorations were becoming increasingly elaborate. Some women had now taken to wearing all sorts of assorted material in their high-piled hair: feathers, vegetable matter and even miniature boats, although Peg settled for a more conservative coiffure. Judging by the two images thought to be of Peg, she wore her hair tightly drawn back from her face in a bun with braids or ribbons around it.[17] Hair was usually powdered to counteract greasiness, from a variety of materials made from the poorest quality in corn and wheat flour, to the best quality in finely milled and sieved starch. Powder was usually white, but it could also be brown, grey, orange, pink, red, blue or violet. The application of white powder over dark hair produced shades of light to dark grey. Both women and men displayed their respectability and status through white skin, and heavy make-up was considered more respectable than naturally light skin. Cosmetics also had the ability to hide disfiguring marks such as scars from the pox, acne and smallpox.

The gleeful pair shot off to the races in horse-drawn carriages with servants dressed in liveries of scarlet and gold. Peg employed Isaac Isaacs, the popular German Jewish musician, to follow them wherever they went, playing on his dulcimer. She had probably first spotted him when he played the theatre in Smock Alley in 1767–8. She had retained him as a patron for fifty guineas a year and said she would have her groom 'with the Dulcimer tied on his back, Isaacs playing on it, and another man on the violin, to play through all the walks'.[18] He also played for her at home at least once a week, often accompanied by a violin player. For the first couple of years of his engagement he played at any place she commanded, but then, as demand for his services grew, he became unresponsive to her requests. On numerous occasions, when Peg had travelled with friends to locations out of town, such as the beauty spots at the Dargle or at the Glen of Downs, she increasingly found him unavailable. As his popularity increased, he was called on to play at various functions and clearly enjoyed the celebrity, so she eventually let him go.

Peg had gone from serial monogamous mistress to infamous brothel-owner. In between she had had another child by her last long-term protector, Thomas Lambert, but since casting him off she had begun a merry-go-round of pleasure. However, Peg's heart was not really in it. She was merely affecting the appearance of bountiful hostess in order to survive. Although she professed to be enjoying the attention showered on her, she had effectively erected a barrier around her heart. No longer open to falling in love, she blocked out feelings for any man who might pay her attention. Next time, she would not let go as easily . . . or so she thought.

Violence and Brothel-keeping

But it is past, that day is spent and done,
And it has long been night, long night with me.

The American Revolution had been underway since 1775 and the British were struggling to maintain control over their rebellious colonial subjects. By June 1776, the Americans were in full control of most areas, but the Royal Navy had managed to capture New York City and make it their main base. Strangely, Peg does not discuss the war in any detail in her memoirs. Yet Lawless was in New York and she must have had her concerns. France, Spain and the Dutch Republic were secretly providing supplies and ammunition to the revolutionaries as early as 1776, with France openly joining the war in 1778, providing extra strength to the American rebels. Spain and the Dutch Republic joined in over the following years and Britain felt under threat of invasion. As the war was playing out in the background, Peg and Sally saw many a young soldier they knew go off to fight. Some would not return. Meanwhile, the women were keeping up their spirits 'on the town'.

It was now 1778, and Peg had not heard from Lawless for four years[1] when, out of nowhere, Peg received a letter from him. The missive came as a shock: he had arrived in Cork and wanted her to come and see him. She was at first unwilling to go running into his arms once again. As she herself confessed, 'I was greatly changed. The time was past when I would almost have given one of my eyes for a letter from him.' How could the man she loved have left her so easily, and failed to write to her once in all those intervening years? She was angry with him for having written at all, but for her to even consider going to him meant that she still felt lingering pangs of attachment. After all, he had fathered five of her dead children and they had shared a loving, if tempestuous, life together living as man and wife for over five years. While she vacillated, her friends voted in favour of her going to see him, not least because he might have brought back some money from America. In any case, as Sally pointed out to her, Peg already had a carriage and she would only have to borrow another couple of horses for the journey, so the expense would be trifling. She would also be happy to accompany Peg on her journey.

What is surprising in the midst of all this dithering is that she would even consider going back to a man who had been violent and left her without means – and when she was pregnant with his child. Peg no doubt knew that her feelings for him were irrational, but she told herself that it was the sensible consideration of money which influenced her final decision. Peg and Sally packed up enough clothes for a month, climbed into the carriage and off they went to Cork.

The journey would have meant at least two overnight stops, so Sally and Peg would have had to find lodgings on the way.[2] It was an uncomfortable trip, although at least Peg now had her own carriage and was not squashed into a stagecoach as she had been on other occasions. On seeing Lawless, she professed to having lost the passion that she previously had for him. She said, 'I did not look upon him with the same eyes as formerly; his neglect (a crime no woman can bear) had penetrated deep into my heart.' She had to let him know, 'I was entirely my own mistress, and was accountable to no one for my conduct or actions.'

Peg's plans were simply to enjoy all the city had to offer, and at Lawless's expense. The thriving city of Cork was bustling with life, though the old quarter was 'very close and dirty'. Arthur Young in his *Tour in Ireland 1776–79* remarked: 'Cork is one of the most populous places I have ever been in; it was market-day, and I could scarce drive through the streets, they were so amazingly thronged: on the other days the number is very great.' The city was dominated by Blackrock Castle, standing in place of the old four-storey tower which had been destroyed by fire in 1722, the new one built by the citizens at the cost of £296. It was now used by the corporation for banquets and 'convivial gatherings'. There was also an English coffee house opposite the

Exchange Coffee House located in Castle Street, near the boot and shoe makers.[3] Young wrote in his diary:

> I must remark that the country on the harbour I think preferable, in many respects, for a residence, to anything I have seen in Ireland. First, it is the most southerly part of the kingdom. Second, there are very great beauties of prospect. Third, by much the most animated, busy scene of shipping in all Ireland, and consequently, fourth, a ready price for every product. Fifth, great plenty of excellent fish and wild fowl. Sixth, the neighbourhood of a great city for objects of convenience.[4]

The huge harbour sheltered the enormous British fleets which were amassed during the American Revolution. Accordingly, sail-making had grown substantially. Economic expansion saw the development of the city as new buildings were erected. Various marshlands had been reclaimed, including Hammond's Marsh on the west of the city where Lawless took lodgings for Peg and Sally. The river channels between the marshes had been filled in to form a web of modernised streets incorporating St Patrick's Street, the Grand Parade, Henry Street, Grattan Street, Cornmarket Street and Sheare's Street. Peg was determined to retain her independence and kept their general monies separate from Lawless. Their lodgings belonged to 'an old stiff Puritan' as Peg called him, and she was highly amused at the thought of how shocked he would be to know that he had a couple of courtesans living in his house. While in Cork, Peg was determined to 'partake of every pleasure and amusement the city afforded' and they made daily excursions to various sites including the pretty village of Cove, Glanmire, the Rock and Sunday's Well.

Despite her protests that she no longer loved Lawless, Peg fell back into an easy relationship with him. She was disappointed to find he had returned from America without a fortune, but the fact that she so quickly fell in with him again points to a strong connection bred by familiarity. However, the commitment was no longer there, and his claim that he had been unable to send her letters because of the war fell on deaf ears. After all, Peg knew he had sent letters to his family.

After about a month, with all three of them running out of money, it was time for them to return to Dublin and attend to business. Within a few months, Peg found herself pregnant once again, this time with her ninth child, her sixth with Lawless. Her pregnancies do not appear to have detrimentally affected her business, as she continued to entertain clients. She may have been simply hostessing at this stage, but she must have been a woman worth knowing for men to continue to frequent her house. There were always plenty of other women in her establishment to choose from to take to bed.

Peg and Sally's establishment, however, was not without competition. Often, places had wine and spirit licences paid for with bribes. One newspaper suggested there were about seventy-four brothels in Dublin in 1776, rising to at least three hundred only nine years later.[5] Newspapers sometimes reported arrests and informed the public of which bawds were operating where. Lower-class whores operated from taverns in the worst areas of town such as the Rose and Crown tavern on George's Quay, and a man with a shilling in his pocket could always find a prostitute. Some brothels were disguised as shops, milliners' premises being particularly notorious for this activity; they also operated from a china shop in Fishamble Street, a hotel in Stephen Street and bagnios on the quays, in Fishamble Street and Smock Alley. Between Dame Street and the River Liffey there was a veritable maze of courtyards and back alleys with brothels patronised by soldiers, sailors, tradesmen and clerks.

Running a brothel was no easy task, particularly when there were gangs of unruly youths roaming the streets. Peg would have read about various assaults on brothels and prostitutes in the newspapers: Norah Beatty aka Mrs Marlow in Ross Lane (Bridge Street) had recently been upset when a riot occurred and prostitute Catherine Neale was assaulted, along with some of her co-workers. Worse was experienced by Catherine Halfpenny of Marshall Alley, Fishamble Street, when she was killed by rioters. Mrs Davis, who ran the brothel in Fishamble Street, would suffer damage to her 'china shop' in 1792 when four bucks pushed a blind horse into it. Prostitutes were frequently hurt when dealing with rough clients.

One of the most notorious gangs in Dublin was the Pinking Dandies, who rampaged through the city wrecking houses, attacking men and assaulting women. Unlike many other gangs such as the

Whiteboys and the Oakboys, the Pinking Dandies were from the upper classes at a time of relative prosperity for Dublin. Kitted out in splendid outfits, they targeted passers-by, jostling them and pricking them with their swords. One commentator wrote of them, 'some were sons of respectable parents, who permitted them to get up to man's estates in idle habits, with adequate means of support; others were professional students, who having tasted the alluring fruits of dissipation, abandoned their studies and took a shorter road to gain supplies, by means no matter how fraudulent.'[6] Often drunk and in bad temper after having lost at gambling, they would 'assail passengers in the street, to levy contributions, or perhaps, take a lady from her protector, and *many* females were destroyed by that lawless banditti.'[7] They targeted women, 'by exacting from unfortunate girls, at houses of ill-fame, their share of what they deemed booty'. Of their thuggery, Peg commented, 'They ran drunk thought the streets, knocking down whoever they met; attacked, beat, and cut the watch; and with great valour, broke open the homes of unfortunate girls, demolished their furniture of their rooms, and treated the unhappy sufferers with a barbarity and savageness, at which, a gang of drunken coal-porters would have blushed.'

In November 1779, Peg became the victim of an attack by the Pinking Dandies when they broke into her house, wrecked everything inside, threw her furniture onto the street and physically attacked her. The gang was headed by balloonist Richard Crosbie (1755–1824) who, along with his cronies, did so much damage that Peg was left severely traumatised. He was to become known as the man who made the first attempt to cross the Irish Sea in a balloon, starting from Ranelagh Gardens in Dublin on 19 January 1785, and became Ireland's first celebrated aeronaut. As a youth, though, he showed no compassionate qualities but was merely a hooligan in dandies' clothing. He had shown a talent for clock-making and mechanical engineering while a student at Trinity College, although he never graduated. According to his friend Irish judge Jonah Barrington, 'He was, beyond comparison, the most ingenious mechanic I ever knew.'[8] However Barrington also gives an idea of the boisterous life for young men at Trinity when he and Richard Crosbie were students. They not only raided houses, but attacked the theatres too:

All the ladies, well-dressed and peaceable people generally decamped forthwith, and the young gentlemen proceeded to beat or turn out the residue of the audience, and to break everything that came within their reach. These exploits were by no means uncommon; and the number and rank of the young culprits so great that, coupled with the impossibility of selecting the guilty, the college would have been nearly depopulated, and any of the great families in Ireland enraged beyond measure had the student been expelled.[9]

The attack on Peg's house was brutal and unrelenting. As Peg lay fitting on the floor, the Pinking Dandies swept through the house on a rampage. Even when the watch finally came, the gang did not run but turned to fight them, leaving them with considerable cuts and bruises. Only when the two sheriffs, Mr Moncrieff and Mr Worthington, appeared with the military in tow did the rioters disperse.[10]

Dr William Vance was called but, even though he was a competent physician, he failed to save the baby who died with its leg broken inside Peg's womb.[11] According to Peg, her two-year-old daughter died from shock as a result of the event, 'so frightened that she took to a fit of screeching, and never recovered of her terror, but died in the consequence of the fright.'[12] The house was wrecked, but Peg managed to have it repaired the next day while neighbours looked on at the disorder. The sheriffs left her with military guards to protect her from further assault. Peg said of her assailants, 'Thus, these magnanimous warriors, actually murdered two helpless infants, bruised and maltreated their defenceless mother, destroyed the furniture of the house, terrified a whole neighbourhood, and wounded some of the watch – for FUN. How void their hearts must be of humanity and true bravery.'

In a similar incident, Peg's friend Mrs O'Brien would also have her house trashed after she had gone to the country one Sunday. Her establishment in Cope Street was seriously damaged after being visited by a gang of soldiers. Although some of the culprits were caught carrying off her possessions, they were acquitted after one of the witnesses stood in the witness box 'having a drop too much to drink'.[13] O'Brien, represented by advocate barrister John Phillip Curran, a friend of Peg, sued for malicious damages for £2,000 against the city.

Although she only received damages of £173 11s. 4½d, with sixpence costs, at least she won her case.

Part of the problem with trying to protect vulnerable people from attacks of this kind was the inadequacy of the police force. The only policing at the time was the local watch, and the official Dublin police force was yet to be established. Each parish had a permanent 'watch' of fifteen, selected and overseen by the minister and church wardens and presided over by a constable. The watch were only employed to police crime between the hours of 11 p.m. to 5 a.m. from April to Michaelmas, then 10 p.m. to 6 a.m. for the rest of the year, meaning trouble outside these hours went unmonitored. Although an Act for Encouraging the Discovery and Apprehending of House-Breakers had been passed as early as 1706, offering rewards for the capture of criminals, not many citizens wanted to risk their lives to do so. It was also a long and arduous process trying to supervise an active watch. Many members of the watch were negligent of their duties, or the board failed to provide the parish with enough fit and able men. Further acts had been introduced in 1715 and in 1721, a report remarking, 'The watches have been much neglected by reasons of many persons refusing to watch when thereunto required', which resulted in corruption by the constable who hired the watch who 'collected from some of the inhabitants . . . greater sums of money than by law were due', yet still did not have as many watches as were deemed necessary.[14] Various other acts failed to get the watch up to scratch. By 1765 a fifth act was introduced, increasing the levy for the watch tax to nine pence, with the hours of the watch increased from 10 p.m. to 5 a.m. in summer; 9 p.m. to 6 a.m. in spring and autumn; and 8 p.m. to 7 a.m. in winter. The seventeenth and eighteenth acts were raised as a response to concern about policing the Liberties and the rest of the city. The governors of the Lying-in Hospital levied a tax on houses in Rutland (now Parnell) Square to raise £128 a year to pay for the constable and eight 'able and creditable watchmen' to police the immediate neighbourhood. Gangs of ruffians could easily over-power these inexperienced volunteers.

The lack of adequate policing meant prostitutes often partnered up to open brothels together, a practice which afforded them some protection from brutality. Attacks on brothels were quite frequent,

Printed for John Bowles at the Black Horse Cornhill.

W. Hoare pinx.   **Miss Plunkett.**   *J. Watson fec.*

A print from William Hoare's supposed portrait of Peg: this is one possible candidate for a real likeness of Peg, though none can be definitively confirmed as showing her (see p.191).

The 2nd Duke Leinster, William Robert FitzGerald, one of the most important men in Ireland and a regular client of Peg's.

Thomas Gainsborough's portrait of Anglo-American scientist Count Rumford (Benjamin Thompson), a supposed spy and inventor of a popular new form of chimney, and a subject of Peg's gossip.

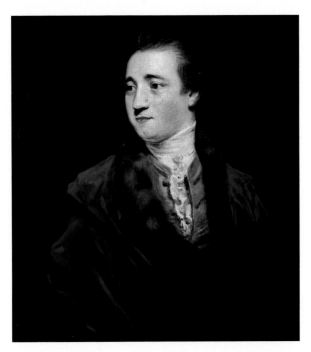

Charles Manners, 4th Duke of Rutland, Lord Lieutenant of Ireland
(1784–7) and one of Peg's favourite clients: this portrait is by Sir Joshua
Reynolds. His wife, Mary Isabella Somerset, Duchess of Rutland,
(below) was a celebrated figure in Dublin society.

JOHN, EARL OF WESTMORLAND.

John Fane, 10th Earl of Westmorland, Lord Lieutenant of Ireland
(1789–94) and a client of Peg's: his wife, Sarah Anne Child
(below) was the daughter of wealthy banker, Robert Child.

Anne Catley, a celebrated singer and actress whose reputation Peg tried to ruin.

Captain John Hayes St Leger, a noted 'rake' and a favourite of Peg's: this print was made from Gainsborough's 1782 portrait of him.

Batoni's portrait of Joseph Leeson, 2nd Earl of Milltown, an important man in Peg's early life.

Pompeo Batoni's *Portrait of a Lady as Diana*, sometimes said to be Peg, but more likely to depict a member of the Leeson family (see p.191).

but it was not unusual for the owner to successfully sue for compensation. However, taking a case to court was no easy matter – harder for a woman than a man, and even harder still for a known whore. Virtually every aspect of English life in the eighteenth century was influenced by perceptions about women's role and how they should behave. In Ireland, poorer women would have had to work hard on the land alongside men if the family was to survive. In the well-off cities such as Dublin, Cork and Belfast, respectability was as necessary as it was in London if a person was to be accepted in society. Even in the *demi-monde* of Peg and her female friends, they would have had to assume a certain air of propriety in order to engage with their upper-class clients.

Long-established views of gender roles permeated society; men might be ruffians, but their behaviour was largely accepted as part of their make-up. It was understood that men were prone to violence, obstinacy and selfishness, but ruled by their minds, while women were perceived to be ruled by their emotions and their bodies, known to be naturally lusty, excessively passionate and unreasonable. Because the law made men legally responsible for women, any financially independent woman was seen as unruly. The fact that a courtesan could do as she pleased because of her financial independence did not sit easily with a group of men of the middling sort expecting women to know their place. These views carried over into the administration of the law. Since women were meant to be seen and not heard, any woman showing up in court was seen as brazen for showing herself in public.

Peg wasted no time in filing her own suit against seven of the ruffians whom she recognised as Trinity College students, including Crosbie. As soon as Crosbie heard that Peg was threatening to prosecute, he started to bully her and made threats against her life. No slouch in defending herself, Peg immediately retorted that she kept a couple of pistols in her pocket and she would blow his brains out if he came near her. Some of the accused youths repaired to the country, worried about court action, while others continued to harass Peg at home. If Crosbie thought he would escape punishment because of his high birth and good connections, he was mistaken. The prosecution saw to it that he was detained for two days in Newgate. As Dublin's main jail, it had originally been one of the city gates situated at Cornmarket, near Christ Church Cathedral, on the south side of the River Liffey. It had become old and dilapidated and, between 1773 and 1781, a new prison was being built in Little Green Street near Smithfield. Thomas Colley, the architect, designed the building, but unfortunately it was so badly planned that a proper sewage system could not be installed. Security was poor, the boundary wall being the rear wall of the cells, and the place was cramped with as many as fourteen to a cell.

The fact that a baby had died during the attack, a detail which her physician was prepared to swear to, meant Crosbie could be charged with murder. The murder of a child in utero was a capital offence, and he was therefore detained without bail. With a possible death sentence hanging over him, Crosbie was quick to try and make amends and ensure some recompense for Peg, pleading for forgiveness. Counsellor Theobald Wolfe of Aungier Street suggested that if found guilty he would hang. The sheriffs prevailed on Peg to drop the murder charge, which she eventually did, but she continued with her prosecution against Crosbie for damage to her home. Judge William Henn, Third Justice in the Court of the King's Bench, oversaw the trial as witnesses came forward to describe the extent of the damage done to the house and to attest to the violence of the assault. The jury returned a verdict of guilty and Crosbie was fined and confined to jail. He could not have served a long sentence, as he was out by the time Peg pursued him for damages in a second trial. This time, Peg received proper financial recompense from him.

Although the other rioters had absconded, Peg issued 'green-wax' processes against them (the summons was sealed with green wax), by which means a court could order fines and forfeiture of goods against known felons. This, of course, ensured they all disappeared out of Dublin as quickly as possible. In the long term, Peg would forgive Crosbie, even shaking hands with him as she saw him off on his first balloon flight from Ranelagh Gardens. Its seems this aspect of Peg's conduct, when she deferred to men who had been violent to her in the past, was a reflection of the times, since most women of her status had to live with violence in their lives.

What became of the Pinking Dandies? Some members of the gang continued to terrorise people throughout Dublin until the establishment of the Dublin police force. Several of them went to London and took to the gaming tables there; two of them were even admitted to St James's Street clubs, one commentator mentioning, 'I have often seen them walking and conversing with high fashionables.'[15] Money, as usual, would protect the guilty.

Spats and Trips

Oh Man! Man! Sex of deceit!

Peg was now in her thirties, a mother nine times over, but with none of her children living as far as can be ascertained. The only child who may have survived was her first, with Dardis, whom she never mentioned after the birth. Evidently, she had kept Lambert's daughter with her in the house at Drogheda Street – hidden away on the top floor with her nurse – but this child, too, had died in the assault by Crosbie's mob.

No longer in her prime, it is unlikely Peg could attract the young men she had in her youth. Nor did she have a wealthy protector. The men she had lived with so far had failed to live up to her expectations, either in terms of money or love. While acting was considered moderately more respectable than whoring, both were thought to be unsuitable professions for a lady. A woman putting herself on public view was viewed with some disdain in polite society, although actresses would still attract admiration for their skills on the stage. Whores, on the other hand, would garner praise only for their wit, looks, personality and ability to perform in bed. For a successful woman, a career in entertainment, be it whoring or acting, depended to a large degree on looks. There was every reason to see why a misunderstanding occurred with a younger, more highly skilled performer who came under Peg's scrutiny.

The celebrated singer Anne Catley often appeared at the Smock Alley Theatre. Born in Tower Hill, London, in 1745, she was one of a number of poor young girls who had turned to entertainment to make a living. She had started off in her youth singing in taverns to officers of the Tower of London and was soon spotted by theatre producer William Bates. While serving an apprenticeship with him, she sang at Vauxhall Gardens before moving on to debut at Covent Garden Theatre company as the pastoral nymph in Thomas Arne's *Comus* in 1762. As with many other women who became mistresses, she was rebellious and threw away opportunities which might well have served her better in the long term. She had reneged on her performance contract to run off with the reprobate Baronet Sir Francis Blake Delaval (1727–71) with whom she had embarked on an affair. She became hugely popular in Dublin, having an impressive run there after Charles Macklin had spotted her and set her up to play at Dublin's Smock Alley Theatre in 1763. Her popularity grew when, in May 1765, she gave a free performance, raising £66 13s. in aid of the Lying-in Hospital, when the usual takings were £6. Of her svelte figure and brown freckled face, playwright and actor at Smock Alley, John O'Keeffe wrote, 'she was one of the most beautiful women I ever saw: the expression of her eyes, and the smiles and dimples that played round her lips and cheeks, enchanting'.[1] Dramatist James Boaden would say of her, 'no other female singer ever gave the slightest notion of her. She was bold, volatile, audacious; mistress of herself, of her talent, and her audience.'[2] The *Morning Post* for 8 October 1776 claimed her portrayal of Euphrosyne was a role 'in which she delighted, and astonished with her vocal powers'. Playing to a full house, she was reputed to have earned forty guineas a night. She had met Lieutenant-Colonel Francis Lascelles (1744–99) around 1768, marrying him in 1771 and bearing eight of his children. It was easy to see why Peg might see her as a rival – a handsome younger woman with a permanent protector, and a talented actress, praised by all who saw her.[3] In short, Catley had it all.

A battle ensued between the two women, and the instigator seems to have been Peg, even as she admits in her memoirs. Through a gentleman of her acquaintance, Peg had heard that a scurrilous attack had been made on her reputation by Catley, although she had not a shred of evidence and must have been used to gossip by this point. Peg lost no time at all in racing round to the actress's house, where, still fuming, she waited to confront her, Catley not being at home at the time. Unsuccessful in her mission on the first occasion, Peg allowed a couple of days to pass before seizing her next opportunity. By chance, as she was passing in her carriage, Peg saw Catley standing at the stage door at Smock Alley so she pulled over and beckoned to her. She then demanded an explanation as to why her name had been sullied in such a scandalous manner. Catley appeared surprised at the allegation, denied it and accused the man who had reported it of being a liar. Thinking no more of it, Catley made to return to the theatre, but Peg, her temper now up, called out from her carriage 'you little street-walking, London ballad-singer'. An hour later, unwilling to let the matter drop – and it sounds as if Peg was now stalking her rival in a bid to humiliate her in public – Peg spotted her walking down Dame Street. She stood outside the mercer's shop at the corner of Parliament Street waiting for the actress to come within earshot, and started to harangue her again. Catley was totally unprepared for such an assault in broad daylight and stood there aghast. In a bid to escape Peg's tirade, she hastily picked up her son who was with her at the time and fled into the nearest shop for refuge, where she promptly fainted. On her return home, she reported the incident to her husband Colonel Lascelles, who, as a long standing member of the military establishment at Dublin Castle, had influential friends. He immediately engaged an attorney to sue Peg for slander, since Catley alleged that Peg had called out that she hoped the postilion would 'drive over her, and her bastards'.

The case went to court and was tried before a judge and jury. The legal system of the time, to a large extent, rested on economics and how much money a person had. Such cases would come before the petty jury rather than a grand jury, used for greater crimes. The fundamental qualification for petty jury service was a man's status as a 'freeholder', with between 67 and 92 per cent of jurors being merchants or artisans.[4] While those who devised the laws and presided over trials as judges were from the elite in the Irish Parliament, as well as the king's representatives in Dublin Castle, it was cobblers, candle-makers and shopkeepers who were entrusted with the responsibility of applying these laws as petty jurors. The Lord Lieutenant maintained personal control over the appointment of most of these positions, but the less public aspects of this infrastructure, namely crown witnesses and informers, offered possibilities of corruption. In this case, the gentlemen of the jury were in favour of Peg, who had spent a small fortune on their wares over the years and were heard to murmur 'it would be a pity not to favour a woman, who, by spending considerable sums among the traders of this city, was of service to it, preferable to a woman who was only a bird of passage; who came here to pick up all she could from the public then carry it off to another country; as it was well known that Catley never laid out a single farthing in Dublin that she could avoid.' The fact that people came over to Ireland, made money and took it back to England was a bone of contention for many in the country. They had long since watched as money poured into the coffers of the richer Protestant merchants. Having been brought up in Ireland within the Catholic faith, Peg's allegiance was with the economically and politic- ally disempowered Irish Catholics. She placed Catley firmly in the enemy camp, the side which had squandered and pillaged all of Ireland's natural resources and hot-footed it back to Britain. Catley had become the scourge of Ireland, and so finished another battle in which the case was thrown out, and as Peg triumphantly declared, 'the Petticoat prevailed over the Sword and Gorget'.

Despite the showy public life she shared with Sally Hayes, Peg was still in mourning. The death of both her unborn baby fathered by Lawless and her infant daughter by Lambert had seriously affected her, particularly since they had been her only remaining children. Her trust in Lawless was gone, but while separated, they remained in communication and their relationship limped on. Lawless left for London after the death of his father in order to attend to his affairs, although unfortunately for both him and Peg 'what he left him was scarce worth mentioning'. Thereafter she frequently received letters from him suggesting she sell all her property and join him, but she reasoned that it was better to stay in Dublin 'immersed in all the pleasures of the world, and be entirely my own mistress'. She could see her own savings would be drained away looking after him. Yet still the biggest attraction of going to London was that Lawless was there – whatever her protestations had been in the past, he was still the love of her life.

Lawless was clearly hoping to inherit some money now his father was dead, but his remaining family continued to refuse to provide him with an annuity. He was obviously a 'ne'er-do-well' in their eyes and they intended to keep the family estate out of his hands. Meanwhile, Peg was 'straining every nerve to serve him, and sending him every assistance' in her power. Although they'd previously had fallings out, Kitty Netterville was helping by making applications to all the army captains they knew in order to put in a good word for a possible commission for Lawless. Peg was even sending him money. He responded with gratitude and wrote to her, 'I am obliged to you and Mrs Netterville, for both your good intentions, and most friendly dispositions to serve me.'

Peg had been left seriously ill after the attack by the Pinking Dandies and he'd supported her in her attempt to sue those responsible. 'It gives me infinite satisfaction to hear you are likely to recover, what I am thoroughly sensible, is nothing more than your right, and that you may be successful is my most ardent wish; it affords me not a little pleasure, to find you have those different miscreants you mention, so much in dread and awe of you.' He ends his letter of Monday, 28 February 1780: 'Great news this day, of Admiral Rodney's success.' Lawless had just heard the news of the outstanding victory of the relief of Gibraltar during the Great Siege, and the prevention of attempts by Spain and France to capture it from the British during the American Revolution. George Brydges Rodney, 1st Baron Rodney (1718–92) had captured a convoy of sixteen Spanish ships on 7 January 1780, off Finisterre, and a few days later, off Cape St Vincent, during the famous Moonlight Battle, had completely defeated Admiral Langara, the Spanish commander. While the uprising of the American colonies had no direct effect on Peg, London was agog with gossip and London was about to be rocked by the Gordon Riots, an uprising by Protestants against Roman Catholic emancipation led by Lord George Gordon.[5]

Feeling in low spirits, with her finances ebbing away and no doubt missing Lawless, finally Peg made a decision to leave Ireland and try her luck in London. She paid off all her debts, left a few hundred pounds in the bank, and sequestered the rest of her money in a secure place. One of the safest spots for a woman to hide the valuables was in a pouch about her person. Most women would have had at least one pocket which served as a place to keep their valuables and immediate necessities. None of these pockets were obvious, but were sewn into petticoats, in skirts or under clothes. In these, Peg discreetly hid most of her money or trinkets to ensure they could not be easily stolen.

The Irish Sea was choppy and the weather mostly poor for her journey. Small packet boats were the main mode of transport for passengers crossing between Ireland and England. One couple of travellers, Mr and Mrs Hall, described such a boat: 'The Sailing Packet was a small trade-schooner or sloop. The cabin, of very limited extent, was lined with "berths", a curtain portioning off those that were intended for ladies.'[6] Formal meals were rarely provided on board. Each passenger laid on their own supply of 'sea-store' to which they resorted when hungry or thirsty. 'The voyage was a kind of purgatory' with only an awkward steward boy to assist the seasick passengers. Although the journey could be made in a few days, it sometimes turned into weeks, as the wind blew back and forth, and ships were forced to dock and wait for the weather to turn.

Peg's fear of sailing was not unfounded. Shipwrecks were common, with ships going down every year or so, sometimes with passengers on board. Many of the wrecks which occurred over the centuries could be seen at low tides on the North and South Bull and on Portmarnock beach north of Dublin Bay, particularly after sand and mud had been stripped away following storms.[7] Only a few years before, on 25 January 1775, a schooner *Polly*, sailing from Newfoundland to Waterford, was lost a mile east of Ballycroneen Bay in a heavy gale on the Cork coast. The captain and three others were lost and four saved. In the same gale the brigantine *Geddes*, laden with wheat and sailing from Maryland to Liverpool, was driven ashore, also in Ballycroneen Bay. The crew and passengers were saved with some difficulty, but it was thought the vessel would be lost.[8] Fortunately for Peg, her crossing was safe, and she arrived in one piece to start her new life.

On her arrival in London, Peg moved into lodgings with Lawless, but she was soon to find out that he was keeping another woman, a Miss Sharman, at another lodgings behind her back. A gossipy friend of the woman with whom she was staying knew about Lawless's mistress, although she tried to cover it up. After all the loving declarations that Lawless had written begging her to come to London, the news came as a shock. She remarked, 'To think, that he had formed such a connection at a time, when he was continually writing in the most affectionate terms, and urging me to come to him, hurt me greatly.' Her venture had been for nothing. Having enticed her to a city where she had no acquaintances, and with no intention of remaining faithful to her, Lawless was simply no longer worth the effort. Thwarted, yet reluctant to return to Ireland so quickly defeated, Peg was determined to move on and fend for herself as best she could. From now on, she would cut herself off from him completely.

In a trice, Peg packed up all her belongings in a trunk and left Lawless for new lodgings. She was determined to enjoy herself in London while she had the chance. She had money, she had a roof over her head, and she was single. Although Lawless found her address, she left his letters unanswered and instead concentrated on finding her enjoyment elsewhere. She hired a companion, an Irish woman who had been the wife of a respectable merchant in Dublin, but who had been turned out after her husband had caught her in bed with another man. Together, they went to live in an elegant house at 4 Cleveland Row, which Peg rented for them. Pall Mall had replaced the ancient highway which stretched from Charing Cross to St James's Palace, and the surrounding area was known for its beautiful buildings, among them the royal residences of Spencer House and St James's Palace, as well as parks where they could stroll or ride. Warwick House formed the eastern extremity of this ancient highway which, to the west of the palace, continued along what is now Cleveland Row, and thence across the fields which are now Green Park to Hyde Park Corner.[9]

As Peg made her way around the city, she would have been familiar with the sight of the wheelbarrow boy who rolled his chestnuts round the streets and the old grey-haired woman who sang ballads on the corner of the Covent Garden piazza. Tinkers wandered up and down the roads crying the sale of their pots and pans, while sooty chimney sweeps wandered past the large houses of Marylebone touting for work. London at this time was one of the busiest capitals in the world. Thousands of people were migrating from the country to try and earn a living – an estimated 675,000 people were living and working in the environs of the metropolis by mid-century. Many of them were visible on the streets. Outside Drury Lane Theatre, young girls sold oranges to passers-by, and tradesmen of all descriptions – knife-grinders, watermen and sedan chairmen – shouted their services. At the bottom of the heap, rag-pickers and rat catchers scavenged the gutters to see what they might find.

Countless brothels were to be found around the city, from the basest in Covent Garden to the richest in Mayfair's St James's Street. Peg would easily have spotted the streetwalkers in their shabby clothes and heavy make-up. All manner of services were on offer, from a quick fumble in the back room of a tavern to the flagellant services offered in Portland Street. With trips to the theatre, dancing until midnight at Ranelagh Gardens, watching fireworks at Vauxhall and drinking until dawn, Peg enjoyed herself as best she could, despite her hurt feelings, using up the remaining money she had brought with her from the sale of her property.

Peg's house was a stone's throw from St James's Palace, where official royal functions, such as receiving visiting ambassadors, took place. The royal family lived in Buckingham House, which King George III had bought in 1761 for his wife and growing family to live in. By the 1780s, the Prince of Wales had become a drinker, a gambler and a womanizer. His love life was the cause of much gossip after a string of affairs with actresses, and was causing great concern to his father. He had fallen for Mary Robinson, known as 'Perdita' after her role in *The Winter's Tale*, then taken up with another actress, Elizabeth Armistead, while she was still mistress to Lord George Cavendish, making further conquests of Grace Dalrymple, Elizabeth Billington and Countess von Hardenburg. Of the latter, he would gush in a letter to his brother Frederick, 'O did you but know how I adore her, how I love her, how I would sacrifice every earthly thing to her.'[10] Once Prince George turned twenty-one in 1783, he was given an allowance from Parliament of £60,000 (over £6m today) and an annual income of £50,000 from his father. He settled into Carlton House, entertaining friends and leading a profligate life. He had yet to meet Maria Fitzherbert – a commoner twice widowed, six years his senior and a Roman Catholic – and disgrace his family still further.

It was in the Strand one day that Peg first encountered the Prince of Wales, at that time around eighteen or nineteen years of age. Supposedly by chance, she had entered the same shop just as the prince was ordering new waistcoats to be made up. Peg immediately ordered the same silk materials, and instructed them to be sent to her shoemaker in Dublin, a jibe at the prince's choice, much to his bemusement. Such tall tales of encounters with royals were common in memoirs of courtesans since it gave readers high-class gossip, but possibly many of them were untrue. Everyone was keen for the latest tit-bit about the prince. Peg would not, however, claim to have had an affair with him, unlike countless others. A further encounter took place as she was out riding en route to Richmond to have dinner with friends and the prince was on his way to his house there. On hearing a shout for her to make way on the road for the prince's carriage, she refused and retorted, 'There is room sufficient, there is one-half the road for him; and I have as much right to the other half, as he or anyone else.' The prince scowled at her 'and looked as sour as if he would have bitten my nose off' as he passed.[11] Not put off, she galloped to keep up with him until he reached the gate of the park to Richmond Palace simply to make a nuisance of herself. Although the palace is no longer standing, the gatehouse can still be seen at the entrance to Richmond Park.

Stealing by housemaids and servants was a perennial problem. At the end of that particular evening Peg fell ill after dinner, and so began a tide of events which would lead her back to Ireland. What started off as a severe pain in her side turned to 'pleuretic fever'. While she had agreed to share a ride in a carriage home from Richmond with one of her friends, she refused to miss the evening's ball. After dancing all night and dissipating most of her energy, the fever erupted. As the night wore on, her breathing became increasingly laboured as fluid began to collect on her lungs. The result was the onset of pleurisy, and a dry cough took hold. As a consequence, she took to her bed for a month. She was unable to get out of bed or to look after herself, still less to keep a check on her household. Unfortunately it was Peg's incapacity which gave her employees the opportunity they had been waiting for. Seven diamond brooches, a gold watch and a trunk of Peg's clothes went missing. The fact that Mrs Green had disappeared pointed to her guilt, but since she could not be found, Peg had two of her domestic servants apprehended and held in Bridewell Prison in Tothills Field. Mrs Green was never found.

On her recovery, Peg thought it time to take stock. The money she had was nearly exhausted, so she had no means of replacing the stolen items. In her line of work, it was necessary to have all the accoutrements of a glitzy lifestyle; without them, she could not attract attention. In any case, she hated London and it had done her no good. Lawless had crushed her feelings irrevocably, her servants had proved disloyal and her health had suffered. She had tried her best to make her situation work, but she had failed and now felt it was time to go home. Without further hesitation, she sold off her furniture and everything in the house, tucked away all her valuables and money in her pocket – bar twelve guineas for the cost of the transport – and made her way to Holyhead, where she took Wybrant's packet boat back over to Ireland. She had never been so glad to set foot on her native soil.

Returning Home

In Dublin's Fair City . . .

Coming in to dock, Peg breathed a sigh of relief at the thought of being back in Dublin. From a distance, Peg could see the Poolbeg Lighthouse, which had first shone in 1767 using candles as its light source. As the boat drew closer to St George's Quay, the South Bull Wall loomed into sight. The quay was the main point of arrival and departure for England, where passengers could book tickets for Holyhead or Parkgate, the two main nearest ports. Famous people had stepped ashore here such as Jonathan Swift in 1723 on his return from London, Handel in November 1741, and John Wesley in August 1747 after a twenty-six-hour journey. Not wanting to delay, Peg hired a sedan chair and headed to the house of her friend Moll Hall in Mecklenburgh Street, where her friends awaited her. She had known Moll for some years, as she ran a similar establishment to Peg's and they shared clients.

Squeals of delight greeted her as she opened the door to the house and Sally Hayes and Moll Hall fell upon her. Both women were over-joyed to see her, and only too willing to help out, a kindness Peg now needed. Most of Peg's money had gone on presents bought in London before she had taken the packet boat over and her belongings were still sitting in the customs house awaiting clearance. Many of the items in her luggage were taxable. A mass of prohibitions, tariffs and taxes meant that few goods could be imported freely. As a result, smuggling had grown extensively, and evasion of levies on imports had become increasingly attractive. A new custom house was being designed by

James Gandon, and work on the building would begin in the summer of 1781.[1] Luckily, most of the custom officers were well acquainted with Peg, so when she returned the following day to pick up belongings, her trunks were let through without search. The officers shouted in unison, 'Oh fie, sure you would not suspect Mrs Leeson for having any contraband goods. She has nothing but her own apparel.' This was just as well, since her trunks were packed with new gowns, rings and silver buckles she had brought back for herself and as gifts for friends – luxury items which surely would have been taxed. It was essential she looked the part for her re-entry into the Dublin *demi-monde*. She had to exude wealth and glamour and put on a show for the gentlemen of the aristocracy. Only her two closest friends could know the true extent of her dire circumstances.

Plenty of people were worse off. By 1780, the population of Ireland had grown to about four million,[2] but many of these were on the brink of starvation, having to steal fuel and timber to keep warm. While living standards in general had been rising since the famine of 1740–41, two-thirds of the population still existed mainly on oatmeal and potatoes.

On the political front, Peg had returned at a time of uncertainty for Ireland. Henry Grattan, as leader of the Patriots (those who supported personal liberty and felt a strong Irish identity, but rejected full independence, advocating strong self-government within the British Empire) and a member of the Irish House of Commons, had watched with interest as the American Revolution spun out of the control of the British. Concerns were raised about possible similar battles for Irish independence from Britain, or invasions from Spain or France. British militia were still fighting in America, and fewer soldiers were left to defend Ireland in case of attack. Since Irish Catholics were not allowed to bear arms, Grattan therefore persuaded the British Parliament to authorise a volunteer Protestant militia to guard against a possible Franco-Spanish revolutionary invasion. This group would eventually back a campaign to prevent imports and promote only the use of Irish-manufactured goods. As a campaigner for legislative freedom for the Irish Parliament, Grattan would have been supported by Peg, as her politics stood in defence of Ireland. Although she did not often express her political ideas, it is evident that throughout her life she would retain a strong affiliation with Irish Catholics and would condemn the constant flow of taxes and goods to Britain at Ireland's expense.

More pressing issues than politics were on Peg's mind as she plotted her re-entry into Dublin society. It was the new decade of the 1780s and the changes were ringing in Dublin. The Bank of Ireland Act had recently made provisions for extending credit,[3] which was always a good sign for business. Peg had few doubts about her potential success. She boasted, 'The celebrity of my name would open up the sluices of profit.' Accompanied by Sally, she decided to try out her new look. Dressing in newly purchased bell-hooped petticoats and expensive gowns, the women cut an impressive sight as they paraded through the town. Despite their inconvenient size and shape, bell-hoops had become popular in England and Peg was about to set the trend in Ireland as she reckoned hers were 'the first ever worn in Dublin'. The petticoats were made up of three or more graduated hoops of whalebone, hand-sewn into robust undergarments. They became the butt of many a joke by male commentators, as one of them complained: 'If the ladies had determined to do their best to excite the wrath of satirists, nothing could better serve the purpose.'[4] This may have been to do with the fact that the hoops were lightweight and easily upended by winds, making the wearer's naked flesh shockingly visible.

In 1741, one facetious article in the *London Magazine* of 1741 entitled 'The Modern Hoop Petticoat' explained:

> I have heard it objected, that the ancient Petticoat must necessarily too much confine the Woman's Legs; whereas the circular Hoop gave the Feet a Freedom of Motion, shew'd the Beauty of the Leg and Foot which play beneath it, and gain'd Admirers when the Face was too homely to attract the Heart of any Beholder; Some polite Defenders of the late 'convex cupolo' Hoops have observ'd in their Favour, that they serv'd to keep men at a proper Distance, and a Lady within that Circle, seem'd to govern in a spacious Verge sacred to herself.

However the virtue of women who wore hoops became the subject of suspicion: 'It was well known that many Ladies, who wore "hoops" of the greatest Circumference were not of the most impregnable Virtue.'[5] The sheer size of the hoop made them a problem for moving around, and carriages and doorways had to be modified – women often had to enter rooms sideways. Small rails were put in place around tables to stem the risk of small objects being swept off the top by errant hoops, and hoops were criticised for taking up too much space and discouraged at large assemblies and balls. At a court ball in 1780, 'the ladies wore such large hoops that one of them kept as much room as four people.'[6] Mr Neal, the treasurer of the Charitable Musical Society, made it a proviso for attendees at his new music hall that women remove the hoops from their skirts and men remove their swords so that 700 people might squash in.[7]

It was not long before Peg heard from Lawless again. On her return to Dublin, she had fired off a letter chastising him for his unfaithfulness. From his response, it looks like Peg had given him a severe reprimand, as he responded, 'On the subject you have been pleased to write, I have only to add, I never entertained the smallest partiality for that person, neither did I see her for full three months before I left Dublin.' He did, however, in his next letter, admit to having an affair elsewhere, presumably the one in London. 'I assure you it hurts me as much, as it nearly can you, your reflections on an affair, that each time I hear of, makes me hateful to myself; however after my candid declarations to you, it is not only unkind, but highly ungenerous in [sic] you, to upbraid me with what I now regret from my very soul.' Peg must have also brought up the topic of him being in Dublin again, as he replies to her, 'As to my being in Dublin, staying there or elsewhere, I am now fully convinced, can be no object to you.' In any case, he was too worried about the 'busy inquisitives at large' since his affairs had been 'been considerably injured by my last stay in Ireland'. His creditors were still after him and it was best to stay out of the country. The stockings he had sent to Peg as a gift she regarded as 'paltry', but Lawless evidently still held a sincere affection for her.

Since Peg had sold her property on leaving for London, she stayed with her friend Moll Hall until she could re-establish herself in Dublin. Gentlemen callers once again began to gather at Peg's door to welcome her home. Many offered banknotes, some brought wine, some came as friends, others out of curiosity. She procured herself a house on Wood Street (probably rented), a favourite area for Peg as it was conveniently situated for the men of Dublin Castle. The house was much larger than her previous one, and therefore expensive, but it had plenty of land at the back which she turned into an elegant garden. Here she lived with one of her old lovers for a year in great comfort, although she says no more about him.

To the delight of audiences, Signor St Giorgio and Signor Carnivalli, both musicians and impresarios, opened a new season of Italian opera at the Theatre Royal in Smock Alley in 1781–2. A new comic opera, *Alcina*, was to be performed, with the music by Signor Gazaniga to be conducted by the Italian organisers.[8] For the event, the latter had introduced new rules barring courtesans from entering their theatre, and anyone with a dubious sexual reputation was now unwelcome. Two of Peg's friends, Moll Hall and Miss Townley, had already been involved in an unseemly eviction on the opening night of the performances, an evening when Peg had been otherwise engaged. Although they had initially gained entrance to the better section of the theatre (the lattices), they had been unceremoniously asked to leave their seats and retire to the gallery instead.

Incensed by what she had heard, Peg was intent on making an entrance and causing such a scene as to convince the Italians to change their minds. Carnivalli had hired bully-boys – whom Peg had identified as Jackson and Wilson – to watch the doors and prevent any questionable ladies from entering the theatre. Accompanied by her friend Mrs Ann Judge, a courtesan and another rival of Kitty Netterville's, Peg was determined to get to her seat. With ticket in hand, she made directly for the stairs leading to the best seats in the house, only to be restrained by Jackson, one of the hired thugs. The two improbable wrestlers tussled for a time, but Peg was no match for such a large man and he simply picked her up and carried her back to the box office. Dishevelled, but infuriated once he had put her down, she turned on him and slapped his face with all her force. She called for Signor Carnivalli and demanded he explain himself. He told her forthrightly that while his season of operas lasted, she would never be permitted entrance. 'Very well, Sir,' she retorted, 'you'll abide by the consequences; and I'll bet you a hundred guineas I will.' With one earring lost and her clothes in disarray, she retired home in tears, furious that her companion Mrs Judge had stood by, mouth agape, watching Peg being manhandled, and done nothing to defend her.

That evening, after hearing about the incident, four noblemen dropped round to see Peg to offer their condolences. One of her clients with whom she had 'been intimate' happened to be a well-known barrister and was only too willing to help Peg procure warrants for assault and robbery; the former charge being the attack made on her by Jackson, the latter for taking her ticket from her for which she had properly paid. The following morning the warrants were drawn up, and George Roe, the keeper of Newgate Prison, acquired four mean-looking rogues with scarred faces to act as bailiffs to accompany Peg on her mission.[9] Just before 6 o'clock that evening, a coach took her to the theatre door where she had one of the men summon Signor Carnivalli on the pretext that a gentleman was waiting for him to pay over some subscription money. As Carnivalli came towards Peg's coach, she called out 'Holloa, boys!' as a sign to the bailiffs to grab the impresario and haul him away. Carnivalli began to protest wildly, but Peg called out, 'Here gentlemen, take this ruffian, and leave him in the centre of Newgate, and I shall accompany you myself.' As the rain poured down, Carnivalli's powdered wig grew damper and his soggy clothes clung to his body, the whole of his person wet through. Since the new prison in Green Street was in the process of being demolished between 1780 and 1782, it was the sight of Old Newgate in the Cornmarket that greeted him.[10]

Next it was the turn of the two thugs, Jackson and Wilson, who had laid their hands on Peg the previous night. Again, at a signal from Peg, the two were arrested and taken off to accompany their employer. All the while, the theatre-goers were watching the commotion. In a show of ingenious contrition, made in order to demonstrate her victory, Peg turned to the people waiting in the lobby, curtsied and apologised, 'Ladies and gentlemen, I am extremely sorry to deprive you of the pleasure you may expect from tonight's entertainment, but I have sent Mr Carnavalli [sic], the first fiddle, to Newgate, and am now sending two of his domestics after him.' She turned and exited, leaving the onlookers flabbergasted.

The incident was related in the *Morning Chronicle and London Advertiser* for Tuesday, 25 December 1781:

> In Dublin, the 10th inst. Sig. Carnevalle [sic], and two of the box-room keepers on Opera nights were committed to Newgate on a charge of Mrs Peg Plunkett, for grossly assaulting and abusing her the Wednesday evening before, and despoiling her of some ornaments during the scuffle of turning her away from the Opera. After remaining for some hours, they were released at the earnest application of some gentleman of distinction to the Sheriffs, and to the Magistrate on whose warrant they were committed; but we hear the affair will be finally determined in a Court of Judicature.

The next day was a Sunday and, after a sound night's sleep, Peg intended to go to see a military review of the Irish Volunteers. The volunteer army, made up of Irish Protestants, was up to 100,000 men strong. Outside of government control, they were armed and self-taught in the military arts, ready to defend Ireland from foreign invasion. They were formed in the Seven Years War (1756–63) when threats from abroad, notably France and Spain (such as the French landing at Carrickfergus in 1760, which Peg had witnessed with Dardis), were taken seriously. Local landlords had encouraged groups of men to come together for the protection of property and to preserve the peace. The units were made up mainly of Anglican Protestants, as under the Penal Laws only they were allowed to bear arms, but gradually Presbyterians and a limited number of Catholics were allowed to join after the Relief Act of 1778; subject to an oath renouncing Stuart claims to the throne and the civil jurisdiction of the Pope, it allowed Roman Catholics to own property, to inherit land and to join the army. Although there had been a British victory over the Spanish off Cape St Vincent in 1780, the Volunteers would continue to maintain their strength by involving themselves in the fight for free trade. They staged regular armed demonstrations in favour of Henry Grattan's reforming agenda under which he was agitating for a more favourable trading relationship with England. After pressure from the Volunteers and a parliamentary group led by Grattan, greater autonomy and legislative independence was given to the Irish Parliament in what some called 'the constitution of 1782'.

Watching them do their drill at the military parade was a popular spectacle, with people of all ranks attending. This particular event was at Phoenix Park, which was regularly used by the military. Inside the park, a number of lodges were used by government officers and other lesser officials involved in park management. As Lord Lieutenant of Ireland, the 4th Earl of Chesterfield had initiated considerable landscaping schemes in the park, including the planting of trees on either side of the main avenue and the erection of the Phoenix Column in 1747. He also opened up the park to the public. Wanting to make an impression after her previous night's performance in the lobby of the Theatre Royal, Peg dressed the part. She admitted, 'I was the great object of attention, and was particularly stared at by multitudes.' She was pleased that her act of defiance had earned her so much praise, reporting, 'I had the satisfaction to be congratulated for my spirit, by most of the gentlemen present', adding with delight, 'Several ladies of the *sisterhood*, also accosted me with their thanks for asserting their rights.'

Not finished with business, Peg prepared for the next confrontation, now determined to obtain free access to the theatre on opera nights. In order to have the most impact, as well as for protection, she asked two gentlemen friends to accompany her. They had been hand-picked with the knowledge they were the sort who liked to 'kick up a dust' as Peg called it – in truth, both of them were good-natured rakes with no money. She explained, 'They were two of the kind of Bucks, that though they were always well drest [sic], had seldom a shilling in their pockets, therefore they could never afford the opera.' She offered to pay for their tickets and they agreed to defend her. That evening, they all arrived at Smock Alley Theatre ready for a spoil. Their plan was subverted when the man who kept the box office at Daly's playhouse, a Mr Tresham, informed Peg that Mr Carnivalli had backed down and offered her the 'freedom of the house'. His hired thugs Jackson and Watson had refused to guard the doors for fear of getting beaten up. Wisely, having won her point, she let the prosecution drop.

In describing these battles, Peg had established a character for herself, and revealed a side to her personality which she wanted people to like and admire. She claimed to be modest yet fiery, extravagant yet charitable, soft-hearted yet determined. Her ability to mould her image was exceptional, and she knew just how to present herself to her public.[11] These public contretemps did not seem to affect her reputation detrimentally– if anything they served as an advertisement that Peg was back in town and raring to go.

The Two Bobs

Then all was jollity
Piping and minstrels, gay and mirth and dancing

During the early years of the 1780s, Peg and her friends enjoyed some of the twice-weekly concerts held in the Round Room at the Rotunda for the benefit of the Lying-in Hospital. The best talent was procured at high fees, and Irish musicians, who had been forced to move abroad for their livelihood, came back in droves.[1] In the summer months, open-air concerts were held in the adjacent pleasure gardens, and firework displays lit up the night. Here all the latest fashions were on display. Apart from the bell-hooped style, the women favoured the Polonaise dress, a popular choice of gown according to the *Lady's Magazine*: 'These dresses are very much the taste, and various are the makes by many worn in assemblies and public places of a full dress.' The gown consisted of an open robe with 'long sleeves, cut in four quarters with a silk braid down every seam . . . trimmed round the train with rich braid of satin ribbon and crape.' Underneath the robe, the petticoat was on show 'festooned with a crape and thick satin cord with tassels.'[2]

Peg could be seen out in her carriage driving round the Circular Road, amidst fellow courtesans supposedly out for an airing, but in truth advertising themselves. The 'women on the town' lost no opportunity to show themselves to their potential clients, or to wave at their current beaux. Mrs Brookes, a rival brothel-keeper and procuress with bawdy houses in Trinity Street and Derby Square, went so far as to flout her business by taking her girls down to Irishtown to bathe, scandalising the family holiday makers. Respectable families were horrified to be confronted with the sight of strumpets parading around. Irishtown was at that time a popular resort thanks to the promotion of sea bathing as a health restorative.[3]

Back in Wood Street, business was flourishing and Peg was now so embroiled in the trade of prostitution that she was deaf to any admonishments. She admitted 'living in splendour, enjoying every luxury of dress, table or shew, no matter from which source they were derived, made me resolve not to quit the means of gaining the end.' Although her earnings were already substantial, she looked for ways to make yet more money, determined never again to feel the claws of poverty. Her clientele included noblemen, judges, bankers and merchants such as the Duke of Leinster, the Duke of Rutland and David La Touche, who would later become governor of the Bank of Ireland. She admitted, 'I had entered so deep into a series of errors, and so plunged in the whirl-pool of dissipation, that I became ingulphed [sic] therein.' As she hankered after schemes for bigger success and income, she hit on the idea of throwing a masquerade.

Masquerades had become a prominent feature in Dublin social life. People would gather together at balls dressed up as a character of their choosing. Masks were worn as a disguise, supposedly to heighten the sexual frisson of encounters between strangers. In reality, most people recognised each other, and it was an excuse for fun. The first masquerade had been introduced in London in 1708 by a Swiss count, John James Heidegger, at the Haymarket opera house. Peg had experienced them herself at the London pleasure gardens. The infamous Teresa Cornelys, Casanova's lover, was known for her magnificent masquerades at Carlisle House in Soho Square in the 1770s. Anglo-Irish novelist Laurence Sterne, famous for his *The Life and Opinions of Tristram Shandy*, recalled that a visit to Mrs Cornelys was 'the best assembly and the best concert I ever had the honour to be at.'[4] No doubt having heard of such successes, Peg wanted to outshine them in her efforts at party-throwing.

A ban had been placed on masquerades in Dublin, according to Peg as a result of incidents a couple of years previously when, in 1779, public disturbances had erupted in the theatres. While some of her friends were applauding her initiative, others were warning Peg of the potential dangers: 'For a fortnight before the appointed time I had above twenty visitors of the latter class, trying to dissuade me, or frighten me from my attempt. They told me, if I persisted my house would be pulled down about my ears.' Peg, however, was unconcerned about the law, as its representatives would be at the party. She was determined her masquerade would be a magnificent display, but was wary of an invasion of riotous young men and uninvited attendees. As a precaution, she invited police officers to attend, placing Mr Henry Robinson, the high constable of Dublin, on the door, assisted by Mr Nathaniel Warren, MP for Dublin and later mayor, and a Mr Smith. With two hundred tickets on offer, the evening was to be one of the most talked-about events of the year.

Worryingly, by six o'clock, the street was packed from one end to the other. A large crowd had gathered and was growing restless. Occasionally someone would call for Peg to show herself. Peg admits, 'I really began to be frightened for fear of the mob.' A ruffian threw a stone through the dining-room window, shattering the glass. Once Peg and Sally had appeared on the front porch, the crowd seemed satisfied and quietened down. Visitors began to flow into the house quickly: Mr Pearson dressed as a fortune-teller, Captain Hamilton as a jockey, Mr Jones as a domino, Mr Cashel as a sweep and Mr McNeil as a sailor. The women were equally amusingly kitted out: Moll Hall as a pie woman, Kitty Netterville as an orange girl, Nancy Weems as a nun, Miss Townley as a flower girl. The guest list included titled men, all in fancy dress: Lord Westport as a blind fiddler, Lord Molesworth dressed as a coachman and Lord Headfort as a drummer. Peg kept her bed free for the Duke of Leinster, William Robert Fitzgerald, who, in the event, did not turn up. An elegantly laid out table enticed guests to eat, and the richest of wines left everyone happy. Afterwards, a band struck up in the drawing room and people danced until dawn. To Peg's relief, no one from authority had shown the slightest interest in disrupting her party.

Over the next couple of years, life went on as usual. Peg continued to run her business, went to plays, concerts and threw frequent soirées. Her profession was her livelihood and she threw most of her energies into entertaining her clients. However while Peg's lovers would include dukes and lords, it was the army men for whom she had a soft spot.

The soldiers from the army garrisoned in Dublin frequented the brothels while serving there or waiting to be shipped abroad. Around 1782, against her own expectations, Peg once again fell in love, this time with a soldier, an 'extremely handsome' man called Robert Gorman. She admitted her fondness for him: 'He was almost constantly with me, and then I despised all the rest of mankind, they became odious in my eyes, which could not look with pleasure or complacency on any but my dear Bob.'

The relationship was not without its difficulties as Gorman's father had discovered the affair and insisted his son come home every night. Gorman senior's intention was to try and curtail his son's profligate life and prevent him squandering hundreds of pounds of his money on gambling and whoring. He demanded his son live with him at his country house in Blackrock. The road itself was somewhat treacherous, as one report stated, 'The Rock Road . . . was in the eighteenth century in a most dangerous state, owing to the absence of a protecting wall on the sea side . . . [and] had also an unenviable reputation for highwaymen and footpads.'[5] Regardless of its dangers, the lovers put it to constant use, racing back and forth for lovers' trysts. Because Gorman sen. so vehemently opposed their meetings, the lovers had to devise a routine: young Gorman would have supper with his father, then slip out unnoticed to race back to spend the night with Peg, before darting back to his own bed in the morning. During the day, they then dined together at Booterstown, another small coastal place nearby. After dinner, Gorman would return to his father's house while Peg awaited his return at night.

Despite keeping his son under lock and key, Gorman sen. was mystified as to how his son was still managing to escape at nights. Unbeknown to him, Bob had managed to take all the servants into his confidence, as Peg explained: 'He went down into the kitchen; and established an ascendancy over the servants, by a few bottles of wine, and some money, till they became devoted to him. It has been well observed, that there is but one road to the heart of a domestic, and whoever is generous cannot miss it.' In order to catch his son in the act of returning home, Gorman sen. sat up all of one night. The unsuspecting son was caught as he clambered in through the window and was apprehended, but the ensuing reprimand only served to push him back into the arms of his lover. Gorman jun. stormed off and stayed away three weeks, all the while remaining with Peg.

As with many other fathers in such predicaments, Gorman sen. considered that the only way to lift his son out of bad company was to send him for a stint in the East Indies. The East India Company had been set up as a trading conglomerate to ship everything from silk, tea and salt to spices and opium, and they needed men to oversee the operation. The company owned large tracts of India, marshalled by its own military camps. A man could easily go out to India with a moderate outlay and live like a king while making his fortune. It was also a last-ditch option for fathers to encourage their errant sons to make good.

At the end of his tether, Bob's father now gave his son an ultimatum: he must go abroad or his allowance would be cut off. Since Bob now had considerable debt, amounting to several hundred pounds, he was left with little choice. He agreed to meet with his brother in Durham's tavern where they laid plans for his future; both of them would go to England and prepare Bob for his trip to India.

Around the end of March or beginning of April 1783, another tearful farewell ensued as the lovers parted and Gorman left for England with his brother. He wrote to Peg on 12 April from London: 'I had this day, the happiness of receiving your two letters; and my love, I have been neither able to speak, eat or drink since I saw them; as the idea of your being unhappy on my account, makes me miserable, my love.' In the event, the ship was held up and, despite her lover's protestation, Peg insisted she come and see him one last time. He told her, 'With respect to your coming to see me, it would be the height of madness, as every one would conjecture you left Dublin for that purpose.' While waiting for his ship to sail, on 13 April he sat to have his portrait painted to leave Peg as a reminder of him; he wrote, 'I only regret, that I am not able to send you some more valuable token; but, my Peggy, I am sure you will take the will for the deed.' Peg was only too pleased to hear his ship would not sail for a while so that she could go to see him. Filled with desire, she lost no time in booking the packet across the sea and then travelling on to London where Gorman was waiting for her. The pair travelled to Portsmouth, and since his ship did not leave for another six months, they managed to pack in many hours of happy amusements. The East India Company had had a profound effect on Portsmouth, which was full of sailors and prostitutes, but there was plenty to do. The port spilled over with coffee houses, taverns and gaming houses where Peg and Gorman might entertain themselves. There was a theatre available, although according to one visitor it was 'very shabby, the company of Comedians as poor as possible'. They might walk the town ramparts, attend the Concert Rooms in St George's Square or sail up harbour to view Portchester Castle.[6] Peg had left her 'nymphs' in charge back home in Dublin, so she hoped business would run as usual. She was loathe to leave, as she called him, 'the second man I ever loved'.

Inevitably, their pleasures came to an end. With the ship ready to sail, Gorman took her back to London and saw her off in a stagecoach bound for the packet boat back to Dublin. He returned to Portsmouth, along with a miniature portrait of Peg which she had given him, and made preparations for the journey to India. Gorman was on the *Eurydice*, a twenty-four-gun ship built two years earlier which had seen service in the American Revolution under the Royal Navy. Co-incidentally, on board ship was eighteen-year-old Fletcher Christian, who had signed up on 25 April 1783 at Spithead and would later become famous as the instigator of the mutiny on the *Bounty*. The *Eurydice* was the first Royal Navy ship that Christian had signed on to.[7] Meanwhile, poor Peg was once again without her true love.

Gorman wrote from his ships en route to India at stops on the way, from Madeira, the Cape of Good Hope and Madras, obviously missing Peg and home. Only five days out of port, he wrote to Peg, 'I wear your picture the whole day; and when I go to bed I have it under my head, lest the heat of my hand should disfigure your lovely face', adding 'my returning to Dublin is quite out of the question, at least for some time'. He was evidently contemplating his future and what to do when he landed. He told Peg, 'I shall go to India either with the commander-in-chief, or with a particular friend of mine, who has been there many years. I shall go with the first introduction, so it will be my own fault if I do not get forward'. Formal presentations were a matter of course when arriving in an unfamiliar place or a foreign country. Often these preliminaries were in the form of a letter or a personal introduction. Once in Madeira, Gorman would be lucky enough to reconnect with a man called Jones, the purser of the ship *Race Horse* whom Peg and Bob had first met when they had dined with him at Spithead. Peg had made him a present of some garters. In turn, Jones would be kind enough to present Gorman to all the top people.

His letters contained news about how the ship had sprung a leak, the good news about Admiral Rodney's success (he earned a peerage for his glorious battles), and about the capture of their friend Mrs Dixon's son in India, who had been taken prisoner with Brigadier-General Richard Matthews during the second Anglo-Mysore War, which ran from 1780 to 1784. This was to be one of a series of wars fought in India over the last three decades of the eighteenth century between the Kingdom of Mysore and the East India Company. A letter was published in the *Town and Country Magazine* in 1788 which had been written by Mathews on his arrival in prison to the officers confined in the prison of Seringapatam, dated 27 May 1783: 'I think that Tippo wishes for peace with us, and that something towards it may take place in November. I am used ill, but not in irons . . . For myself, and two European servants, and one black, I am allowed one fanam [twelfth of a rupee] and a half per day; with one sear of meat, three of bad rice, and one of ghee. I am compelled to receive what they give, and not allowed to buy anything from the bazaar.'

Gorman wrote to Peg again on 25 December 1783, having arrived safely at the Cape of Good Hope. Conditions on board ship were tough because of the heat, which he said 'has been so great that it was almost impossible to stay below'. While at sea the passengers were obliged to close every air hole, resulting in a suffocating atmosphere. His thoughts were mainly on Peg, and he was as affectionate as ever, 'the farther I am from you, the more deeply your image riveted in my soul'. He confessed that he thought and dreamt about her constantly. The ship was bound for Madras, which would take a couple of months (given a smooth passage), and from there he planned to go to Bombay, head-quarters of the East India Company.

On 14 March 1784, a year after he'd left England, Gorman would write again, telling Peg of the problems he had encountered. Servants were a particular bane in his life, one having stolen his watch, shoe and knee buckles, his hat and twenty-five pounds. Another had stolen four guineas, most of his linen and his pocket-book. Other

misfortunes had befallen him as he failed to obtain the introductions
he needed; General Matthews to whom he had been recommended
was now dead, as was Mrs Dixon's son, both poisoned in captivity.[8]
The Treaty of Mangalore had just been signed between Tipu Sultan
and the British East India Company only three days before, bringing
to an end the second Anglo-Mysore War. Gorman had intended to
join the 36th Regiment, but it had already lost a number of men
though they had only been there six months. En route he had lost a
friend in a duel in the Cape of Good Hope. He provided Peg with
details of the sights of India, but he was most proud of his attire:

> I wish you could see the dress I am sitting in, as I am sure you would
> like it; a white waistcoat, with sleeves, edged with red; long breeches
> to my slippers, which are of white linen, bound with red; and a straw
> hat, the crown covered with muslin; and adorned with the feathers
> you gave me, which I shall never part with, but with my life.

He had become browner and fatter from the sun and his lack of exer-
cise. If his commission was successful, he planned to be home in three
years. As he wrote, he was stationed aboard a huge seventy-four-gun
defence ship but the heat continued to be unbearable, 'I sleep generally in the open air, with no covering than a pair of drawers.' He
mentions that a mutual friend of theirs, Miss Scriven, 'who lived at the
Green' [St Stephen's Green] had arrived that week, married to a writer.

On her return to Dublin, Peg found her friend Sally Hayes in a
similar state of distress, having just lost her favourite captain, who had
gone to rejoin his regiment. Both women were determined to pull
themselves out of their heartache by plunging into pleasure. Peg's next
distraction came in the form of Mr Simon L. Cunynghame, curiously
nicknamed by her as Bobadil.[9] This was probably in teasing reference
to the character of the military braggart in Ben Johnson's play *Every
Man in His Humour*. The play had been successfully played at the
Smock Alley Theatre in 1751, so the joke would have been obvious.[10]
Peg's nickname also comes from the diminutive, as she saw him as a
smaller version of Bob Gorman. She would eventually lose him too
when he received a commission in the 67th Regiment to serve in
Barbados and St Kitts in the West Indies.

Drunken soldiers continued to be a disruptive element for brothel-owners, but Peg now knew enough senior officers to call to help keep their men in check. One evening, a group of three soldiers from the local garrison came to Peg's house with the intention of extracting money from her. First they asked for a drink, then they went and searched through her house on the pretext that she was hiding a deserter. She refused to serve them and sent her servant off to the barracks to inform the authorities what was happening. The officers obviously took the accusations seriously as they directed the gates of the barracks to be shut and took a head count to establish who was missing from the compound. The next morning Peg received a note from Colonel Crampton requesting she come to the barracks in Arbour Hill to identify the men. Of eleven soldiers missing the previous night, Peg identified her three visitors. Only the one who had been rude and obnoxious was sent for court marshal and subject to a hundred lashes. For days following his confinement, begging letters came through to Peg asking forgiveness. He even sent his wife to plead on his behalf. Her tears flowed as she stood in Peg's doorway entreating Peg to intercede on behalf of her husband. Peg, having had her revenge, wished to take the matter no further, and contacted the Colonel to request the prisoner's release without further punishment. Various friends from his regiment called over the following few days to thank her for her intercession.

Peg was full of tales about her magnanimity, whether it was forgiving violent ruffians or saving a young forger from a death sentence. Forgery touched the lives of most people at some point and, if caught, the culprit might well hang, particularly if they had a history of similar offences. If a person was lucky, transportation might be substituted for the death penalty. A young beau of Sally Hayes, a man called Gibbons, embroiled Peg in such a scam when he presented an £80 promissory note supposedly made out by Mr Macquay, the sugar baker in Thomas Street. He asked Peg if she might advise him as to who might cash it for him. In good faith, she directed him to an upstanding gentleman who said he could give Gibbons thirty pounds now, and would obtain the rest to give him the following day. The gentleman, being of a cautious nature, went along to Mr Macquay, and showed him the note to check it was, in fact, his signature. On finding out that it was not, he took off to find an officer of the law and raise a warrant against Gibbons. Finding him at Peg's house, the officer arrested him, but Peg pleaded with the gentleman for the release of young Gibbons and agreed to pay the thirty pounds in cash on his behalf.

Part of the problem was that banking was still in its infancy, with only eleven banking establishments opened between 1760 and 1797.[11] If coins were in short supply, rather than hold up business, merchants often carried out transactions by issuing promissory notes or bills of exchange. The Bank of Ireland Act in 1781 eased the situation, and the Bank of Ireland opened for business on 25 June 1783.[12] The Bank of Ireland's own note issue grew slowly at first, but other banks were starting to issue notes too.

Along with her role as defender of poor criminals, Peg also took on the mantle of protectress of vulnerable young women. When a young, beautiful fifteen-year-old girl came to her house late one night telling her how her parents had been cruel to her, she tried to help. The girl related how she had been sent to live with an old aunt by her parents, but found to her horror that the old lady was a vicious old crone who merely wanted a slave. Not only had the young girl worked her fingers to the bone, but she had been locked in a small room, her food sent up on a plate. Her gowns were taken away and she only had the white darned maid's dress she stood up in. She had heard of Peg's similar ill-treatment by her family, and so came to her to implore her to let her stay, not as a whore but as her servant. Throughout the conversation, Peg attempted to find out who the girl's parents were so she could take her home, although the girl was extremely reluctant. She believed her parents 'would tie her with cords, and use her still worse than before'. Peg threw a cloak round her shoulders and took a coach for them both, back to the girl's parental house. After giving the girl's father a severe scolding, Peg extracted a promise from him that he would look after his daughter better, or she would advertise his faults to the whole of the city.

From a young girl with uncaring parents to the poor young army man, life was often hard in eighteenth-century Dublin. Setbacks or hardship could throw a person off balance and into a life of infamy, vice or poverty. Even men lucky enough to gain a commission in the army might be sent off to war at a moment's notice. This was especially likely in the turbulent times of the American Revolution and the wars in India. For the women who fell in love with them, their task was just as thankless. Not knowing when her lover might be sent abroad, or whether she would ever see him again, a woman might be called upon to give up her loved one so he could go off to do his duty. Both Peg and Sally would experience the personal loss of men they knew being sent abroad in the line of duty.

The Army Men and Some Disagreeable Adventures

What gudgeons are we men,
Every woman's easy prey?
Tho' we have felt the hook, again,
We bite and they betray.

While around 4,000 British soldiers had been sent to fight in the colonies, there were still 9,000 left behind in Ireland.[1] Fears of invasion were ever-present, and reports of spies were everywhere. Peg had recently heard that Sir Benjamin Thompson, Count Rumford, was a spy sent to Ireland and England by the French, but she laughed at the idea. The rumour had spread because of Rumford's friendship with Thomas Pelham, Chief Secretary at Dublin Castle in 1783, a key political position in the British administration in Ireland. Peg nicknamed Rumford 'the chimney doctor', declaring, 'By Jupiter, he has fairly *smoked us all*, peeped into our private recesses, and will shortly perhaps pay us another visit, and send us to his country seat Rumford to get our Arses new bottomed.' The joke was based on the fact that Massachusetts-born Thompson has been educated in the sciences and had become famous for creating the Rumford fireplace. The chimney was a clever design which modified the domestic fireplace by inserting bricks into the hearth to make the side walls angled. A choke was added to the chimney to increase the speed of air going up the flue thereby producing a streamlined air flow which meant that all the smoke went up into the chimney rather than lingering in the room and choking its inhabitants. Rumford was evidently well-known during the 1780s and his 'Rumford fireplace' became fashionable worldwide.[2] During the American Revolution, he had sided with the loyalists and opposed the rebels. As a result of his loyalties, his house was attacked by the rebel mob and he had to flee to Britain, deserting his wife in the process.

While interested in the local gossip about spies, Peg had her hands full with soldiers garrisoned at the Royal Barracks of Dublin. The three-storey complex was situated just to the north-west of the city and dominated the landscape. It housed two foot regiments and three horse troops, with several parade grounds where the men could be heard drilling every morning. The erection of the building had started in 1701 as a base for the British army on a site originally intended for the mansion of the Duke of Ormond. An Act of Parliament of 1707 stated that 'all officers, soldiers, troops and companies in her Majesty's Army . . . shall be lodged in the barracks . . . instead of being accommodated in the public taverns and alehouses within the city'.[3] This was perhaps not a bad idea, given the soldiers' propensity for drink, but evidently did not stop them from over-imbibing. The barracks were designed by Thomas Burgh, who also created plans for Trinity College and St Steven's Hospital across the River Liffey. Much of the complex was rebuilt in the 1760s to make room for the ever-pressing need for extra soldiers.[4] The granite-faced, neoclassical building was an impressive sight, with its large squares opening out to the south side and its magnificent arcaded columns on the east and west sides.

The soldiers were very much involved in the life of the city, and were members of various clubs, hunts and Masonic lodges.[5] Officers were in demand at elite soirées given by the gentry, despite many being known for their drunken behaviour.[6] However, there were strained relationships between the army, the Volunteers, the Parliament and the general population. Resentment against the British saw a fevered political situation in the city, with British profits viewed as being made off the backs of the Irish people. A minor concession for the Irish had been made with the passing of the Renunciation Act on 17 April 1783, which finally allowed the Parliament of Ireland the exclusive right to self-legislation. The rowdy behaviours of the soldiers in the Dublin garrison resulted as much from high spirits as it did from the knowledge that the tasks they were performing were a risk to their personal safety. Guarding Newgate Prison or escorting unwilling recruits could be life-threatening. Also, the presence of a sizeable military garrison created a tense relationship between the soldiers and the community, which frequently erupted in scuffles and aggressive behaviour, even bloodshed. By the late eighteenth century, the Dublin garrison had become so integrated into the rough-house life of Dublin's streets that the soldiers acted as much like one of its gangs as an instrument of peacekeeping.[7] Many of them lacked a basic gentlemanly code of conduct. Even officers might behave badly, as Peg was about to experience.

Dublin was simply too full of potential beaux for Peg to stay grieving for Gorman or Cunynghame for long. No longer tied down by personal attachments, Peg decided to throw a supper and ball at her house to help her get over yet another lover's departure. Around midnight, they were entertaining a hand-picked selection of guests and all the company were merrily dancing. Sally and Peg had just left the ballroom and were overseeing the setting out of supper in the dining room when they heard a violent rapping at the front door. On entering, Captain Stephen Freemantle of Dublin Castle, aide-de-camp to the Lord Lieutenant, pushed past the servant and demanded to be admitted to the party. Some months before, in April of 1783, Freemantle had been assigned to the 2nd Regiment of Horse in Ireland. That night, he was accompanied by John 'Dicky' Dillon of the 5th Dragoons and two other men. Peg came into the hall to deal with the noisy confrontation and immediately recognised Freemantle and Dillon as men from the upper ranks of the army who were often in her establishment:

> These bucks wanted to be of the party, and to be admitted where they were dancing. I told them it was a select party, if it were not I should be glad of their company as of any others; but as this was not the case, I begged they would depart, as the supper was ready to come down, and I wanted the room clear.

Instead of backing out and apologising for their rude interruption, Freemantle answered in such an impertinent manner that Sally Hayes, who had been looking on, took up a horse whip and began laying into him, a sight which was to be the occasion of much mirth in the coming days. Anyone with less grit might have succumbed to the overbearing intruders, but Peg and Sally were tough and experienced enough to deal with them.

Freemantle was obviously a troublemaker, and he caused difficulties again some months later. He started a riot in Peg's house along with captains Boyle, Hanger, Cradock, Monck and McGuire when they arrived drunk outside and demanded to be allowed entrance.[8] Peg was elsewhere entertaining some army man in his lodgings at the barracks, but Sally recognised them, it still being daylight, and refused them admission. In retaliation, they smashed all the windows and wrecked part of the house. Once again Peg had to obtain the services of a lawyer in order to serve writs. With the officers pleading for forgiveness and offering her money by way of reparation, and having covered all her expenses and a little besides, Peg dropped the charges.

Such bad behaviour by soldiers was commonplace, and dealing with it an unfortunate drawback of running a brothel. Peg found her own methods of sorting out such problems, sometimes with dramatic consequences. An incident took place after one of Peg's clients, Captain Henry Monck (one of the troublemakers at the ball), had encouraged Peg to try on his uniform. For fun, she decided to stroll out for an evening's entertainment at the Rotunda dressed up in his outfit, to see the effect. Instead of admiring her, one of the officers, called Hunt, began haranguing Peg. She recalled, 'He kept following me, and calling me *Peg*, and being piqued at my not vouchsafing to speak to him, he asked me aloud, how I dared to wear a uniform, and threatened to pull it off my back.' Miffed at such treatment, Peg returned home immediately and wrote a letter of complaint about Hunt's behaviour, as a result of which he was court-martialled. The unlikely consequences were dramatic, as, according to Peg, 'This disgrace had such an effect on Mr Hunt that he died a few weeks afterwards.'[9]

Even officers who had been introduced through personal friends managed to surprise Peg with their poor conduct. One navy lieutenant who visited her was an acquaintance of Cunynghame, so she had presumed he was a trustworthy man. It was around one o'clock in the afternoon and Peg was having her hair dressed in the dining parlour, the officer standing behind her. As her back was turned she glanced at his reflection in her mirror and was horrified to see him pilfer two silver tablespoons and some teaspoons from her sideboard. She wrote, 'I was so amazed at such an action, by a gentleman and an officer, that I really had not power to utter a word.' Rather than challenge him there and then, she let him leave with the stolen goods in his pocket. She soon discovered that he had taken them to sell in a shop in College Green, but the shopkeeper recognised them as Peg's. He had been about to apprehend the officer when Peg sent word that she had given them to him, knowing that the officer would be court-marshalled at the very least, if not imprisoned or hanged, if convicted of such a crime. The severity of punishments for crimes often prevented victims from prosecuting.

Yet part of the British military was made up of criminals and debtors. The government had an arrangement to release prisoners on condition they joined the army, a method which had raised three entire regiments during the American Revolution. Lower positions might be obtained in the army, and a man could work his way up the ranks, but officers had to buy commissions. Talent was unimportant, and there was no set time before a soldier might increase his rank – it was simply a matter of money.[10] Soldiers placed advertisements in the newspapers in bids to swap regiments, switching from poor commissions to higher-paying posts, selling their own commissions, and swapping commissions in British regiments for Irish equivalents. The favourite newspaper for these notices was the *Freeman's Journal* (government-funded from around 1782), but adverts could also be found in the *Dublin Evening Post*, and the *Volunteers' Journal*.[11]

At this stage, Cunynghame came back into Peg's life. He had just obtained a commission with the 67th Regiment and was now obliged to live in Dublin's Royal Barracks.[12] Although previously he had prevaricated, he was now more decisive about taking her into his keeping, and asked her to move into his elegantly furnished apartment. However Peg was loath to give up her independence totally. Instead she consented to spend four days with him and three at her own house, where she could see whomever she pleased. He wrote to her affectionately when he could not get away from his duties: 'Nothing, my dear Leeson, would have prevented me calling today, if it had not been for my indisposition; and I am sure, when I tell you, I have been unwell, you will not be angry with me.' He gave the excuse that he had gone out the previous night 'without a surtoot' or overcoat, and the cold had affected his bones and limbs. In his letters, he professed to love her, but she meanwhile retained her cool. She had sent a letter to an acquaintance of Cunynghame's, but had failed to ask after him. Her lover complained how upset he became 'when I think of the coolness you treated me with last night, and sending a letter to Mr Barret, without ever enquiring for me'.

There was, in fact, more to it than a simple chill – both his physical one and her emotional one. The real reason for his absence was financial, as he admitted in his next letter to her: 'Part of the money I got for my exchange, I lost at hazard [a card game]; and to compleat my misfortunes, I saw the gentleman I lost the money to, at Tralee.' As a result, he had gone off to the country with his friend Mr Warren to see if he could raise some money. He was obviously worried she had taken offence, 'I hope you will not imagine I have used you ill, as I assure you on my honour, you would be the last person in the world, I would offend.' Perhaps as recompense, he was having a miniature portrait made for her, concluding, 'There is only one sitting for my picture, and you may expect to see it tomorrow.'

For her part, his lack of money gave Peg every reason to remain reserved. When at the end of the year Cunynghame was called by the army to the County Quarters and stationed in various places around Tralee and Clarecastle, south of Ennis in County Clare, he entreated Peg to go with him. Although she was fond of him, she was reluctant to leave Dublin for a man of such middling income. In any case, she preferred the delights of Dublin. After he left, Cunynghame continued to write. On 11 June 1784, he sent her a letter telling her he had marched to Kildare with the troops but had managed to shirk his duties to see the races; they had then all marched on to Roscrea. He sent his respects to Sally Hayes and Nancy Weems.

The couple would meet again once more at the port of Cork as Cunynghame was about to leave with his regiment for the West Indies in 1784. From Barbados, on 26 May 1784, he wrote, 'My dear Leeson, from the time we parted with you, your heavenly person never left my sight, you image was *allways* before me, and thought of nothing but the blissful moments we spent together.' Evidently they had swapped miniature portraits before he left. He had got hers set in a ring as a reminder of her. 'I constantly wear it on my finger, and kiss it an hundred times a day.'

He sailed via Madeira, where he had picked up a cask of wine. 'We arrived here yesterday, after a remarkable fine passage of about six weeks from the time we sailed from Cove [the port near Cork].' That evening he was to dine with the governor of the island and then go on to a ball. From there he was going on to Antigua. He would again write from Brimstone Hill, St Christopher's on St Kitts on 4 November 1784, evidently homesick. 'When you mentioned Circular Road, *Rotundo*, Plays and all the public amusements, I sighed, and brought to my recollection the many times I have been with you.' Peg had included news about Bob Gorman, probably to make Cunynghame jealous, and the ploy worked. 'But when I came to the part of your letter, where you mentioned BOB [Gorman], all my hopes were blasted; and every pleasing reflection my poor heart could possibly suggest, were *totally* vanished!' He professed to love her sincerely. He told her that Gorman was in India but his regiment was about to return home 'for I know that all the troops that are in the East Indies, are to be relieved in Spring.'

Meanwhile, Peg was finding other distractions to keep her occupied. A Captain St Leger had gained her approval, as he could afford to indulge her excesses and pay her well for her services. As with many of her beaux, she does not give his full name, but this is likely to have been John Hayes St Leger (1756–1800), army officer and courtier with properties in Grangemellon, County Kildare (from his mother's side) and Park Hall in Yorkshire.[13] He began his career after receiving a commission in 1778 as captain in the 55th Regiment of Foot, going through various promotions through to major, and being made lieutenant-colonel in the 80th Foot in 1782 (Peg was notoriously unreliable with her dates and titles). Known as 'Handsome Jack' St Leger, he was a close friend of George, Prince of Wales, who described him as 'one of ye best fellows yt. ever lived'.[14] It was said of him, 'Already an accomplished rake, having some years earlier cut a swathe through the *demi-monde* of Louis XVI's court in France, St Leger's roistering incurred the disapproval of George III, who warned the prince against emulating him.'[15]

He moved between Ireland and England, but eventually outran his income and was forced to retire to Ireland to recoup his fortune. Peg said, 'He visited me very frequently whilst he was in this kingdom.' When in Dublin, he revelled in the company of Buck Whaley, with whom he revived the Dublin Hell Fire Club, notorious for its debauchery and irreligious meetings. He was a favourite with Peg's lover-in-waiting Charles Manners, the 4th Duke of Rutland, and paid extravagant compliments to the duke's beautiful wife, Mary Isabella, going so far at one dinner party to drink the water with which she had just cleaned her teeth. Gossip had it that they were having an affair at the time. Certainly, after the duke's death in 1787, they became lovers before the duchess went after the king's brother Frederick, Duke of York.

Peg welcomed soldiers such as St Leger with open arms as they were so free with their money. Others such as Buck Whaley's young brother John,[16] though she liked them, caused her trouble. She complained, 'He would often break my windows, and pull the rails out of the kitchen stairs, whenever he could not meet me at home.' He was young and had little income, but she bore his behaviour so long as she could extract payment from him. The end came with a slap to his face, when his money finally ran out and he admitted he could not afford to pay her.

The havoc caused by the soldiers was as bad outside her house as inside it, but the potential dangers of walking the Dublin streets after dark did not seem to deter Peg. Coming home with Cunynghame one evening, he, Peg and Sally ran into trouble. They had just spent a pleasant evening at the home of one of Sally's friends in French Street. It was snowing, but warmed by wine they were enjoying themselves kicking up the snow. Halfway up the street, they encountered a city councillor they knew, accompanied by an officer.[17] The officer addressed Cunynghame belligerently, 'You have two ladies, and one is sufficient for you, you may therefore give me the other.' Although the officer had no sword, the councillor drew his and thrust it at Cunynghame, cutting his waistcoat and grazing his breast. A fight broke out, and Cunynghame grabbed the sword and snapped it in two, while Peg and Sally rained blows on the villainous pair. Neither women would shirk from a fight, and had become good hands in battle, a necessary accomplishment given their career path. As soon as the councillor called for the watch, Peg packed Cunynghame off home, knowing he would get the blame. The remaining four fell into a slanging match as they each accused the other of assault. Eventually, as the cold seeped in through their clothes, tired and dispirited, they agreed to let the matter drop. The councillor later called on Peg, requesting Cunynghame's address, but she refused to give it as a duel would have ensued.

Duelling was common throughout Europe, whether with swords or pistols. Codes had emerged in early Renaissance Italy and France and by the eighteenth century had become frequent in Great Britain; one commentator stated, 'Duels have become so common, that we cease almost to hear of their immediate causes. It is now deemed, by those who record passing occurrences, while sufficient to say, that a meeting took place between two gentlemen, as it were an interview or pleasant courtesy, instead of an arena.'[18] In Ireland in 1777, duelling had become so frequent as to warrant its own set of codes enshrined in *The Practice of Duelling and the Point of Honour*. The book outlined the regulation of duels drawn up by the gentlemen delegates of Tipperary, Galway, Mayo, Sligo, and Roscommon at the summer assizes in Clonmel, County Tipperary, and prescribed for general adoption throughout Ireland.[19] Seconds were nearly always present to ensure that protocol was followed, few duels being fought without them. These were usually friends or colleagues of the dueller, a man who could be trusted to carry their pistol and to observe proceedings.[20] One notorious dueller, George Robert Fitzgerald, to whom Peg referred in her memoirs as the 'fire-eater' (meaning 'a person of recklessly defiant disposition, especially a persistent duellist'), fought twenty-six duels and was afterwards hanged for murder. According to one anecdote about Fitzgerald, 'Having teazed Lieutenant Thompson, on his return from a review, and trodden on his toes at a ball the same evening, they proceeded unattended to a garden, and locked the door inside. After an ineffectual effort on the part of Thompson to obtain a competent apology for the offence he had received, he desired Fitzgerald to choose the ground and distance. "Here I am," said Fitzgerald, "fire away." At the second fire Fitzgerald was struck above the temple, upon which he staggered, groaned, and fell. Some neighbours, hearing the reports of pistols, forced the garden door to find Thompson prostrate, weeping over the body of his adversary. He accused himself of the murder, and offered himself a willing victim to the law. On Fitzgerald's removal, it was found that trepanning was necessary; and the patient begged of the surgeons, in the most pathetic manner, that his toupee might not be injured in the operation.'[21]

Fights over courtesans were common, particularly on evenings when much drink had flowed. However, there are few recorded instances of women ploughing into physical affrays. If in trouble, Peg and Sally gave everything they could – bashing, scratching and horsewhipping. However, such scenes of bravado, while enhancing the image of the pair as female warriors, may have been glamorised, as no doubt some incidents resulted in a much worse experience for the women.

Violent scuffles frequently broke out on the spur of the moment. In March 1784, a soldier brutally attacked a drunken brush-maker with a hanger. In August that year, after the arrest of Captain Palliser of the 9th Dragoons for debt, his mistress pleaded with his associates to rescue him, resulting in a shooting which left one dead, three mortally wounded and five seriously injured.[22] The result of such skirmishes involving soldiers led Charles Lucas, co-founder of the *Freeman's Journal*, to rally public opinion against the army.[23] Other newspapers merely inflamed already established anti-military sentiments. The *Hibernian Journal* called the army 'our present monstrous Peace Establishment' which was 'composed mostly of the Dregs of the People'.[24]

That soldiers were frequenting brothels was only to be expected, yet the newspapers took a prurient interest. In 1784 the *Volunteers' Journal* pressed Colonel Lumsdale to delve into the goings-on at a well-known bawdy house at 12 Barrack Street. Here, late at night, soldiers consorted with the lowest of prostitutes. 'It alleged that, these sons of Mars, to retain the smiles of Venus, when the scanty pay is exhausted, must, and actually do, attack their supporters, the public, and plunder those, whom they are destined to defend.'[25]

Although Peg's establishment was high class, she still had to contend with drunken officers. She had clawed her way out from poverty, escaped from various unsuitable relationships, managed to survive the death of most, if not all, of her children, and now she was about reach the pinnacle of her career. She would meet some of the most eligible and wealthy nobles in the land and throw some of the most successful parties in Dublin. Now in her early forties, Peg found herself at the height of her profession, 'the reigning vice queen of the Paphian Goddess'.

Lords, Ladies and Gentlemen

The very zenith of my glory.

Despite being fitted up at great expense, Peg's house in Wood Street had quickly fallen into disrepair. With water penetrating into its foundations, the house was now unsafe and Peg had ordered a new one to be built in Pitt Street. Her status had risen to the extent that she was attracting some of the wealthiest men in town. Lord lieutenants, judges and politicians were flocking to her door. Her house was acknowledged as the best entertainment establishment in town, and all kinds of fashionable gentlemen came calling, bringing gifts and spending money. She had accrued enough to be able to invest in her business and to ensure her position as the 'Paphian Queen' of Dublin. At the beginning of that year, she had thrown herself into setting up her new establishment by choosing the most luxurious goods, and decorating the house in the most up-to-date fashion. Elegant hangings fell from the panels over shuttered windows, embroidered cushions lay on elegant sofas and lustrous candelabras hung from the ceilings. French girandoles stood flickering with an array of candles on the mantles, mirrors behind reflecting the flames back into the room. Lascivious prints hung on the walls, to be admired by customers and to inflame passions in order to do justice to 'the greatest variety of elastic beds'. Smart footmen kitted out in embroidered liveries met arriving guests, and a coachman and a fleet of servants were on duty. Hand-picked young women were on hand to entertain with witty conversation and gratify clients' sexual demands, many of the prettiest prostitutes being specially imported from Covent Garden and

Drury Lane.[1] Here, along with her constant companion Sally Hayes, she began to run the most elite establishment of its kind in Dublin.

Dublin social life tended to revolve around its castle. The Lord Lieutenant lived in the Viceregal Apartments in Dublin Castle, and members of Parliament and the aristocracy flocked to the city for the highlight of the social calendar known as 'parliament winter'.[2] In the castle's various halls the Lord Lieutenant held his hospitality and social events; there was a ball and a drawing-room night each week, and most of the composers who lived in Dublin arranged dance music for such occasions. The Great Hall, built in 1741, was the main place for large public concerts, and it was here that the annual ode written to commemorate the birthday of the reigning monarch was performed. On state occasions, the Lord Lieutenant dressed in his regalia and was accompanied by a Colonel's Guard of Horse and the Battle Axe Guards, the streets lined with foot soldiers. An added boon to Dublin's social events came with the founding of the Most Illustrious Order of St Patrick by King George III in Dublin Castle. This was at the suggestion of the 1st Marquess of Buckingham, then Lord Lieutenant, George Nugent-Temple-Grenville. The knighthood was intended as a reward for for serving the Irish Parliament, and a magnificent inaugural dinner had been given the previous year on 7 March 1783. Parades, church services and banquets were also held on special occasions, adding to the atmosphere of excitement and activity of the town.[3] Large churches and St Patrick's Cathedral would frequently be used for large public concerts. St Andrew's Round Church, for example, provided the setting for the annual benefit concerts for Mercer's Hospital when Handel's *Utrecht Te Deum and Jubilate* and his *Coronation Anthem* were performed every year. Tickets were half a guinea each and raised over £200.

By the winter of 1784, having said goodbye to old lovers Gorman and Cunynghame some months before, Peg was beginning what she would call 'the most memorable epoch of my unfortunate life', a period which would place her at the peak of her profession. She boasted, 'I still increase in celebrity and was esteemed the first woman in Ireland in my line. I was visited by nobles and gentlemen of the first rank in the kingdom.' In short, it was now fashionable to be acquainted with Mrs Leeson.

It was during this period that Charles Manners, 4th Duke of Rutland, arrived in Dublin, and he was to make a great impression on Peg. He had just been made Viceroy of Ireland on 11 February 1784 by Prime Minister William Pitt, an appointment (already declined by Lord Cornwallis) worth a basic £20,000. Still under thirty years old, Rutland was perhaps somewhat young for the post. Nonetheless, noting the recent disturbances, he sensibly made his will on 15 February, before taking up office in Dublin two weeks later. While enthusiastic about Pitt's aim to achieve Anglo-Irish union within twenty years, he was unsure of its feasibility. Soon after his arrival his staff became embroiled in an affray with Irish protestors in Dublin, which, though he suppressed it successfully, led to him being threatened with tarring and feathering.

The entrance of the Duke of Rutland into Peg's life was dramatic. Peg was enjoying a cup of tea with her friends Mrs McClean, Miss Love, Mrs Stevenson (alias Brooks), Mary Read and Kitty Netterville, discussing the highlights of their week and exchanging local gossip. The house was relatively quiet that evening. Suddenly a commotion was heard in the street – trampling horses, neighing and a hubbub of voices. The doors were flung open, and a grand introduction was announced as Rutland stomped in, flanked by two of his aides-de-camp. On guard outside was a mounted troop of men in full military dress, armed with swords, protecting the entrance. There they remained for the next sixteen hours while Rutland and his aides drank copious amounts of champagne and were serviced by the 'impures' of the house. Peg recalled, 'His Grace would take no partner but myself, and in the morning he paid me a profusion of compliments on the happiness he enjoyed in my company.' So impressed was he that he promised to put her on the government Pension List, under an assumed name, for the sum of £300 a year.

While Rutland would frequent Peg's establishment, it was never quite with so much panache as that initial visit. Indeed, he admitted to being drunk that first evening and had forgotten he had left his guardsmen outside. Peg had had the sense to send out a large supply of Maddock's Irish porter and some 'pure native' (her best Irish-made whiskey). Irish whiskey was immensely popular in both Ireland and Britain. In 1779 an astonishing 1,200 distilleries existed in Ireland;

most of them were unlicensed. Expensive obligations came with high official posts, but Rutland exceeded expectations with his lavish hospitality. Indeed, he was credited with a record for dining out unequalled by his viceregal successors. Sir Jonah Barrington recalled: 'The utmost magnificence signalled the entertainments of the vice-regal court, and the duke and duchess were reckoned the handsomest couple in Ireland.'⁴ Rutland's wife, Lady Mary Isabella Somerset, whom he had married in 1775, was the daughter of Charles Somerset, 4th Duke of Beaufort, and was, according to Peg, unfazed by his affairs. A celebrated beauty, she bore him six children while putting up with his philandering and passion for gambling.

The newspapers were full of the exploits of 'Peg and Charley', and reported an incident which had taken place a few nights earlier at the theatre. As Peg had entered the auditorium, the crowd roared, 'Peg, who lay you with last?' to which she wittily replied, 'Manners, you blackguards, Manners.' While the duke supposedly laughed at her retort, his long-suffering wife, used to his intrigues, simply ignored the commotion.⁵

In July 1785, Rutland would receive the infamous Richard Crosbie (he of the Pinking Dandies who had wrecked Peg's house and caused her miscarriage) for breakfast. Only the day before, Crosbie had attempted to balloon to the skies, leaving from the Duke of Leinster's lawn, but his balloon had failed to make its proper ascent and drifted into the sea.⁶ Rutland would sink into poor health after a strenuous tour of Ireland in the summer of 1787, during which he was seldom sober. From then on the duke steadily went downhill. His claret consumption was well known, and for breakfast alone he was reported to have consumed six or seven turkey eggs a day. Inevitably his excesses cost him his health. In the end, Rutland's increasing popularity as viceroy was bought at the price of both his pocket and his health. He was to fall into a dangerous fever while at Phoenix Park Lodge in Dublin, and died of incurable liver disease on 24 October 1787. There was no doubt he was Peg's favourite noble, both because of his genial personality and the fact that he had placed generously her on the Pension List. Of him she was to declare, 'the gay, the witty, the gallant, the convivial Rutland, whose court outrivaled that of Comus himself'.

During this time, Peg had made the acquaintance of an assortment of titled gentlemen. One of these fresh-faced gallants who came calling at the house was young Lord Guilford, otherwise known as Richard Meade and heir to the earldom of Clanwilliam, to which he would succeed in 1800.[7] He was about eighteen years old when he first visited Peg, taking with him the man who managed his family's fortune, his attorney Crosbie Morgell of Tullilease, County Cork. The contrast between the two men was striking to Peg. After an evening's conversation with them, having watched as they downed a pot of porter, she was satisfied to see the affable young Guilford throw down a guinea and entreat his companion to do the same. Morgell was less inclined to throw his money around, and instead declared defiantly, 'Not I indeed, My Lord. I think your guinea sufficient to pay for fifty pots of porter. What two guineas for a pot of porter! I have not such a fortune as you have to throw away my guineas in such a way.' Somewhat taken aback, Lord Guilford responded, 'Why, Morgell. I thought you would give five guineas for sitting in that lady's company. But I suppose you have no change about you. Come, come, I'll pay one for you.' For Peg, this was the difference between a man 'noble and generous' and another 'sordid and mean'. The fact that one had a fortune and the other had to earn his living meant nothing to Peg. She preferred those clients who could afford her or were more likely to be generous.

Some of these errant young lords were less amiable and thought themselves rather grand. In most instances, Peg humoured them in order to encourage them to part with their money, but occasionally she indulged herself in a little mocking play. Such was the case when Walter Butler paid a visit, a youth hitherto unfamiliar to Peg. He would eventually become an Irish peer and politician, 18th Earl and 1st Marquess of Ormond.[8] Peg described him as a 'young lad of seventeen or eighteen years', but he would have been only fourteen at the time.[9] When he arrived in Peg's drawing room, Peg sent Sally and Moll Hall to go and see if they recognised him, but neither did. Unwilling to entertain anyone without a proper introduction, Peg politely addressed the youth:

> Sir, I have not the pleasure of knowing you, nor can either of the ladies I sent in. I therefore must wish you a good night, and desire whenever you shall do me the favour of another visit, that you bring

some gentleman with whom I am acquainted to introduce you, for I
never admit any strangers unless they are properly recommended.

To such a young man without the nous to withdraw as a gentleman,
her words simply provoked his ire. Digging into his breeches, he
pulled out a handful of guineas which he flung on the sofa as he
roared, 'Madam, am I not a gentleman?'

To which Peg retorted, 'I can not tell whether you are or not'.

'What, does not my appearance look like one?'

In the face of such youthful bravado, Peg bristled, her retort sharp
with sarcasm. She exclaimed, 'Why really, Sir. Your scarlet frock, in
my opinion, seems rather against you; as I assure you when I first
came into the parlour, I took you for some English *flashman*, such as
the ladies in London have about them.' She continued, 'They are
commonly hair-dressers, or waiters, dressed every Sunday in just such
another frock and small cloathes, as you have on now.' The youth had
not expected such treatment, but he was unwilling to leave without his
coins, and groped about on the floor for his guineas. He then stum-
bled out, swearing he would never enter the house again.

Two years later he was back, and this time, both Peg and Moll Hall
recognised his noble connection. Money and titles frequently had the
effect of destroying those who had no restraint, and Ormond was to
be one of them. Between the years 1789 and 1796, he would represent
County Kilkenny in the Irish House of Commons and lead an increasing extravagant lifestyle. He would eventually relinquish his hereditary
right to the grant of the prisage of the wines of Ireland for an enormous amount of money.

As ever, it was money which held the most interest for Peg. For
this reason she was also was fond of young David La Touche, later
governor of the Bank of Ireland, a frequent client at her establishment. The success of La Touche's banking business meant he was
well-heeled enough for Peg to encourage his patronage. According
to Peg, he spent much of his time admiring his youthful good looks
in her large mirror. Posing in her drawing room, he would declare,
'Well Leeson, arn't [sic] I a damn'd handsome fine fellow?' His
family banking business was well established, and run from Castle
Street in Dublin. La Touche's father had succeeded to his position

in the bank after the death of his own father, David's grandfather in 1745. His clients – many of them the same as Peg's – included nobility: the Dukes of Leinster and Rutland, the Marquesses of Buckingham, Headfort, Cornwallis, Lansdowne and Westmeath, as well as an assortment of earls. Clients either wrote their drafts upon pieces of ordinary writing paper, or had their own cheques privately printed. When he died in 1785, La Touche's father was reputed to be one of the richest bankers in Europe, a fact reflected in his will, in which he left his eldest son, David, a huge estate and £12,000 a year. The Bank of Ireland had been established by Act of Parliament in June 1783, and in order to gain a good name for the enterprise and make its stock attractive to the public, David La Touche had been appointed governor for the first three years. La Touche's bank initially adhered to the legitimate and simple business of receiving money on deposit and in current accounts, and making advances,[10] but eventually began to issue paper currency.

Peg's trips to the theatre sometimes caused a stir, with jealous spats played out in full view of the audience. About a week after the incident of Peg's banter with the crowd about Charles Manners, she was back at her favourite spot in the auditorium when she saw two ladies of the Stratford family, Lady FitzHerbert and Lady Queade, sitting in the box where Peg usually sat. Enraged by their audacity, Peg immediately went up to them and seated herself between them, arranging her friends around them. The intruders, now aware they were sitting amongst a bunch of whores, rose to leave. Peg, however, was not about to let them off so easily. She addressed them in a loud voice:

> Ladies, don't be ashamed to be seen in my company, no doubt half the house knows I am a whore, the other half are as well convinced that you are arrant thieves, and pray tell me now, who are so fit to go together as whores and thieves. Though you must confess the whore is a much safer acquaintance than the thief.

Peg may have been alluding to the fact that the ladies had stolen her seats, or possibly she was referring to the dishonesty in the Stratford family; Edward Augustus Stratford, 2nd Earl of Aldborough, an ardent Whig, had been elected member for Taunton to the British Parliament in 1774, but had been unseated with his colleague Nathaniel Webb, on petition, on 16 March 1775, for bribery and corruption.

One of Peg's close friends was Mrs Brookes, a woman who had been with her when Charles Manners first made his appearance at her establishment. She had started off as a fruit hawker, selling apples and oranges as well as her sexual favours on the side, but had turned to running a successful brothel in Belfast. She had been forced to leave the city after being threatened by a mob who believed her to be an accomplice to the murder of the wife of one of her clients, a Mr Donnelly. Because Brookes was his favourite whore, it was thought that she had encouraged him to kill his wife. The only person to defend her was Amyas Griffith, a printer of whom Peg was rather fond, who had started the prosecution against Mr Donnelly, believing him to be the true culprit. Thanks to Griffith, the mob believed Brookes's innocence and her life was spared. She had hastily moved to Dublin, bringing with her a bevy of her girls – Jenny Neilson, Polly Dalzell and a couple of others.

Now running a whorehouse in Derby Square, Brookes's clients included Richard Wellesley, Earl of Mornington and brother to the Duke of Wellington, and Waddell Cunningham. Brookes, despite suffering many losses in the past, had made her fortune, and would retire a rich woman. One potential impediment had been a surgeon[11] who had been her constant bedfellow, but had run up unpaid debts of nearly a hundred pounds. Another time Mrs Brookes's house was set on fire when one of her girls, Miss Mary Russell, and a client were so in the throes of passion they knocked over a candle. This set alight the bed, their clothes and all the furniture in the room. According to Brookes, they were going at it 'buff to buff' or 'bare breeched', 'as 'twas once practised in the Garden of Eden', an incident of naked sex, a rarity at this time. Most sex took place partially clothed, with breeches left half on and petticoats simply lifted up for easy access. Since no underwear was worn, there was no need for its removal. Perhaps because of her colourful background and resilience, Brookes would remain a friend of Peg and often take tea with her.

The area of conviviality centred on a small group of people; peers of the realm mixed with printers, bankers and barristers, all of whom frequented the brothels of Dublin. One of the least liked by Peg was

Waddell Cunningham (1729–97). He had been a visitor to Peg's establishment as well as a patron of Mrs Brookes's house in Belfast. A leading merchant of a Belfast-based slave trading company, his status was buttressed by his position as founding president of the Belfast Chamber of Commerce and first president of the harbour board.[12] He had been charged with various crimes relating to his business activities, including trading with the enemy during the American war, but managed to bribe his way out of it as witnesses refused to testify, and even custom house officials cooperated with the defence by falsifying documents. Greg & Cunningham held its position as the city's pre-eminent Irish trading house.[13] Cunningham was embroiled in a further scandal when he was elected MP for Carrickfergus in 1784 in controversial circumstances, including suspicion of corruption and bribery. Now in his fifties, he was a wealthy Belfast Presbyterian merchant, a leading member of the Volunteer movement and a radical. According to Peg, Cunningham was 'an ungrateful lecher' who, 'while his amiable wife lay barren by his side, for forty-five years and more, made a shift to knock triplets out of his kitchen maid'. Another female contemporary would conjecture, 'I would shudder if WC's interest, ambition, and therefore inclination and abilities were combined against me.'[14]

More popular by far was the printer who had been of such help to Brookes, Amyas Griffith. He was probably Peg's lover too; he features greatly in her life and she obviously had affection for him. He explained in his own words how he felt about the situation:

> Upon my arrival here, with my family, early in May, 1780, from a province where I was adored by all degrees and ranks of people, and where every compliment, civility and respect were paid to my wife and children, I took it into my head that a particular class of people who should have been the first to pay us attention, being for the most part revenue officers and the agents and the dependents of Lord Donegal, had treated me and my family with great disrespect.

In fact, Griffith had been ceremoniously ignored. As a tribute to Peg's loyalty to him, he addressed his pamphlet *Truth and Falsehood, A Fable* to 'Mrs Leeson'.

Griffith was just one of the casualties in the politics being played out in Dublin. A cyclone of business, politics and social events brought together people from a wide range of backgrounds. The brothel was their meeting place, the Rotunda and theatre their playground. Peg's house in Pitt Street was to some extent a social leveller, although all of the men had to have money. While Peg did not much involve herself in politics, of those she saw as Irish Catholic sympathisers she made loyal friends, and those whom she saw as traitors, such as Cunningham, she abhorred. She was also to prove a good friend to her sisters in prostitution, but she was about to suffer the loss of a very close companion.

The 'Impures', or Ladies on the Town

Where the girls are so pretty . . .

For the next few years Peg was to rule over Dublin's world of courtesans. Women would come and go from her brothel, some of whom she remembered with more fondness than others. Every evening was spent continually entertaining clients. With this came the unenviable job of picking, training and overseeing the women she employed. Women fell into prostitution for a number of different reasons – some were 'seduced' at an early age, a broad term which might include rape. Natural waywardness, abandonment by lovers and husbands, being tricked out of money, or simple poverty were all precursors to a career in a brothel. There were various names given to these women, such as 'courtesans', 'women on the town', 'demireps', and Peg's own favourites, 'nymphs' and 'impures'. They were also called the less polite names of whore, harlot, slut and strumpet. Those who managed to procure a well-known, wealthy keeper sometimes took his name as their working alias, as had Peg when she took Mr Leeson's.

It was some time in October 1784, after a protracted illness, that Sally Hayes, Peg's long-term friend and companion, died. Peg was to say of her, 'Miss Sally Hayes was my constant companion whilst she lived, and the woman I loved best, as she had a spirit congenial to my own. But alas, I lost her; for . . . she contracted some bilious complaint from vexation, at the loss of a favourite captain who went abroad, which carried her off.' Rather than a broken heart, as Peg suggests, Sally's death was more likely connected with some sort of venereal disease which had previously laid her low. Indeed, Peg may well have been exposed to the same condition herself as she had been experiencing ill health off and on for some time. Lawless was evidently still in contact with her, as he wrote her a letter in which he expressed concern for her health as well as sending his condolences on Sally's death. 'It concerns me not a little, your relation of your frequent fits of illness; however it must be of some consolation to you for the loss of your poor dear little Sally, as you say, whenever you are afflicted in the manner you mention, you have one with you, who alleviates your pain and anxiety.' Peg had written to him about another lover, perhaps Cunynghame, in order to pique his jealousy. But Lawless knew Peg all too well and did not rise to the bait. 'Whether you mention that by way of causing me uneasiness, I shall not take it upon myself to say.' Instead he merely hoped she would never want for a friend.[1]

Over the years, many women came to Peg for financial assistance or for the chance to work in her establishment, and Peg peppered her memoirs with their stories. One woman of Peg's acquaintance, Mrs Wynne of Summer Hill, had managed to escape prostitution through marriage to an Englishman. Soon after Sally's death, she introduced Peg to a young woman called Kitty Gore. This type of introduction was helpful in sifting out the more reliable girls from the rest – or so it should have been.

While Mrs Wynne may have been acting in good faith, Peg's other friend Miss Ross knew Kitty to be of the worst character imaginable, and her mother to be ten times worse. On her advice therefore, Peg initially refused to employ the girl. Yet only a few days later, after much persistence on the mother's part, Peg relented and permitted Kitty to take up residence in her house. Peg herself admitted, 'In truth, I was an easy fool, who suffered myself to be over-persuaded.' She was even taken in by Kitty's mother, who informed Peg that her daughter had been lodging at the house of Mrs Burnett at 22 Whitefriar Street for the last two months. Kitty could not leave until the amount she owed for her clothes was paid off at the princely sum of seven guineas. The bawd Mrs Burnett, it seemed, had done the usual trick of binding her employees to the brothel by putting her in debt for the clothes suitable for business. Peg duly paid off Kitty's debt to allow her to move in with her, but on arrival that night, the mother and the daughter came back with no clothes and no trunk. Even the cloak Kitty wore was borrowed, and immediately snatched by her mother to be restored to its rightful owner. Peg enquired as to the true circumstances of Kitty's current plight and lamented, 'she owned she had not a shred more than was on her back, but what was in pawn'. As Peg prepared her for work, she told her, 'Well child, you are a likely girl, and may do very well, if you take care of yourself, and behave properly; but you can't keep my company without making an elegant appearance. If I should take proper things for you, will you be honest, and repay me?' Kitty swore she would, and promised that she would never forget how kind Peg had been to her.

The following day, Peg took her to the most exclusive shops to purchase anything the girl wanted up to the amount of a hundred guineas. No sooner was Kitty dressed fit for business than her mother was round to the house asking for money. Although Kitty said she had none, after much tiresome haggling, Peg made Kitty give her mother £10 just to get rid of her. It was not long before Kitty's old keeper re-entered her life and realised she was now in far better circumstances than when he had left. He induced Kitty to return to him, taking along all the clothes Peg had bought for her, which foolishly Peg gave up on the promise that he would pay her. As time went by with no sign of repayment in sight, she decided to sue, as was Peg's usual practice.

> After waiting three or four months, and no money coming in, I sent to the gentleman for payment. The answer was, that he would never pay me a farthing . . . I then took out a writ, and arrested Miss Gore; the surgeon [her keeper] got bail for her, and defended the suit. After a short time, her attorney came, and offered to pay half but I thought it too bad to loose £26, for my foolish good nature, refused and the case came to trial.

Peg's litigious nature made her press on, and she was unwilling to give in without a full fight. At the trial, despite bringing in the shop owners to give evidence of the bills Kitty had run up, and much to her anger, Peg lost her case.[2] According to Peg, the jury were dishonest men selected by the defence, 'a set of picked-up fellows, hired, like hackney coaches, for a shilling fare each, who valued neither soul nor body;

and probably had not the price of a dinner, till they received their hire from Kitty Gore's honest friend and protector.'

Other reasons induced Peg to let her impures go. One whore she let go for becoming too bawdy. The woman was a Mrs Porter and had been a friend of the mistress of the Duke of Westmorland, a Mrs Sinnot who, although not a personal friend of Peg's, was someone whose opinion she thought reliable. Sinnot appeared to think highly of Mrs Porter, as she had been happy to befriend her and introduce her to rich men when she was seeking a protector. However, Porter was not of a discreet nature, and her vulgarity soon excluded her from the *bon ton*. Peg noted, 'before she was two months on the town, she became so common, that Mrs Sinnot broke off all connection with her'. She sank so low that she was 'happy to share her favour with every ruffian who can "a crown afford"'. Although Mrs Porter had been at the Pitt Street brothel for only a short time, she had become so uncouth that Peg, concerned that Porter's failing reputation would reflect on her own good establishment, had asked her to leave. However, Peg perhaps underestimated Porter's allure, as she was later taken to live in Mark Street under the protection of William Robert Fitzgerald, 3rd Duke of Leinster.

At the beginning of 1785, it was announced that a masquerade was to be held at the Rotunda on behalf of Peg's friend, James William Hughes, proprietor of the Hughes gambling house in College Green. Concert and balls were often held to raise funds for the hospital. In order to make an impact on the crowd, Peg employed 'four of the prettiest *impures* in all Dublin': Fanny Beresford dressed up as Venus overseeing Mary Read, Miss Love and Mary Neilson as the three Graces. Having already appeared at other masquerades as Cleopatra and Messalina, this time Peg chose the character of Chastity, Diana the Huntress. The men made equal efforts with their fancy dress, if not with their behaviour. Beau Myrtle came as Beelzebub, drunk as a lord after imbibing too much champagne and burgundy. While Peg castigated his behaviour, she thought him handsome: 'not bad for a young divine, and being inflamed by beauty and heated with Champagne and Burgundy, of which he tippled too freely, he took most indecent liberties with the beautiful Vice Queen, by thrusting his black hands into her fair bosom'. He was promptly ejected from the party. According to Peg, some time later he was thrown out of college for his drunken behaviour (other sources say he received a Masters Degree)[3], having to make a living writing for the 'Man of Ireland, poor Jack Magee!'

Jack Magee was the proprietor of the *Dublin Evening Post*, running a column under the heading 'Man of Ireland'. According to Peg, Magee had married his wife (or '*Woman of Ireland*', as Peg called her in a skit on the name of her husband's column) 'in one of his *paroxysms* of insanity', in great style in 'a certain house in Great Britain Street', and for two months she was kept with her 'own chariot, footmen, and coachmen in laced livery'. He had taken a house for her in College Green and another at Blackrock, squandering over £3,000 on her in all. Her pleasant way of life was to come to an abrupt end, by her own admission, due to bad conduct, when her husband whipped her and turned her out of doors at two o'clock in the morning 'like a common prostitute'. However, before leaving him, she had managed to extort £300 while agreeing to release him from his marital obligations. When Mrs Magee left him, she was to become one of Peg's boarders for a time and proved problematic. Once settled into Peg's establishment, it became evident that Mrs Magee was drinking too much whiskey. Her drinking habits, however, were no impediment to finding a keeper. Despite her frequent state of inebriation, Buck Whaley, a client of Peg's just back from Jerusalem, was to take Mrs Magee into his protection. His excursion to the Middle East two years previously had started off as a jest at a dinner table but, as he explained himself, 'I instantly offered to bet any sum that I would go to Jerusalem and return to Dublin within two years from my departure. I accepted without hesitation all the wagers that were offered to me, and in a few days the sum I had depending on this curious expedition exceeded £15,000.' Peg had been there to see him off at the quayside, along with all his supporters.[4] Now back and looking for a mistress, Whaley paid off Peg for Mrs Magee's board and lodgings, as was the custom in these exchanges. Peg admits, 'I was not sorry to get rid of that exalted lady, as she became extremely troublesome, and beside was too fond of the native [Irish whiskey].' John Magee's 'insanity' was in fact a form of mental illness so acute as to land him in Swift's Hospital for Incurables by his own choice. Peg had a soft spot for Magee, saying 'he is one of the best men', and was fond of all his family.

Peg was willing to take in all sorts of unfortunate women who applied to her establishment. Mrs Palmer, another of Peg's 'tribe', had started off her career bound to a milliner for three years. Milliners, with their reputation for turning good girls bad, were known for supplying prostitutes to clients, acting as a kind of pimping service. Other whores Peg knew came from the foundling homes; with no security from family or friends, once they came of age, they were out on the streets. Red-haired temptress Mary Fagan Crosbie had been taken from the Foundling Hospital in 1775 to work for a mantua-maker. After various keepers, she had ended up with a Captain Misset. After Crosbie had squeezed him dry, he was incarcerated for two years for debt, while she lived it up on all the money she had taken from him. These girls sometimes became petty thieves, understandably, in a world where women had such a precarious existence. More often than not, men had already taken advantage of them, then turned them out on the streets with no means of survival. Some like Peg had made their way through brothel-keeping, a career which, if handled properly and extended into the realms of the titled men, at least allowed for a comfortable and stylish life.

In order to keep up connections and extend her business, Peg made various trips to soirées out of town. One particular gathering was held at the Donegall Arms in Belfast, a place which had started its life as the New Inn, standing at present-day Castle Place, with some small accommodation.[5] Here the party got underway, headed by Tom Greg, the famous merchant of the town and brother-in-law to Waddell Cunningham. He was assisted by his sister-in-law, Mrs Anne Pottinger, whom Peg described as 'a diminutive deformed hobgoblin'.[6] One of the women there was Greg's daughter, Jenny, who although very beautiful was also haughty and rude. Wanting to deflate her, Peg commented to her companion in loud stage whispers, 'Pray has not that tall awkward thing a great deal of *Black* about her countenance?' Her companion answered: 'Hold your tongue you rogue. Don't you know her Papa, the king there, was a blacksmith?' These exchanges were in reference to the slave trade, in which Greg was embroiled with Waddell Cunningham; the suggestion being that Jenny was the illegitimate offspring of a slave. Presented with snobbery, Peg was apt to show the boorish, and sometimes childish, side to her nature. She wrote on the window:

Jenny Glen they say has wit and some, they add, have felt it:
She walks as if she was beshit and looks as if she smells it.

While distressed women were constantly applying to Peg, she admitted only to taking in those who had been seduced, had an adulterous past, or who were already on the town. She consistently denied ever having procured girls. While Peg's establishment frequently saw newcomers pass through its doors, these women, to Peg's thinking, had already been down the path of sexual immorality. Not all bawds were so scrupulous, and went out of their way to procure young, innocent girls, a practice Peg abhorred. Vicious and violent procurers were legion: Anne McDonagh of Little Booter's Lane had her premises ransacked on October 1781 after the killing of a thirteen-year-old Belfast girl who had refused to work there; another riot erupted in summer 1782 when McDonagh blinded one of her workers. Mrs Docas Kelly of Copper Alley was executed in 1788 after five corpses were found in her brothel.

The rescue of such unfortunate women had been undertaken by a woman whom Peg professed to admire greatly, Lady Arabella Denny. Denny had opened the first Magdalen asylum in Ireland on Leeson Street in Dublin in 1766, after she had noted how poverty encouraged prostitution, but it admitted only Protestant girls.[7] Her aim was to help those 'unfortunate females abandoned by their seducers and rejected by their friends, who were willing to prefer a life of penitence and virtue to one of guilt, infamy and prostitution'.[8] When they entered the asylum, the women had to abandon their previous identities, and were forced to assume new names. The daily routine consisted of strictly controlled and regimented chores. A chapel attached to the asylum, opened in 1768, was patronised by some of Dublin's elite and served to raise funds for the institution.[9] Denny was also a member of the ladies' committee of the Rotunda Lying-in Hospital, and she used her social standing and family connections to promote her charitable schemes. Some of her activities caused controversy, but Peg admired both Denny and fellow philanthropist Mrs David La Touche, referring to them each as 'a paragon of *charity, piety* and *humanity*'. David La Touche held a pew at the hospital's Magdalen chapel where his wife was a member of the committee. He was also treasurer of the Lock penitentiary for the treatment of venereal disease, possibly having a vested interest as a regular client at Peg's establishment.

Prostitutes were at constant risk of being apprehended while walking the streets, as Peg was to experience. One night, after seeing a play, she was about to go and dine with Moll Hall, a friend who ran a brothel in Johnson's Court within walking distance of Pitt Street. Since it was a fine light night and her friend's house was not far, Peg decided to walk. However, Peg was about to fall foul of the new system which had been introduced under the Dublin Police Act 1786 (some forty-three years before Robert Peel's 'Peelers' were established). Prior to this, keeping the peace and local governance had been overseen by the Church of Ireland parish. It was responsible for key aspects of local administration including burial of the dead, providing welfare for the poor, lighting, street-cleaning and overseeing parish security through the employment of constables and watchmen. Provision of these local services was all financed by the parish through a levy administered by the parish vestry (the committee responsible for the upkeep of churches and welfare of all the people within the parish boundaries irrespective of religion). However, policing of the growing metropolis had become a problem, and new measures were implemented to establish a professional police force under the direction of commissioners appointed by the lord lieutenant.[10] A special police force would oversee Dublin, responsible for the four divisions of the Barracks, the Rotunda, St Stephens Green and the Workhouse, with each area under the command of a chief constable. The police could now enter public houses, arrest people for 'drinking, tippling or gaming at unreasonable hours', apprehend vagabonds and try and keep order.

Since 'respectable' women would not be seen wandering the streets at night, and although she was accompanied by her footman for safety that night, Peg was a prime target. She was hardly out of sight of her house when a policeman came running up alongside them as fast as he could.

'Where are you going?' he asked.

'What's that to you?' Peg retorted.

Her servant intervened and asked the policeman, 'What assurance do you have to stop my mistress?' The policeman ignored the question but continued to insist that they accompany him to the watch house.

Peg demanded to be told why, but he merely reiterated that she must go with him. Peg was becoming increasingly irate.

'My good fellow! Remember you will pay for this, and I advise you to be quiet,' she warned.

The constable insisted he was only doing his duty.

'Do you know me?' Peg asked, exasperated.

The policeman responded, 'No I do not. Nor do I care who you are.'

'Well my fine fellow. I am Peg Plunkett and this is my house and I don't think you can have any orders to take me up. But come, let us go to the watch house, and you shall pay dearly for your conduct.'

The policeman was no doubt angling for a bribe. Many of them were corrupt and made extra income from extracting money from arrests. As Peg remarked, he was trying 'to squeeze half a guinea or a guinea out of me, but he was mistaken.' She had little choice but to accompany him to the watch house in Aungier Street, where she immediately asked the guard to show her to 'the best apartment they had'. Peg sent her servant to find one of her friends, either Captain Carleton or Captain Atkinson, to inform them what had happened.[11] It was handy to have connections with officers, as they could help in times of trouble, despite the occasional contretemps Peg had had with the less reliable men in the army. The officers came along immediately, put her in a sedan and sent her home. Captains in the army evidently had authority over ordinary policemen, as the officers sent the policeman to the 'black-hole', the worst pit in the prison. They had every intention of making him sweat for a couple of days. The outcome was that the policeman lost his job and was soon round at Peg's house begging forgiveness. While she wanted people to admit their wrongdoing and pay for it, she was not one to bear a grudge – she simply needed to put people in their place. She eventually took pity on him and helped him regain his former employment. Inevitably, this experimental police force failed, as it was inefficient and too expensive. Not until 1795 would there be a return to a decentralised police force coming under the control of the local parish.[12]

Women would sometimes repay their female benefactors with interest as a 'thank you' for saving them from dire situations. Peg recalled the generosity of spirit of many of the women in the business. A whores' 'sisterhood' existed, which allowed for a subscription or kitty, from which women could withdraw funds during hard times.[13] A squib entitled 'The Humble Petition of the Sisterhood' was mentioned in the *Dublin Evening Post* in 1779 with the supposed authors as Sally Hays, Anne Judge, Peg Plunkett and P. Austin, endorsed by Kitty Netterville.[14] Indeed, Peg and Sally had attended a prostitutes' union meeting in October 1776.

For Peg, the period between 1784 and 1789 saw a series of women coming to and leaving her establishment. Having lost her best friend and co-worker Sally, she had done what she knew best to keep herself occupied. She had kept her grief at bay by throwing herself into her business. She had also managed to enjoy some offbeat jollities, including the Mugglin festival in late August or early September of 1788, involving the mock coronation of the Mugglin King of Dalkey, as well as a celebration of Prince George's birthday at Fiat Hill involving 'racing pigs, dancing girls, grinning hags and cudgelling-blades' – the last two probably being grimacing competition and hand-to-hand fights with blunt weapons.[15] She had even had a racehorse named after her. According to the *General Advertiser* for 13 October 1786 'fifty pounds [prize money] for 4 year old of 8 stone 7lb' Mr Dunn's grey mare, Peg Plunkett, coming in third place.[16]

While Peg's business vied for clients with her friend Moll Hall's brothel in Johnson's Court, as well as Mrs Dillon's in Fishamble Street, Mrs Johnston operating in a house in Fownes Street, Mrs Sterling in Jervis Street, Mrs Wynne on Summer Hill, Mrs O'Brien in Longford Street and Mrs Burnett in Whitefriars Street, clearly there was enough business for them all. These women had many different types of beauty and talents to offer. While Moll Hall was a plump woman to whom Peg referred as a 'little fat Pretty creature', she was popular, indicating that some men were not averse to a surplus of flesh. Despite their rivalry, most of these women forged friendships which would carry them through the best of times and the worst of times together.

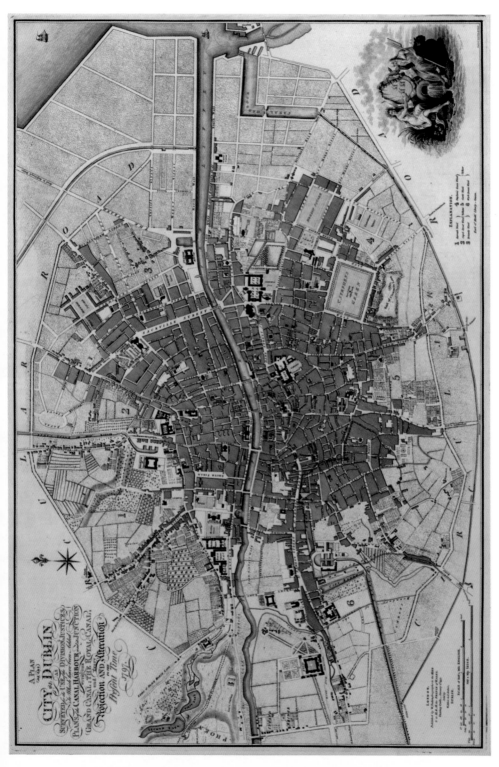

A map of Dublin as it was during Peg's lifetime.

The Custom House, Dublin, built in Peg's lifetime and still a major landmark of the city.

Trinity College, Dublin, where many of Peg's clients were students.

Dublin's foundling hospital, established in 1729 and familiar to many women in Peg's profession.

Russborough House, one of Ireland's most important stately homes, built by the Leeson family and owned by Peg's keeper Joseph Leeson.

A contemporary satire of the fashion in the 1740s for the enormous 'bell hoop' dresses: many found them absurd, but Peg was an enthusiastic adopter of the style.

'A woman of pleasure' – the popular view of women of Peg's status as dissolute and drunken: detail from *Progress of a Woman of Pleasure* by Richard Newton, 1796.

Hogarth's *Beer St*, the companion to the more famous *Gin Lane*, showed an idealized kind of contemporary London life: Peg did not find the city so welcoming.

'The Fountain', built on James's St by the Duke of Rutland: Peg lived near here in her final years, and her funeral procession likely passed it.

The title page of the 1798 edition of Peg's memoirs.

THE

L I F E

OF

Mrs. MARGARET LEESON

ALIAS

PEG PLUNKET.

WRITTEN BY HERSELF:

In which are given *Anecdotes* and *Sketches* of the LIVES and
BON MOTS of some of the most CELEBRATED CHARACTERS

IN

GREAT-BRITAIN AND IRELAND,

PARTICULARLY OF ALL THE

FILLES DES JOYS

AND

MEN OF PLEASURE AND GALLANTRY,

Who usually frequented her CITHEREAN TEMPLE *for these*
Thirty Years past.

THREE VOLUMES COMPLETE IN ONE.

A NEW EDITION WITH CONSIDERABLE ADDITIONS.

" She was 'tis true MOST FRAIL, and yet so JUST,
" That NATURE when she form'd her knew not where——
" To class her."——
" A Dame of highest VIRTUE and of TRUTH,
" Or the POOR WRETCH that she has chanc'd to be."

ANONYMOUS.

DUBLIN:

PRINTED AND SOLD BY THE PRINCIPAL BOOKSELLERS

1798.

Price sewed, 5s. 5d.

The parish record of Peg's burial (named as 'Margaret Plunkett', listed 4th).

St James's graveyard, Dublin, where Peg is buried, though the exact site of her grave is not known.

15

Masquerade and Marriage

I looked upon the connection with such loathing . . .

To perk up the season in 1789, Peg decided to throw another masquerade, seemingly egged on by Moll Hall, who revelled in such excitements. It was a couple of years after Kitty Netterville's death who, according to the *Evening Post*, had died a virtual pauper on 17 May 1787 at Broadstone, Dublin. If Peg were to celebrate her pre-eminence in the world of courtesanship, a magnificent masquerade seemed in order.

For the party, Peg decided she would invite all of Dublin's Freemasons since they were known to be generous and fun, if a little unusual. She claimed, 'The gentlemen of that ancient and honourable fraternity in this city gave sumptuous entertainments, fandangoes and coteries, by inviting their friends and acquaintances to roast meat, and beating them with the spit; that is clubbing them *sans ceremonie*', an obvious mockery of Masonic membership rituals. Peg would charge an entrance fee of two guineas, with any extras such as the sharing 'of one of our fair guests' bed' to be added to the bill. The beds had been updated with the finest springs and properly stuffed mattresses.

Among the women attending to the men's needs were Fanny Beresford and Mary Neilson of Ballyclear, as well as Mary Read.[1] Others in attendance at Peg's masquerade were Jack Plunkett, Daly from Kerry, Captain Kelly and politician Peter Seguin, as well as literary folk such as the author Jane Elizabeth Moore, the playwright and author of *Democratic Rage*, William Preston, and blind Bartholomew Corcoran, a Dublin printer specialising in chap books and ballads. Some of the gentlemen were picked as stewards on the door to ensure everyone entering had a ticket. Henry Blennerhassett,[2] the old keeper of Miss Grove, one of Peg's girls, was there, having lately impregnated his kitchen maid with triplets while his wife of forty-five years remained barren. Also present was Ebeneezer Radford Roe or Rowe 'of convivial, cleanly and generous memory', a first cousin of Frances Griffith, Amyas Griffith's wife.[3] Surgeon Bolger, a friend of Peg, had offered her the use of the Lock Hospital near Donnybrook for the party, but she politely declined as she preferred to use her own establishment. Michael Kelly, who managed the Ménage in Capel Street and subsequently ran a brothel in Whitehall, County Dublin, was also at the party. Ned Nowlan, editor of the *Freeman's Journal*, made sexual overtures to Peg at the party, along with a host of other eager suitors. However, the gentleman of the evening who turned Peg's head was the son of the perfumer Peter Le Favre of Grafton Street, and she spent most of her evening dancing with him.

Peg's list of attendees acts as a roll-call of everyone she knew: Mrs Robinson, who could generally be found operating from Mrs Grant's brothel, came as 'The Blue-Eyed Nun of St Catherine's', accompanied by her lover Lord FitzWilliam, as well as Mrs Grant herself; Miss Archibold, currently being kept by a gentleman reputed to be tight with his money, but one that Peg had always found 'quite a generous fellow'; and Mrs Vallance, who despite a respectable upbringing, had fallen into the lifestyle of prostitution through idleness. Alderman Worthington and Moll Hall came dressed as Father Paul and Mother Cole; Henry Blennerhassett and Miss Grove came as the Mayor of Coventry and Pretty Maud; Waddell Cunningham and Mrs Brookes came as Alderman Smuggler and Diana Trapes; Mary Neilson was accompanied by a reverend (possibly George Phillips)[4], she dressed as Miss Hardcastle and he as Tony Lumpkin respectively, characters from Oliver Goldsmith's play *She Stoops to Conquer*.

Another old friend of Peg joining the masquerade was Mrs Wrixon, who had taken refuge in Peg's brothel after stealing 200 guineas from a man injured in a duel in England. She had escaped with her lover on Captain Harrison's packet boat, landing in Dublin in August 1789. Nancy Hindes also joined the party. She had similarly escaped poverty after swindling her lover's captain of all his money (when the captain was recalled to join his regiment, he had foolishly given power of attorney to his officer and he and Nancy spent everything he owned; the good captain, on finding himself in dire straits, had blown his brains out). Many of Peg's guests appear to have been in some sort of trouble in the past, living off their wits or their wiles. Now the whole gathering was making the most of Peg's hospitality.

Peg threw open five or six rooms to make one large space to accommodate her guests for the grand occasion. Chandeliers glistened, candles flickered, glasses shone and champagne flowed. More and more guests arrived, including John ____ S____, a 'little whiffling old gentleman', husband of the lovely Kitty Attridge. Kitty was from Skibbereen, County Cork, and had previously boarded in Peg's house, having sought refuge from a blighted life. Peg said of her, 'She had a charming taste for poetry and the Belles Lettres in general, sung like a Siren, played inimitably well on the pianoforte, and was in every respect one of the most accomplished and beautiful women I was ever acquainted with.' She had come up against unfortunate circumstances after a disastrous marriage to Mr Attridge, an infamous gentleman with an estate in Cork. Despite the couple's separation, he had continued to pay her maintenance, but after she'd formed a connection with John Gahan, then Surveyor General of Munster, he cut her off. When Gahan was ruined during an election, he ended up in prison, and Kitty became a boarder at Peg's house. Gahan was mortified that he could not support Kitty, and refused to take the money she offered him. Unable to persuade him to live with her, she eventually returned to Cork and married a gentleman who had been enamoured of her many years previously and had recently come into an estate of five hundred pounds a year.[5] She had returned to Peg's for the party.

According to Peg, after the masquerade, the radical printer Amyas Griffith 'gave a flourishing account of that whimsical entertainment, with all his own *hyperbolic* embellishments.' After his earlier ruin, he had set up the *Phoenix* newspaper, running it as its owner and editor. At the masquerade, he had watched as William Alexander English of Ranelagh Road had taken Peg into one of the recesses for sex while the party carried on around them. This gallant had spent his youth in dissipation, 'a profusion so lavish, as to procure him the name of *Buck English*'. He had spent the middle years of his life in Four Courts Marshalsea, then his final years suing for the recovery of his estate.[6]

In the event, the Masonic Masquerade lasted from nine o'clock at night to five o'clock the next morning. It was the success of the season, attended by authors, representatives from both sides of the Houses of Parliament and all the 'impures' in town. Although bawd Margaret Lewellen and Father Patrick Fay had attempted to buy tickets for the event, they had been refused because of the recent scandal surrounding them. Fay had recently been served a sentence for forgery, while Lewellen of Blackmoor Yard, Angelsea Street, had been sentenced to hang for her complicity in the rape of Mary Neill, aged thirteen, by Lord Carhampton and Francis Higgins. The incident had occurred only the year before, in a brothel run by Lewellen and Robert Edgeworth, and had shaken society. Barrister Archibald Hamilton Rowan had taken up the case and Lewellen had been pardoned and released in April 1789.[7]

After the excitement of the masquerade had died down, by chance Peg was presented with an opportunity of obtaining both wealth and status when Barry Yelverton jun. called on her and offered to marry her.[8] As second son to the chief Baron of the Court of the Exchequer who was about to be made a peer,[9] Yelverton jun. was in a position to inherit both money and a title. Yelverton sen. was an Irish judge and politician, a charming man and convivial companion, popular among his colleagues at the Irish Bar. Despite frequent courtroom clashes with barrister and wit John Philpot Curran (often visited Peg's house), they seem to have got on personally, both co-founders of the popular drinking club The Monks of the Screw. This was an Irish drinking club to which many of Peg's clients belonged, active over a decade from around 1779 onwards. The 'screw' referred to the corkscrew necessary for opening a bottle of wine. Around 1785, at great expense, Yelverton sen. had built a mansion, Fortfield House in Terenure, County Dublin, which no doubt Peg had her eye on when she accepted the marriage proposal of his son. Although he was not first in line, Barry jun. was set to come into a sizable inheritance.

For most young women in the eighteenth century, marriage was aspired to and expected. It was a process through which respectability was gained and a way in which a woman entered society. Nuptials were a sign of maturity, an acceptance by a woman of her allotted role as a wife. Generally speaking, though, the women of the *demi-monde* had difficulty persuading rich men to marry them and lived on the tail end of respectability. They might mix with some of the *bon ton*, mingle with lords and earls, but they would never be invited into respectable homes. A way round this exclusion was to marry a wealthy or titled man. This would ensure a ticket out of the world of whoredom and allow a woman to gain some respectability and security. To this end, some of the whores wanted nothing more than to 'marry up'. Others preferred to keep their liberty and not lose their separate identity in a world which legally only recognised men and saw women as men's property. As Sir William Blackstone wrote, 'By marriage, the husband and wife are one person in law: that is, the very being, or legal existence of the woman is suspended during the marriage, or at least is incorporated and consolidated into that of the husband: under whose wing, protection and cover, she performs everything.'[10]

Peg had always made her feelings clear to Yelverton; she had resolutely refused him and professed to despise him. No doubt her constant rebuttals acted as a spur to his advances. A marriage proposal was not to be taken lightly, and now the sound of 'the Honourable Mrs Yelverton' was becoming increasingly attractive to Peg. Yelverton jun. was, after all, set to inherit a title and a fortune. Without further consideration, Peg agreed to his proposal, and his friend Philip Hatchell, the apothecary of 45 Grafton Street who had accompanied Yelverton to Peg's house, was immediately dispatched to find a couple beggar (a defrocked minister who made a living performing the church rites for a cheap fee) to marry them. It was obvious that Peg was an unsuitable match and that his father would never consent to such a marriage. The couple therefore intended to keep the wedding a secret and to marry in haste – a couple beggar would best suit their needs. The necessary papers were hastily drawn up and duly signed by Hatchell, Peter Le Favre and James Warren, the three men acting as witnesses. The newspapers announced their marriage, and all the 'impures' of the town gathered to congratulate Peg on her good catch. Ballads were composed about the newly weds, and well-known musicians Charley O'Gallagher and his father-in-law Mr Kinselagh sang songs fêting them. Unfortunately, and perhaps unsurprisingly, the union was not to last.

As with many men of the day, for Yelverton the chase had been more interesting than the catch. He quickly grew bored, as it was not in his nature to hold an interest for long. He was a profligate, more interested in spending freely and running up debts. He also appears to have been slightly mad. Jonah Barrington said of him in his memoirs, 'Barry was rather too odd a fellow to have been accounted at all times perfectly compos mentis.'[11] After his nuptials, he lost interest in Peg almost immediately and, according to her, 'grew as cool as a cucumber'. He even groused about the lip salve she wore, complaining she was 'always so plastered with *slave* [salve] or *spermaceti* ointment'. The marriage was so obviously undertaken by Peg as means of squeezing money out of the Yelvertons that she admitted, 'I looked upon the connection with such loathing, that for a very trifling consideration I was ready to relinquish every claim I had on *young hopeful*.' When Yelverton's father offered her 500 guineas to dissolve the marriage, Peg had no hesitation in accepting. Yelverton sen. had the necessary legal papers drawn up to revoke the marriage and Peg duly signed them. Only a few months later, Yelverton jun. was hauled into the sheriff's prison for non-payment of debts, where he languished until he was declared insolvent and released. After that, he often came to call on Peg but she refused to see him. According to Barrington, Yelverton came to an unsavoury end, 'The poor fellow grew quite deranged at last, and died, I believe, in rather unpleasant circumstances.'[12]

With her new husband dispatched, Peg returned to the life she knew best. Peg often supplied girls for parties at various men's secret societies. One of these clubs was the Anecdote Club of Free Brothers, otherwise known as the States of Castle-Kelly. The society had 500 members and was similar to the Beggar's Benison of Scotland, formed in 1732 by John McNaughton and consisting of wealthy Scottish lairds who came together to protect their interests.[13] It seems that a similar men's club had been set up in Ireland for those with an interest in carousing, dining, drinking and sex. Peg visited the 'Free Brothers', taking along her 'nymphs and nymphlings' to their private meetings. She was so popular with its members that they presented her with an elegantly embossed parchment in a beautiful silver box and made her an honorary member of their society. According to Peg, the box was stamped 'with all the emblems of the beggar's benison.'

The Scottish branch was known to have given out similar silver boxes containing female pubic hair. Along with her membership and silver box, Peg was presented with a popular bawdy poem, 'Guide to Joy', written by 'a Mrs H of Drumcondra',[14] mistress to the Prince of Wales. According to Peg, the poet was as fat as she was beautiful, 'her person rather too much in the *embonpoint* order'. On arrival in Dublin, the plump Mrs H. had hired the Exhibition Room in William Street, advertising that she would be reading her poem for the evening's entertainment at half a guinea a ticket. She spent about £6 of her own money on posting bills and puffs, but no one paid to see her, the only attendees being a group of hacks who had been given complimentary tickets. After the failure of the event, she sank into obscurity. However, Peg and her girls often went to visit her, now living comfortably in retirement on a pension from the prince.

As well as reading bawdy poems, Peg liked to read pornographic verse and prose such as Lord Rochester's *Poems*, *The Cabinet of Love* and *Kitty and Amynter*.[15] Pornography was frequently left lying around in brothels for perusal by clients. More mainstream reading was discussed at literary gatherings where Peg and her friends shared their interest in poetry and novels. Literary women impressed Peg, and she counted a handful among her friends. One, 'a pretty little smart Brunette', now being kept by an eminent attorney, she respected for her skill in poetry and novel writing. Another female poet of Peg's acquaintance had taken to the stage for a living after squandering a fortune of £2,000 a year in debauchery and dissipation. Rumour had it that she was the illegitimate daughter of Buck English, delivered after he had gone to stay at the family mansion in Thurles. Mrs Robinson, whom Peg had helped in the past, forwarded Peg £50 worth of calico and an edition of John Cleland's *Memoirs of a Woman of Pleasure* or *Fanny Hill*, a book published in 1749 which gained infamy for its pornographic text. The edition was evidently an expensive one, as it contained glorious images which Peg described as 'some of the finest cuts I ever beheld'. These were fine drawings depicting sex scenes inserted into the text, often hand-tinted. Though we rarely hear about women reading pornography, they seem to have done so with as much pleasure as men.

One of the writers Peg counted among her circle was playwright William Preston. He was known for his play *Democratic Rage: Or, Louis the Unfortunate*, a tragedy about the events of the French

Revolution and its adjutants, the *sans-culottes*. Peg often enjoyed his company of an evening. Having graduated from Trinity College in 1766, he had been called to the Irish Bar in 1777. He assisted in the establishment of the Royal Irish Academy, being elected its first secretary in 1786, a post he held for the rest of his life. An active member of the literary community, he also helped to found the Dublin Library Society and was a contributor to its *Transactions*, as well as being a member of the Monks of the Screw. Preston outlived Peg, dying on 2 February 1807, and was buried in St Thomas's churchyard.

In their early years, many of Peg's girls had suffered poverty, seduction and abandonment, their only recourse being the brothel. In taking these women in, Peg had provided them with an alternative lifestyle. In writing about them in her memoirs, she not only provided her audience with a view of the sexual underworld, but shed light on the sordid behaviour of many husbands and the plight to which society and the legal system had abandoned many women.

With no man lording over her, with money in her pocket and her own roof over her head, Peg saw that her quickly dissolved marriage had in fact been a lucky escape.

Summer Trip to Killarney

Heavens! What a place was here for love!!

One quiet evening, the women of Peg's establishment were gathered round the table for a game of cards. Playing with Peg were her board-ers Fanny Beresford and Miss Grove, and brothel-keeper at Eustace Street, Mrs McClean. Little was happening in the way of business and the women found it a soothing occupation to while away the time with the odd game of quadrille.

It was not unusual for women to play cards, and it had become a popular form of entertainment during the eighteenth century, with games such as whist, quadrille and piquet becoming part of a new leisured culture. Although slower to catch on in Ireland than in England, card-playing was adopted by the fashionable set, and while reckless young profligates frittered away their families' fortunes, middle-class ladies were also sitting down to play in polite house-holds, often playing faro late into the night.[1] Meanwhile, public figures in England such as Charles Fox and Georgiana, Duchess of Devonshire, were winning and losing hundreds of pounds at the gaming table. In establishments such as Peg's, card games were used to pass the time while waiting for gentleman callers to turn up.

The evening was to take a sudden turn as a group of four young blades burst through the doors and demanded their attention, but the women added another game to the evening. They insisted, as Peg explained, that 'they should deposit ten guineas each, and we agreed on our part that for every *perfect enjoyment* [ejaculation], one should be returned'. Because of the state of inebriation of the youths, the women believed they would prove impotent, or at the very least fall asleep on the job. All present company agreed they would discuss the consequences next morning as the eight of them coupled off to bed. The women were proved correct, and the inebriated men failed to exert themselves – all except for Peg's young blade, Mr Purcell. Peg announced, 'This whimsical affair caused great laughter, and poor a figure as my hero cut in the groves of Venus, yet he certainly was the conqueror by a long chalk.' It turned out that he had managed a singular successful congress, but, said Peg, only 'owing to my own exertions'. This was no hardship for Peg, as Purcell was handsome and extremely generous.

The next day Purcell, along with his friend O'Brien, decided with Peg and Mrs McClean to take off for an excursion to the lakes of Killarney, also visiting Youghal, Mallow and Limerick. The two men knew many respectable people in the country, and they thought it would be fun to pay them a visit, and an even greater lark to trick them all by posing as married couples.

The first stop was Killarney, a beautiful and popular tourist destination. Lakes and mountains covered in purple heather provided the perfect scenery, while the ruins of the fifteenth-century friary at Muckross added historical interest. On his tour of Ireland, Arthur Young remarked of Killarney, 'The lakes that I have seen can scarcely be said to have a rival.' Estate tourism was an important feature of upper-class sightseeing, with letters of introduction and personal connections opening doors to spectacular landscaped gardens and historic paintings. On arrival at Killarney on 1 June 1789, Peg and her companions booked themselves into the best inn available – a superior lodgings owned by Lord Kenmare which he provided for his guests. Kenmare was largely responsible for developing local tourism, hiring guns for shooting, and employing men to play horns and bugles which echoed among the lakes and valleys. But it had taken them 190 miles to get there, a journey considered 'too fatiguing and long'.

Purcell had a friend living close by, a Mr Walter Eager, and sent word to him that they were in town and requesting that he join them for a drink. Eager proved generous enough to make arrangements for the following day's entertainments; Lord Kenmare's barge was placed at their disposal and the coxswain, Mr Barry, would be only too happy to ferry them. While the arrangements were being made, Peg took take time out to visit her old friend Mrs Elizabeth O'Falvey.

Mrs O'Falvey had previously worked with Peg in her establishment, when she was known as Elizabeth Bennet (also Betty Quigley). In the past, her keeper had been Mr Bennett, a pedlar who became the laughing stock of the Masonic world after applying to enter the most prestigious lodge existing. Although he was eventually accepted, he appears to have undergone a more than usually degrading initiation. His humiliation was publicly revealed when printer Tommy Wilkinson of Winetavern Street published a ditty in *Ahiman Rezon*, the book of the constitution of the freemasons, dedicated to 'Masters, Wardens and Brethren of the Orange Lodge of Belfast':

> How Bennett was made, by pedlar a trade
> A Mason of whimsical order;
> We stript him quite bare, deprived him of hair
> And painted his skin like a border, &c, &c

At the time, Elizabeth Bennet had 'a face like an angel, a complexion equal to the lily and the rose, bewitching eyes, and a bosom of hillocks of driven snow'. Plumpness was 'all the rage', and Bennet fitted the picture perfectly – then forty and *embonpoint*, according to Peg, just like Prince Regent George's object of affection, Mrs Maria Fitzherbert, now 'fat, fair and forty' (in fact Fitzherbert would have been in her early thirties).[2] Peg's clients had wanted similar types of women, indicating a fashion among the gentlemen of the day to emulate the Regent's taste in women. In the case of Bennet, her lilting Kerry brogue was an additional attraction to gentlemen callers. On her first meeting with Peg, Bennet had pulled from her pocket a piece of exquisitely embroidered muslin, along with other valuables she had smuggled in from the Indian fleet docked at the River Shannon:

> Arrah, my dear Mrs Leeson, or Mrs Plunkit – but by my soule I know
> you better by the name of Plunkit, for I have been hearing of you
> since I was dat high, you see I have come all the phay from Waterford,
> to be after spending a few days in your mighty agreeable company,
> and I have brought you a *prisant or two* to ensure my *whelcome*.

A previous act of smuggling had led to Bennet's downfall; she had been caught red-handed by revenue officers and had her goods confiscated. Since her husband was in Cork Prison, and she had few effects upon her, she had traded her body with one of the principal officers in order to have her goods restored to her. With nowhere else to go, she continued to live with the officer in Tralee for some eight months, finally returning to her husband with all the contraband, but also pregnant. Within the month she had given birth to a strapping son, and although her husband was upset, he seemed more accepting when he was told that the gentleman responsible was the master of Masons of his initiation ceremony at Cork. After her husband was released, they opened a shop in Waterford, but as the years passed, her husband grew increasingly bad-tempered, constantly reminding her about her indiscretion. Eventually he also started beating her and, unable to bear him any longer, she collected all the valuables and cash she could lay her hands on and came to Dublin to try her luck. This is when she arrived at Peg's establishment.

Knowing herself to be 'a damn'd good piece', as she phrased it, Bennet told Peg she had no doubt about succeeding in the business. Peg admitted, 'I never saw, with all her vulgarity, a more dashing looking woman, nor with all, a more innocent or generous creature'. She charmed the clients with her quaint introductions, saying in her broad Kerry accent, 'Haw dau you dau, my sweet friend'. Peg thought her quite the '*je ne s'ai quoi*'. Her popularity was instant, and men flocked around her. It was no surprise when Mr O'Falvey fell desperately in love with her and took her off to live in Killarney. About a month later, Peg received a letter from her friend stating that not only had her awful husband died, but her new beau had married her and she had borne him a child. Her good fortune had found her a secure life, a decent coach and respect from all her neighbours. Despite her temporary stray into the *demi-monde*, she was one of the lucky ones who managed to find a way out.

On Peg's arrival at her house in Killarney, Mrs O'Falvey was overjoyed to see her, brimming with tears and clasping Peg to her bosom. While the two friends gossiped and caught up with their lives since they had last met, both agreed they must keep their previous association a secret, for Mrs O'Falvey was now considered a respectable woman. The two friends resolved that Mrs O'Falvey would visit Peg and then formally present her to all her Kerry friends as a woman who had been a great friend. However, her husband was totally against the idea, fearing for his wife's reputation. He boasted a great lineage, his family supposedly connected to Conaire, King of Ireland during the beginning of the Christian era.[3]

Aware of the need to distance his wife from any scandal, Mr O'Falvey made a suggestion to Peg. 'My dear Peg', he said,

> Mrs Falvey's reputation would be totally ruined, amidst a circle of respectable acquaintance with whom she must always side, if your story should be blasted, which may be the case, considering the variety and extent of your connections, and the number of people who visit this place at this season of the year; whereas, my dear woman, if you should be found out tomorrow, you can return to your own house at will, and the only consequence that might result from the discovery, would be a few tilting matches, which your supposed *carasposa* might be engaged in, in consequence of his introducing a lady of your complexion, under the character of a wife, to the hospitable and genteel inhabitants of this village.

Thus the whole idea was rendered impossible. The social negotiations in weighing up acceptable and non-acceptable sexual misconduct were complex to say the least, but all three of them were well aware of how a woman's reputation might be affected by a stain upon her name. Mr O'Falvey was acutely conscious of the fickle nature of scandal, saying to Peg, 'Had Purcell been married to you, though a whole camp, pioneers and all, had tasted your sweet body, it would not have signified.'

This suggests that a woman might philander all she liked, and marriage could cancel out all prior indiscretions, but this was not always the case. The matter had more to do with the husband's status than any other consideration; if a man was titled, his wife's previous indiscretions would indeed be wiped out, but if a man was only in a trade, his position was more precarious, and any prior indiscretions of his wife, if exposed, would reflect upon him detrimentally. Therefore, instead of agreeing to the women's suggestion, Mr O'Falvey added one of his own: 'Would it not be better for you and my sweet Betsy, to appear as total strangers to each other, except what may arise from your intercourse here.' The two women agreed to meet as strangers.

The following day, as the couples gathered at the shore for the day's boat trip, they were all in a gay mood. They chatted idly as they waited at the lake where the boat stood anchored. When all had arrived, the O'Falveys, McClean and O'Brien, Peg and Purcell were in high spirits, looking forward to their gentle cruise across Lough Leane to Ross Castle.

The party was joined by notable persons from the surrounding area, such as Mr and Mrs McIllicudy, Mr and Mrs Blennerhassett, Mr and Mrs John Lewis Fitzmaurice, Sir Barry Denny, MP for Tralee (Crosbie Morgell's son-in-law),[4] and his wife, and 'Beau coup de Tournack'. Some of the day-trippers lived on the edge of respectability, while others had been involved in scandals.[5]

The sun shone as they ferried the boat across the lake, shooting at the Eagle's Nest rock as they went. They used the boat's patteraroes, or light cannon-like guns on swivels, which they charged with an ounce or two of powder, then rammed them full of clay to add to the effect. The gentlemen bought three of the largest salmon for only half a crown from the fishermen out selling their catch. In the distance the sound of the horns following a stag hunt echoed on the mountains. Once on the island of Innisfallen they all disembarked. One later visitor described its beauty: 'Imagine an island rising from the bosom of a lake, commanding a view, on one side, of immense mountains, whose wild sublimity is contrasted on the other with a green and cultivated shore.'[6] The island itself was about a mile in circumference, broken into undulating swells, with a rocky point stretching far into the lake, and a little bay encroaching on the land. No visit to Innisfallen was complete without a trip to the monastery, founded in the seventh century.

The island had become a popular spot for the various guests of the Earl of Kenmare to stop for some wine and food and enjoy the surroundings, and Peg and her companions found it a romantic getaway. One of the visitors commented, 'If I had enjoyed the pleasures of the Lake, for a day, with the ugliest old hag of four score, and that there was no other object near to satiate my desires, I could not possibly help being enamored with her, nor could I avoid enjoying her, if enjoyment could be obtained by force or otherwise.' Amorous feelings gave way to thoughts of food, and Peg and her companions went to the banqueting hall on the island to eat. Their salmon was divided into large steaks and roasted on skewers. While she was waiting, Peg scratched her name on the window pane with her diamond ring (she was partial to this form of vandalism to establish her presence). As well as salmon there were other tasty offerings – ham, fowl, cold sirloin of beef, cold tongue, mutton pie, apple pie and cheesecake, all topped off with strong cider, porter, Madeira, sherry, port, a fine claret and brandy. The feast was finished with 'gun-powder tea' imported from China, which had been provided by Mr Eager, the revenue officer. Mr Eager had bought a large parcel of it a few years earlier for five shillings a pound and was generous enough to offer a couple of pounds each to Peg and Mrs McClean at cost price. After the meal, Peg went off with Mr Purcell into the woods to find a space where they could enjoy each other 'under a lofty oak'. After dark, the couples all re-embarked onto the boat and were ferried back to town to enjoy an elegant supper and a dance at the inn.

The following morning the group were joined by Mr and Mrs Gunn, the former suggesting that the coxswain should land each couple on a different island to enjoy themselves, so 'each lady and gentleman might [im]personate Adam and Eve in the Garden of Eden'. The coxswain would then return to pick them up three or four hours later. Those who wanted to could stay on the boat and idle the time away enjoying the trip. Each of the couples landed on a different island with Peg and Purcell choosing the delightful 'Miss Plummer's Island'. The lovers wandered about for more than three hours. Peg later recollected in her memoirs that Purcell had romantically carved an elegy to her on a great oak tree they admired:

> Be it remembered, that on the third day of June 1789, the divine Margaret Leeson of Pitt-street, in the city of Dublin, with her lover, enjoyed every pleasure the most refined love could imagine, in this luxurious spot, with her own Purcell; her enraptured lover, humbly presumes to alter the name of this enchanting island from Plummer to that of Leeson.

Of course, this would have taken him far too long to carve, and Peg was recalling it incorrectly. That evening the couples returned from their boat trip to the inn to share a final meal together.

The following morning, the Dublin foursome said their goodbyes to the other couples and set off at dawn to continue their journey to Cork. They dropped off at a nearby village for breakfast at Shine's inn, and by the evening were dining at the town of Macroom, about half-way between Cork and Killarney, on the south of the River Lee overlooked by the small mountain of Muskerry Beg. Thousands of people from all parts of the country descended on the area for devotion and penance on Midsummer's Day.[7] The river ran down to form a lake in the valley, surrounded by perpendicular rocks of an amazing height.

Leaving the picturesque town behind them the next morning, they all set off for Cork. Once in Cork, the foursome settled into their inn, intending to stay the week. The port had expanded considerably, particularly during the American Revolution, exporting large amounts of butter and beef to Britain, the rest of Europe and North America. The year 1789 saw the first mail coaches between Cork and Dublin. Cork's social life was also expanding. While Peg and her friends were there, Richard Daly's comedians were playing at the theatre. Only a few years previously, in November 1786, Daly had obtained a patent from the crown for a theatre royal at Dublin, with important rights in relation to theatrical performances throughout Ireland.[8] In 1788, he had opened the Crow Street Theatre, after an expenditure of £12,000 on its rebuilding and decoration. It was members of that theatre company who were playing at Cork in 1789, and every night, Peg and her companions sat and watched the group of pantomimists perform.

During her stay in the city, Peg chanced upon an old acquaintance, Edward 'Ned' Townsend from St James's Island and Whitehall, County Cork. He had formed a corps of Volunteers, mainly men of eccentric tastes, who called themselves the Jolly Dogs. They wore white coats faced with green, with white waistcoats and breeches, all embroidered with silver. The most striking part of their outfits were the curious bawdy epaulets, sewn in black and silver in the image of a man's penis. These went totally unnoticed by the public but were enjoyed as a shared joke between the Volunteers. Peg and her friend attended a regatta organized by the Volunteers, after which the company of friends were entertained by Mr Thomas Green, who took them to the stunning island he owned. The ladies in the company gradually began to admire the uniforms and came to see what the epaulets actually represented. On recognising what the image represented, Miss Fleming[9] declared she would buy a uniform and become a Jolly Dog, but a thunderous response from Ned cut her short. He roared, 'That, you can't Betty, by God, but I'll tell you what will answer the same purpose and you'll be *up to it* to a shaving, you may purchase the uniform, and call yourself a proud bitch.' Poor Miss Fleming, being an innocent young woman, burst into tears. Peg, on the other hand, made up a riding habit in the same style and colours and was to sport the outfit around when out on her jaunts back in Dublin. She displayed her allegiances, telling everyone that she had joined the corps of proud bitches in the barony of West Carberry, County Cork.

With Peg so easily recognised in Cork, and her reputation well known, it was inevitable that she and her companions would attract attention. After being approached in the theatre on numerous occasions by various young blades, and exasperated by the unwanted attention, the foursome decided to return to Pitt Street. The fact that the four had played a great hoax on the local gentry did not go unnoticed. Many of the gentlemen to whose wives Peg and McClean had been introduced by Purcell and O'Brien were infuriated that they had been conned, and their wives' reputations compromised by association with whores. The blame fell squarely on the shoulders of the two men involved, and the duped gentry queued up to challenge them to duels. Peg remarked, 'Our sparks were called out two or three times, by some spirited gentlemen in the country of Kerry, for presuming to introduce women of our description under the colour of their wives, into their families.' Purcell bravely addressed the challenges, although he suffered in the process. One of the duels resulted in a wound to his right shoulder.

It was now time for Peg and her companions to return to Dublin. After such a pleasant trip, what awaited Peg was not what she might have hoped for.

Problems and Pleasures in Pitt Street

Such a life of riot and dissipation . . .

Having enjoyed a splendid summer in the company of friends, Peg returned to find her establishment in disarray. During her excursion, two of her boarders, Miss Grove and Miss Philips, had taken advantage of Peg's absence and indulged in such drunken, riotous behaviour that the neighbours had complained. Grove had even sold off some of Peg's best furniture with the fib that Peg was replacing some old for new. The auctioneer and cabinet maker, Mr Robin Fannin of Bride's Alley, was taken in, and bought the furniture at a fraction of its true value.[1] The incident gave Peg pause for thought.

Peg had been in the business for 'thirty years and upwards' and was now in her fifties. While she was still a good-looking woman, with an edgy wit and convivial conversation, she knew her life could not go on as it was. The business had had a good run, but the time had come to think about retiring. Having sensibly invested in a plot of land on Blackrock Road some time ago, Peg now set about having a house built to which she might retire. She instructed a builder to begin work on the project, which would cost 500 guineas. For the moment, though, Peg was determined to squeeze every last pleasure out of her last year in business. It was time to start weaning herself from the constant round of company and dissipation.

Having dispensed with the services of Grove and Philips, Peg took in the sweet-natured Fanny Beresford to board. Although new to Peg's house, she was a familiar face on the town and had been employed before by Peg. She was a woman of good education from a reputable family who was to prove herself a worthy companion, and eventually would edit Peg's memoirs. Peg had first met her when she attended Hughes's masquerade dressed as Venus. Beresford had been living with a lieutenant stationed in the barracks at Arklow on the east coast of Ireland, but their relationship had ended when his regiment was ordered back to Scotland. She was evidently not too upset by his departure as she had not been entirely faithful to him. Her dalliances had included once running off to Dublin with the son of Philip Higginson, a prominent tea merchant.

After settling in easily, Peg and Fanny rubbed along well together. As usual, parties and get-togethers were held most evenings, and the house was filled with music and laughter, with food and champagne on offer. At one such evening, part of the entertainment included stories told by both ladies and gentlemen. Lieutenant-Colonel John Mercer of the 49th Regiment told the tale of a soldier who was court-martialled and facing the death penalty for desertion. The soldier extracted a promise from Mercer to deal with his remains as he requested, to which Mercer agreed. To his horror, the soldier requested, 'that when I am *shot dead*, you will instantly in presence of the whole regiment, *turn up my body and kiss my arse*'. Mercer was understandably miffed, but as a man of his word, he had no option but to have the soldier pardoned instead.

Many of Peg's customers were already in a state of advanced intoxication before they even landed at her door. In this condition they frequently 'forgot' to pay for the wine they imbibed. To keep track of these occurrences Peg kept a ledger with the names and amounts owed. Since so many people passed through her establishment, she often could not recall the men's names, so in order to identify them, she noted down a description. 'Mr Blinker, the old country man from Thurles' left owing £4 6d, for 'Money lent, Wine and sundries'; 'Captain Longnose, the whiskered hero with the county Limerick brogue' left owing £18 6s. 6d., having told Misses Groves and Beresford that he would not swindle them; and 'Brown Billy from Kerry with the yellow spencer' left owing £5 13s. 6d. for 'a week's Board & Lodging'. When she decided to go after someone, particularly those who did their utmost to avoid paying their debt to her, Peg never hesitated in suing them. This was the path she would follow yet again when one seafaring man left owing her money after she been kind enough to help him.

The sailor had been arrested for a debt of £18 and, knowing no one in town, he had asked to be taken to Peg's house. Although Peg knew him only vaguely, having seen him once before with a friend of hers, she sent for the plaintiff, a grocer in Grafton Street, who accepted Peg's promissory note for the discharge of the seafarer's debt. In return, the sailor wrote her a note promising to pay her off within twenty-one days. When the time had elapsed and there was no sign of him nor the money he owed, she showed his note to a captain from Belfast who was visiting her establishment. The captain recognised the man from the handwriting and his description, a somewhat easy task as the sailor had only one leg. It turned out he was a midshipman in the navy going by the name of Heighland and, according to the captain, was an honest fellow and must surely have made a simple mistake in leaving his name and date off the note. Now armed with a name, Peg made some enquiries. To her disgust the sailor was working as a ship's mate on a revenue cruiser, a boat employed by the revenue officers to catch smugglers. On being challenged, Heighland denied ever having been to her house. She duly sued him and he was obliged to pay £60 including court costs.

While private entertainments such as parties, card playing and storytelling were much enjoyed, people were always on the lookout for new diversions. With the development of the new sciences came a new, wondrous form of public amusement in Dublin. Experiments in electricity in the early 1770s had shown the amazing effects of magnetism, with gentleman scientists such as Luigi Galvani performing publicly in London lecture theatres. Here he had demonstrated how dead frogs' legs could be seemingly pulsed back to life with the use of an electric shock, an effect which was to influence Mary Shelley's writing of *Frankenstein*.

Galvani's experiment was one of the first forays into the study of bioelectricity, a field that examined the electrical patterns of the nervous system. From this developed mesmerism, supposedly an ability to hypnotise people using magnetic forces. The name of Dr Franz Anton Mesmer was to be on everyone's lips in Dublin, although interest would take some time to filter into Ireland. Mesmer, a German physician living in Vienna, had connected the experiments in magnetism to the more esoteric aspects of medical health, and had begun to practise on humans. When he tested his magnetic treatment on one of his female patients in 1774, he believed he felt a fluid flowing through the woman's body whose flow was affected by his own will. He developed a theory of 'Animal Magnetism' and asserted its beneficial effect on health. At his performances, people became hysterical, experiencing sweats, fits and palpitations. The purpose of the treatment was to shock the body into convulsion in order to remove obstructions in the circulatory system that were causing sicknesses. One London publication of the day explained Mesmer's theory of the vital fluid: 'all bodies moving in the world, abound with pores, this fluid matter introduces itself through the interstices and returns backwards and forwards, flowing through one body by the currents which issue therefrom to another, as in a magnet, which produces that phenomenon which we call Animal Magnetism.'[2] No doubt Peg would have been aware of the novelists and playwrights who satirised mesmerism, including Elizabeth Inchbald's farce of the late 1780s, *Animal Magnetism*, involving a plot of multiple love triangles and highlighting the absurdity of animal magnetism.

The mesmerism craze had hit Dublin by 1790, when Dr John Bell, a follower of mesmerism, was a visitor to Peg's house. As a member of the Philosophical Harmonic Society of Paris, he was certified to lecture and teach animal magnetism in England.[3] This and similar societies effectively made animal magnetism into a secretive art, its members unwilling to reveal their secrets.He charged a small fortune to various gentlemen of Peg's acquaintance to initiate them into his secret art, or 'occult science' as Peg called it, and squeezed the last guineas out of them for his lectures on sleepwalking. In his oval wooden machine filled with coal ashes and dirt, heated with iron bars, the patient would sit opposite the doctor in a chair conveying the 'animal fluid' with their hands in the 'system'. Despite its popularity, many remained sceptical of its purported beneficial effects. In 1790, one pamphlet declared, 'No fanatics ever divulged notions more wild and extravagant; no impudent empiric ever retailed promises more preposterous, or histories of cures more devoid of reality, than the tribe of Magnetizers.'[4]

Dr Bell gave Peg and her friends tickets to see his demonstrations and she thought it all too incredible: 'It was really astonishing to see how the people (and the most sensible and best informed too) were *gulled by this foreign* Chevalier d'Industrie.' He made experiments on women and men in the audience, among them Mrs Fitzmaurice, a titled lady and a friend of Peg, and Mr Charles Craig, a watchmaker of Fishamble Street. Craig was blind in one eye and wanted Dr Bell to heal it. Calling him up to the stage, Bell took his guinea and made Craig squat on the floor. He stroked his magnet over the blind eye, closed the lid, and opened the other eye. He dipped the magnet into the water and poured a drop of this water into the good eye. He then said, 'Rise, Sir. I pronounced you a cure [sic].' Urging Craig to take the magnetized water, he instructed him to expose it to the rays of the sun every morning and to use it as a lotion to strengthen the cure. Within a few weeks, Craig was completely blind. Much to Peg's disgust, Bell went on to perform in Cork, where his supporters formed another society there.[5] He had left Dublin in a hurry after being caught having an affair with a woman he had conned. Despite his many supporters and an apparently thriving business, he was thrown into jail for non-payment of debts. Peg, recognising him for the quack he was, referred to him as 'a libidinous little dog'.

During the same year, John Fane, the Duke of Westmorland, came to call on Peg. The duke, who had been appointed Lord Lieutenant of Ireland by Pitt in 1789, had arrived in Ireland in January 1790 and would hold office until he was replaced in December 1794. His political stance was anti-Catholic, and he would prove reluctant to allow for the makeshift relief measure of 1793 when faced with Irish Protestant concerns about the possible invasion from France. According to Lady Holland, who abhorred his politics, Westmorland was 'coarse in mind, manners and language'.[6] His long-suffering wife, Lady Sarah Anne Fane, according to Peg, 'languished until she died' because of his poor treatment. Her marriage had been opposed by her parents and the couple had eloped to Gretna Green in 1782. Unfortunately she was to suffer the mortification of her husband carrying out a very public affair with Mrs Sinnot, a demirep of some notoriety. At some point Westmorland became embroiled with William Cairns, otherwise known as Patrick Joyce from Kilkenny.

Joyce was proprietor of the Dublin Baths on Batchelors Walk, who had fashioned himself as a Turk under the name of 'Dr Achmet Boromborad'.[7] Peg mentions him in her memoirs, and she would probably have seen him strutting about the streets of Dublin in a colourful turban and flowing robes. His Turkish baths were part-funded by a group of parliamentarians who frequented the establishment. His popularity decreased when he got a group of them roaring drunk and they all fell into the water fully clothed.

On the night he visited Pitt Street, however, Westmorland was accompanied by Edward Cooke, the then undersecretary at Dublin Castle. Cooke had an extremely poor opinion of the Irish judiciary, and sent jaundiced letters to London describing nearly all of them as insolent, ignorant or biased. Peg detested the duke, no doubt because of his politics as much as his unpleasant manners. She severely upbraided him and, much to her annoyance, the pair left without even paying for the champagne they had ordered. Her venom towards the duke was in contrast to the fondness with which she remembered Rutland: 'Pitiful! Despicable! mean wretch! what a contrast to the excellent, generous, noble Rutland, whose like we shall never behold again.'

Peg was to be fleeced once again after being imprudent enough to take in Mary Roberts to board. Roberts was one of the many prostitutes who had fallen in with a gang of thieves, and being smart and pretty, had become the ideal decoy duck for their felonious pursuits. No gentleman was safe walking around Jervis Street or Boot Lane if he wanted to hold on to his clothes and money. The leader of this gang of robbers, Larry Lynch, became Roberts's lover, and was soon sentenced to hang in Newgate Prison in 1791.[8] Looking for somewhere to re-establish herself, she introduced herself to Peg and moved into her Pitt Street brothel. Peg quickly became appraised of her boarder's thieving tendencies through an old acquaintance. She admitted that if this had not been the case, she 'probably would have plundered me of the whole of my property.' She warned 'I hope the wary will be on their guard against her.' Peg was always gullible when young women came to her with their stories of ill-treatment and ill-fortune, and could never keep a keen enough eye on her new recruits.

As a welcome break from their hectic (and sometimes unpleasant) lives, the whores of Dublin took time out to enjoy themselves on summer excursions. In July 1791, along purportedly with her companions Miss Grove,[9] Mrs O'Brien, Miss Beresford, Mrs Burnett, old Mrs Sterling, Mrs Bennis and a handful of other female friends, Peg took the opportunity to ride out of town and take in the country air. The plan was to travel to Rathfarnham to visit the country retreat of Captain William Southwell in Little Dargle. The women were accompanied by a squire of their acquaintance[10] and enjoyed the sights before retiring to Laughlin's tavern for some much-needed food and drink. One of the local attractions was Rathfarnham Castle with its four imposing towers; the house was remodelled in the eighteenth century, both William Chambers and James 'Athenian' Stuart having an input.

The inn where the women were staying was by the river and, at the time, around fifty of the members of the Printers and Booksellers collective were holding a meeting there. After guzzling several bottles of champagne, the women took tea in the garden and sat chatting with a handful of the printers. As Peg described the scene, 'I ordered more wine, and after finishing two or three coopers, the lads of the *Frisket* insisted on treating us, which I peremptorily refused, telling them, in my company on such an occasion, they should not pay a farthing.' One of the printers, the son of Bartholomew Corcoran[11] the Dublin ballad-seller (or as Peg called him 'the Hibernian poet laureate'), took a shine to Peg, but jealousy flared up as the squire accompanying her intervened and a fight broke out. In the furore which followed, the printer's wig was pulled off and tossed to Fanny Beresford who, with presence of mind, quickly took it aside and surreptitiously pissed in it, thereafter gently returning it to its rightful owner. Corcoran hastily thrust the wig into his pocket only for his breeches to be filled with Fanny's contribution. To his embarrassment, and much to the amusement of all the onlookers, in his race to sluice his wig in the stream at the bottom of the garden, he dropped it in the water and it floated off, never to be seen again. The printer returned to town with only a handkerchief covering his bald pate.

After the afternoon's diversions, the party adjourned to Peg's house in Dublin, accompanied by some other, less troublesome, printers. The men threw in a guinea each for the evening's entertainment, with a couple of Peg's male companions[12] keeping them in an uproar all evening.

But time was marching on for Peg. She had had her fill of rude lords, pilfering servants and pillaging ruffians. With her face aging and her energy fading, it was now time to quit the business.

Retirement and Debtors' Prison

Musty morals, grave declamation, dolorous lamentations and puling penitence.

The maid lit the candles, shook out the throws and plumped up the cushions. As usual, Peg sat idly chatting with a couple of her girls while waiting for the gentlemen callers. She was dressed in a beautiful brocaded dress with a simple string of pearls at her throat and two matching pearl studs on either ear. The champagne was on ice, the oysters lying open ready to be eaten for their supposed aphrodisiac effects. The maid suddenly announced the arrival of two gentlemen, and Peg looked up to see Charles Brenan and Richard Wogan Talbot enter the room.

She disliked both men intensely, as they had led her friend Amyas Griffith to ruination. Brenan was a journalist with the *Dublin Evening Post* who had acted as an election agent for Talbot when he was MP for Dublin County from 1791 to 1792, but had been ejected from Parliament after a rival candidate, John Finley, had filed a suit against him for 'undue election'. Peg blamed Brenan for the collapse of the *Phoenix* newspaper, which led to Griffith's bankruptcy.[1] He had set up the paper in order to support Talbot's election campaign at a cost of around £60, but Brenan and Talbot had failed to reimburse him. Such gross dishonesty riled Peg no end and she refused to entertain the two men, giving them a lecture on their despicable behaviour and packing them off into the night. Meanwhile, Griffith had been thrown into Marshalsea Prison for debt.[2]

Peg was always loyal to her friends. When, on 22 July 1792, the bawd Moll Hall died at the age of only forty-nine,[3] Peg was to come to her assistance in death as she had in life. Once Hall's creditors heard of her demise, they raced round to her house to cart off everything inside it – chairs, tables, even the bed on which she had been lying. A Mr Dignam was the first trader to invade her premises. Unwilling to see her friend treated so badly, and determined Moll should have a fitting send-off, Peg hired chairs and a kitchen table for the wake, and ordered in candles, pipes and tobacco, cake, cold meats, wine and some of Hutton's bottled porter. She hired six mourning coaches, each carrying four whores in full mourning. Peg's carriage led the funeral procession along with several others belonging to the more respectable people who had been Moll's friends. Her body was interred in St Anne's churchyard. Peg inscribed her epitaph:

> Here lies the body of Moll Hall
> Who once had a great call
> And a fig for you all.

Peg was still taking in new boarders at Pitt Street. Some time after 1793, she was visited a woman who had been living with a titled man. While initially this sort of arrangement might have seemed beneficial to the women involved, frequently it meant they were left with no means of subsistence when their protectors tired of them, or they died. The worst men would simply turf a woman out, but the better sort would provide her with an annuity or pension. Others might marry her off to a lower-class man. This was the case with Miss Molly McPherson from Banbridge, who had arrived on Peg's doorstep in great distress. She told Peg how she had been seduced by Wills Hill, Earl of Hillsborough, an aged libertine who had the title Marquess of Downshire created for him in 1789. He had doted on her and paid to have her painted by Joseph Wilson of Belfast[4] in various poses, both clothed and naked. So enamoured was he of her that he introduced her to the staff on his estate (he owned Hillsborough Castle in County Down) and all the surrounding minor dignitaries and country squires at the Hillsborough balls and, as she became one of the household, she took on the title of Marchioness of Downshire. Once the Marquess tired of her, he married her off to a revenue man for whom he had procured a post. While she was happy to accept the proposal, the old man did not give her up entirely and she was obliged to have sex with him once every so often when he called for her to spend the night.

Meanwhile, Molly's sister had been seduced by the Marquess's son, Arthur Hill (1753–1801), who inherited the title on the old Marquess's death in 1793. He had infected her sister with the pox. In this case, the venereal disease in question was probably syphilis rather than gonor- rhoea, the more dangerous of the two (although at the time, they were thought to be one and the same disease). While most quack potions purporting to 'cure' venereal disease were ineffectual, some treatments did at least alleviate the worst of the symptoms. However, the 2nd Marquis was significantly less generous than his father had been, and offered Molly's sister no medical assistance, allowing her to languish with the disease until she died. Molly made no mention of her new husband, but presumably with no money coming in from the Marquis, he had simply disappeared. Those sycophants who had previously craved her attention now despised her, the jealous and fickle minor gentry of the area unwilling to continue to befriend a whore now her benefactor was dead. Keen to bestow benevolence on all women who had fallen on hard times, Peg was only too happy to invite McPherson to join them at Pitt Street, supplying her with £5 for the purchase of a necessary change of linen and introducing her to her clients. In turn, McPherson introduced Peg to other clients.

While Peg was used to most men's sexual proclivities, she was surprised when she was told about one in particular. The source was a friend of McPherson who had come to visit. She was being kept by John James Hamilton, who had been created Marquess of Abercorn in 1790, and she enjoyed his company.[5] His only problem was imbibing too much brandy with anyone who cared to sit with him, from his friends to his servants; he started in the morning, and by the after- noon he was too drunk to walk the streets. Indeed, he had frequently visited Peg's establishment while in this state of inebriation. But what really intrigued Peg was this woman's confession that he had never had sexual intercourse with her. In fact he had an obsession with feet.[6] His 'unspeakable pleasure', her friend told her, was 'of picking, wash- ing, and cleaning my pretty little toes, which he took great delight in, and in which pleasurable innocent, and inoffensive pastime he has often spent hours.' She admitted, 'He was never even rude enough to give me a kiss.' In recompense for the lack of physical ardour with the old aristocrat, she turned to another man, a respectable employee in La Touche's bank, but unfortunately he was already married so he was unable to live with her. Peg, after listening to her story and seeing the affection the woman had for Molly McPherson, offered a place *en famille* in her establishment and she became a great favourite with her clients. Not only was she beautiful, but she sang with humour and was witty enough to tell amusing tales at the dinner table.

There can be little doubt that former mistresses of titled men were a boon for the brothel. Other clients were drawn to them because of their previous elevated status and, as a consequence, business flourished. Peg admitted, 'neither of my Marchionesses ever slept a night unoccupied while they remained in Pitt-Street, which was near nine months'. In the end, they left for England together, having become besotted with two veteran officers, one a major in the army, the other a lieutenant colonel.

The story of McPherson's abandonment perhaps gave Peg reason to think about her own career. Maybe she saw Hall's death as a portent of her own doom. 'I took a horrible retrospective view of the course I had run, and all of my past life.' Looking back on her profession, she was now full of fear. Although she had abandoned her Catholicism and churchgoing while running her business, now retired, her old religious beliefs were pushed to the front of her mind. She became wracked with guilt over her past life. In a fit of penitence, she fell to her knees and began to pray to God, crying out, 'O Omniscient Father of all, does Peg Leeson (or rather Peg Plunkett, for I could have no legal claim to Leeson, having never been really married but to Yelverton) set up for a reformer of Men and Manners?' She saw herself as having abandoned all dignity, declaring, 'for there's not creatures of the four-footed tribe, would go indiscriminately from male to male, and suffer perhaps a score in four and twenty hours to enjoy their favours.' She was filled with morbid notions and thoughts: 'in all my life I have not secured a real friend; the prostitutes my associates, and the libertines whose caresses I submitted to, all despise me'. In a fit of delirium, she drank four ounces of an opiate tincture in a bid to kill herself, but it was not enough – she simply became sick and vomited it all up. She then languished in a stupor for eighty-four hours. When her female friends Mrs McClean and one of her lively girls, Miss Sands, called to see her, they were unaware she was ill. They had hoped they might have a trip to visit the soldiers at Loughlinstown camp. The camp had been opened in June 1795 to defend Killiney Bay from a possible French landing. All Peg did was give them a lecture on their wayward lives. Not understanding the sudden change in Peg, they both burst out laughing and left the house convulsed with mirth.

Determined to shake off her past vices, Peg decided to return to her religion and repent. However, she had no understanding of how to go about it. She lamented that were Arabella Denny still alive, she would have given all her money and possessions to the Magdalen asylum and gone to live in it. Revd Dr Leonard, a Catholic priest, continued to comfort her, but the tenets of the Catholic faith were too narrow for Peg. She had a much broader sense of religion, and her opinions showed an enlightened attitude with which few Irish Catholics would have agreed. She declared, 'All religions were alike to me . . . I would also worship the God of nature, in spirit and in truth, no matter whether in a Mosque, a Meeting-House, Chapel, Church, Synagogue, bed or field.' She considered that simply to believe in God was not sufficient to get to heaven, but that charitable works were important too.

Seeking further solace, Peg picked up her pen and wrote to two of her friends, a 'Mrs S' and Mrs Betsy O'Falvey. Both sent her letters commending her on her reformation. They advised her to quit Ireland for good and move to England or Scotland, to go far away from her old life and start afresh. They had no doubt she might meet a nice companion and, in another country, no one would know about her past. Peg was against the idea, not wanting to get married, nor liking the idea of living a lie by passing herself off as a virtuous woman. However she was in need of a companion and prevailed on her friend Mrs O'Falvey to contact the 'sweet black-eyed sentimental girl' she had met some years previously in Killarney, Miss Betsy Edmonds.[7] Betsy had returned to Killarney after a rape ordeal on board ship from Paris in which her female companion had died. The girl had requested that Peg employ her as a maid-in-waiting, but Peg had refused, believing her establishment in Pitt Street was no fit place of employment for her. Now, having given up her life of debauchery, Peg realised she needed people like mild-mannered Betsy around.

How Peg thought she would make a living once she had retired is hard to imagine. Few women in her position retired wealthy, as they tended to spend the money they earned. Without marriage, Peg would have to find an income, but she seems to have given it little consideration. Although Peg had invested in a house in Blackrock, the only other indication of forward planning was the idea that she would cash in her IOUs or live off promised annuities but she had made no serious provision for an income. Having previously rented her house to tenants, it is surprising that she had not thought of property as an investment. She might even have asked her old client La Touche for his advice, but the idea does not seem to have occured to her. Such was her nature that she rarely made provision for the future.

Soon after Betsy's arrival, Peg realised that her money was fast running out. 'I certainly had in bonds, promissory notes, and IOUs, upwards of two thousand pounds due to me; but what value could be set upon the obligations of unprincipled men of fashion, and a parcel of abandoned prostitutes.' None were any use. When presented with such papers, her unprincipled debtors simply refused to pay up. She found her finances 'so very much deranged' that she was forced to sell her house in Pitt Street, along with all of her furniture.

Sometime late in 1793 or early 1794, Peg moved to Blackrock, taking Betsy with her. It was here she had hoped to live out her retirement 'in ease and independence'. The house had cost her £500 to build and she had spent at least another £100 on it. The town was on the outskirts of Dublin, its name derived from a rock formation found under Blackrock Park. It was a popular bathing resort for day-trippers from Dublin on Sundays and holidays. Peg's house was situated near those built as summer boltholes by some of the most prominent nobles of Ireland. It was claimed by one contemporary that at certain times of the year, when the Lord Lieutenant was in resident in Blackrock House, the Rock experienced 'the sweets of dissipation to so high a degree that even Bath could scarce take the lead for more gaiety, amusement, and bon ton.'[8] Nearby Maretimo House (now demolished) was erected by Sir Nicholas Lawless, MP, 1st Lord Cloncurry, and Frescati House built for the provost of Trinity College, John Hely Hutchinson, in 1739, were both known as magnificent houses.

As debts mounted, Peg hit on the idea of writing her memoirs. It is possible that her printer friend Amyas Griffith had suggested it to her as a means of making some money. But for Peg it was also a means of subjecting some of the men who had refused to honour their debts to public exposure. Her efforts had already been successful after she sent the first two volumes to the tradesmen of Dublin who owed her money. Not one of them came back to her without a guinea or more, and by these methods she managed to raise 600 guineas in all. With this, she paid off her debts, then managed to squander the remainder in a matter of months on extravagant living. The first two volumes were published in 1795 and earned her another £500, but Peg quickly ran through that money as well. Even at this stage, it seems she was incapable of reining herself in. A lifetime of indulging in excess had left her unable to budget.

Betsy and Peg struggled on for a while. Bit by bit, all Peg's luxury items were pawned. Off went her gowns, her miniature pictures, her gold and diamond rings, all for a pittance. Betsy and Peg sat in their near-empty house, with no money to buy food for a simple breakfast, nor fuel for their fire. A handful of people showed kindness. Mrs Deborah O'Dowd, from whom Peg had bought East India goods, called round to visit them. Seeing the pair in such straitened circumstances, she gave Peg half of the money she had on her – amounting to ten guineas. She also made them presents of gunpowder tea and a beautiful shawl each. Other visitors included a previous black footman of Peg's who said to her, 'I hear you are writing books, Madam', placing before her a quire of gilt paper, a bottle of ink, a penknife and a bundle of pens. On seeing his former mistress in such dire straits, he sobbed, 'Good Heaven! Did I ever think it would have come to this. You my ever honoured mistress, who were good and charitable to every creature who appeared distressed.' He also provided her with a quarter of his wages, amounting to two guineas. Peg and Betsy both burst into tears at such generosity. He had been an honest young lad, and when working at Pitt Street, he had gone down with a long fever. At the time Peg had afforded him every possible care and he had not forgotten her kindness.

Inevitably, Peg's creditors caught up with her. As she was travelling to Fleet Street to pay a debt she owed to Mr Cornelius O'Brien at his wine shop at number 2, she was stopped and arrested. Her crime was another debt of £15 owing to the grocer's in Grafton Street. She was carried off to a sponging house without a shilling in her pocket.

Sponging houses were often dirty and dingy places, but if a person had the money, they could rent out a superior lodging and even entertain guests. On hearing of her mistress's plight, Betsy immediately gathered up a supply of cakes, wine, tea and sugar and took off to the debtors' apartments. While inside, Peg met another woman in similar straitened circumstances, and the pair formed an attachment. Mrs Mulligan had been arrested for the sum of £11, which she had spent on buying food for her feckless husband, who was by then languishing in Four Courts Marshalsea.

The bully men for the sponging house were ruffians, and keen to earn a quick shilling however they could. Mrs Mulligan had been arrested by Lawrence Mooney, a miscreant with 'the look of a hangman, and the manners of a Yahoo'. Upon her arrest, he had threatened to take her back to his own sponging house in Angel Alley if she did not give him five guineas immediately, but these methods of extortion were well known to Mulligan, who refused to go with him. She also knew that in the sponging house which he ran prisoners were subjected to all sorts of horrors. Instead, she insisted on going to Mr Matthews's sponging-house where the owner was a much more generous man and treated his prisoners with respect. This was the same man who had been Peg's client in her better days. In the event, Mulligan was released when her father came to rescue her, having heard of her circumstances.

Betsy remained at Peg's side, refusing to leave her and sharing her bed. Rather than ask them for extra money for Betsy's lodging, which he might have done, Matthews took pity on them and invited the distressed pair to dine with him and his family. Peg appreciated his kindness: 'I must acknowledge Matthews's civility, who relaxed much from the severity of the character of the keeper of a lock-up house with regard to me; suffering my poor friend to share my bed, without any extra charge, and inviting us to dine, sup or breakfast, whenever he observed us in want of cash.' One particular evening, as Peg and

Betsy sat drinking tea with Mrs Matthews, Peg suffered a shock to see her old lover Purcell sitting opposite her, the man with whom she'd had such a wonderful day on Plummer's Island in Killarney. He had also been incarcerated for debt, but looked less worn than she did. He barely recognised her, as she was dishevelled, in worn-out clothes and wore no make-up. Peg knew she looked awful: 'I was so entirely altered both in dress and appearance, that it was impossible for him to distinguish the gay, the volatile Peg Leeson, in wretchedness, misery and rags in a lock-up house.' Recalling all she had experienced with him in the past, 'our guilty commerce' as she called it, was too much for her and she fainted in a heap, but quietly came round.

As they chatted and caught up, Purcell felt miserable on Peg's behalf and was upset she had ended up in such a quandary. 'You will never want of a shilling, Peg, while I have one. Here, I will divide my last guineas with you.' Peg gave a deep curtsey but retired to her bed. Purcell, though a gentleman, was not so keen to give her up again, and Peg must still have been attractive. Not long in her apartment, she heard a knock on the door. Purcell had come to ask if he could once again share her bed. 'How could I be displeased with such a request from a man who had so often enjoyed all my charms unrestrained? – A man whose caresses I met more than halfway,' Peg asked herself. Nonetheless she held to her resolve not to return to her old life, informing him of her pledge to remain chaste from now on and her penitence for her past career. He kindly replied without pressing her, but he said, 'If you will not share my bed, then you must share my purse', and tipped half of his guineas into her lap. With thirteen guineas, she could now redeem some of her property from the pawnbrokers, and so she sent Betsy out to redeem clothes and essential items. Purcell stayed with them that evening, entertaining them with amusing anecdotes, singing and reciting poetry. After a visit by an admirer, he was set free a few days later. Peg heard he had married his woman of fortune and they had settled in Ennis.

Economising was not within Peg's capabilities, and when she did manage to raise some money, she just as quickly spent it. At least she tried to raise funds while in the sponging house and wrote pleading letters to all those who were indebted to her. While many ignored her, others sent contributions.[9] Some of the men she knew sent her money, and a float was set up for her which netted enough to keep her going for a while.[10]

The worst was yet to come. Her loyal friend and companion, dear Betsy Edmonds, fell ill and died, probably as a result of syphilis. She was thirty-five. Since Peg was without the means to pay for a funeral, Captain Eyre, a prisoner in the Four Courts Marshalsea, kindly stepped in to pay for it. Grief-stricken over Betsy's death, she reflected, 'No human misery could equal mine, I gave myself up entirely to despair and often invoked the Almighty to take me to himself.' Her only consolation at this time was visits from her spiritual advisor, Revd Dr Leonard,[11] and from her friend Mr O'Falvey. O'Falvey had discovered her circumstances by chance when visiting another friend in the same sponging house. When he heard about the death of Betsy and Peg's reformation, he resolved to get her out and immediately set about raising money to pay off her debts. He approached his friends in the Whig Club, a group of radicals and reformers, and managed to raise sixty guineas. Unbeknown to Peg, he consolidated all her debts and paid them off. Most of her creditors were delighted to be paid off, as many thought she was already dead.

Feeling despondent, Peg left the prison and stepped into the coach Mr O'Falvey had called, ordering the driver to head towards Blackrock. At this stage Peg had managed to rent out her house at Blackrock to attorney Mr Charles Fleetwood of 13 Whitefriars Street for £30 a year, which should have been enough for her to live off for the rest of her life, but Peg was never good with money. O'Falvey had taken new apartments for her in the area, where his wife was patiently waiting for them. Her friends looked after Peg for about three weeks, before returning to Kerry in the Limerick stagecoach. They moved her to a comfortable lodging house in Clarendon Street and ensured she had enough money to tide her over for a couple of months or so. She realised she had to concentrate on writing the third volume of her memoirs if she were to raise some more money. Meanwhile her friends promised to try and find subscribers in Limerick, Cork, Kerry, Waterford, Tipperary and Clare. For now at least, she had her head just above water.

Final Days

I shall leave nothing behind me but the traces of my own infamy.

As Peg settled into her new lodgings near St Stephen's Green, she could contemplate starting work on her third volume of memoirs. With no secure income, she knew she could not rely on the future sales of her first two volumes, as she had already taken subscriptions from so many people (and had already spent the money). Within three months of leaving the sponging house, she had enough material for her next book. During this period, the only person she saw regularly was her priest, Revd Dr Leonard, a well-educated man who offered to look over the manuscript. He told her that the public had not been best pleased with her editor's previous efforts, as the script had been full of errors. While some members of the clergy may have been shocked by Peg's memoirs, many others had mistresses of their own. From Peg's accounts, Leonard was a sensible and benevolent man and was only too willing to help Peg as best he could.

The only friend she had left from her old business was Miss Love, who sent Peg several presents and offered an apartment in her house, if Peg thought proper to accept it. However, Miss Love was a kept mistress, and Peg felt she had to decline. To go to a recognised house of ill-repute would undo all the efforts she had made to lead a virtuous life. Peg knew her own limitations and recognised that she must avoid temptation. Since she thoroughly regretted her past, she preferred to suffer her retirement at home alone. Even the theatre lost its appeal for her, and she no longer frequented the lattices at the Theatre Royal, where she had so often enjoyed herself in the past. Over the last year and a half, she had lived a quiet, retired life and kept her routine simple. She had abandoned silks and ribbons for more modest dress, foregone jewellery and worn her hair plainly. For her book, though, she had other plans.

To attract maximum public attention, she worked through *Wilson's Directory* and *Watson's Almanack* and wrote to everyone who she thought might be interested in her third volume. Her proposals were popped in the penny post and, in return, she received a handsome number of subscriptions. While going through this process, Peg compared herself to other female writers. She lamented 'I often wished I had as much bronze [money] in my face as Mrs Jane Moore, the English poet, who certainly is a credit to the kingdom she came from; but poor Mrs Battier herself, that elegant charming sentimental writer, was never more timid or backward in forwarding a subscription than I was.' These two female writers were on Peg's mind as Jane Moore had visited Dublin in 1795 on business and met with Henrietta Battier. The latter was known to have approached Samuel Johnson to ask his advice about publishing a manuscript collection of her poems, and Johnson had assisted her in building a subscription list. He told her, 'Don't be disheartened my Child, I have been often been glad of a Subscription myself.'[1] While Peg was certainly not as rich as Moore, it is hard to believe that she felt she was more timid than even Battier had been. She professed 'Indeed I became so bashful . . . I absolutely was ashamed to be seen abroad', and believed herself to be 'one of the most timid mild creatures on earth'. Peg had now become so reserved that she was afraid to be seen in public. When she *did* go out, further misadventures befell her.

Braving the night air one evening, Peg muffled herself up, dressed in her dowdiest and oldest clothes, and went for a walk in Stephen's Green. To her horror, when she got back to her lodgings she found every item of clothing had been stolen by her servant, along with the thirty guineas she had raised from subscriptions. The culprit was Mary Neill, allegedly the victim of a rape by the Earl of Carhampton and Francis Higgins in May 1788, as mentioned above. At the time, the then fourteen-year-old Neill had been lured into a brothel run by Mrs Lewellen and Robert Edgeworth. The radical barrister Archibald Hamilton Rowan had taken up her case, publicly denounced

Carhampton and published a pamphlet, *A Brief Investigation of the Sufferings of John, Anne, and Mary Neal*, in the same year. Hamilton Rowan's notoriety grew when he entered a Dublin dining club, threatening several of Mary Neill's detractors with his massive Newfoundland dog at his side and waving a wooden club in his hand; some people evidently felt that Neill was a liar and had fabricated the whole story for her own benefit.[2] Peg thought he had made 'such a ridiculous rout about' Neill, obviously not believing her to be credible, particularly since she had filched all her belongings.

Now all Peg had left were the clothes on her back and the two guineas in her pocket. Her landlady did her best to comfort her, but then all suddenly became right when she received a letter from the Earl of Bristol, Frederick Augustus Hervey, with £50 enclosed. He was a man Peg had encountered some sixteen years previously when she had been in London, and was among the list of people she had written to in the hope of receiving a little money. In truth, few responded, and none so generously as the earl. Her friend Deborah O'Dowd, who had come to her rescue when Peg and Betsy were in prison, called by to see if Peg needed anything. Peg bought a few yards of muslin from her and some gunpowder tea, and offered to return some money she had loaned, but O'Dowd would not accept it. Since they'd last met, O'Dowd's situation had vastly improved – her husband had died and she had remarried a respectable shopkeeper, Mr O'Connor, in Castle Island. To celebrate their reunion, the pair took a day's excursion out to the Three Tun Tavern at Blackrock for fun, and were looked after by the landlord, Mr Bishop.

Blackrock Road was known as a haunt of villains. By the late 1780s and early 90s, the area had become known for highway robberies. In response, the locals had held a meeting in Jennett's tavern, chaired by Lord Viscount Ranelagh. One of the resolutions was 'that we will give a reward of £20 to any person who will apprehend and prosecute to conviction any person guilty of a robbery upon the Blackrock-road, from Dublin to Dunleary, Bullock, Dalkey, Rochestown, Cabinteely, and Loughlinstown'.[3] Unfortunately this did not avert an incident which was seriously to affect Peg and her companion.

While returning home with O'Dowd rather later than expected, the carriage was stopped near Bagatrot Castle by three armed robbers, who commenced rifling through the women's pockets. By chance, two gentlemen they knew were riding by and rushed to the ladies' assistance, shooting and chasing off the villains. The incident was reported in the next day's newspapers, but no names were mentioned:

> Last night as two ladies were returning from the Rock rather late, their carriage was stopped by three armed foot-pads, who would have robbed them, had it not been for the timely assistance of two gentlemen who happened luckily to ride up, just as the miscreants were proceeding to violence; one of whom was desperately wounded, notwithstanding which they all escaped, though closely pursued for a considerable way.[4]

Old theatre friends also rallied round to help Peg. Mr Daly of the Theatre Royal suggested they give a benefit performance for her, but under an assumed name so as not to put off the *bon ton*. The performance raised £90, although some of her old acquaintances who had offered to sell tickets at the door pocketed the money. No doubt in an attempt to shame them, Peg listed them in her memoirs, including Mr Simpson of Upper Quay, Mrs Newburgh, widow of Colonel Thomas Newburgh (neé Blacker) and a Mr Johnny Ging, shoemaker of Castle Street. Despite Peg despairing that she had no friends, she had enough support from them to help her out of further trouble. Even she admitted, 'I was now as to pecuniary matters tolerably easy.' The attack had left Peg shaken up and feeling in low spirits, but she gradually recovered from the shock. Her state of mind became more peaceful, and Revd Dr Leonard remained on hand to offer what guidance she might require.

For a servant and companion Peg had employed thirty-year-old Margaret (known as Peggy) Collins, the daughter of a respectable farmer in Roscrea, whose hair was already quite grey; Peg suspected this was a reaction to being deserted by her husband. Collins had run an alehouse with him for three years, but it had failed and they ended up in debtors' prison. When they were released under one of the Insolvency Acts,[5] he fled the country, leaving Collins with little choice but to take up with a gentleman who had helped them while in prison. She found that she was pregnant and had to leave her son in the poorhouse while she took up domestic service with the man's sister, who died within the month. Peg said of Collins, 'I found her intelligent, faithful, sober, discreet and honest; indeed when my distress became too severe for human nature to bear, I found every consolation in my poor dear Peggy Collins, who never forsook me.'

But life had not yet finished with Peg. One evening she decided to go out and visit her friend 'Mrs H' in Drumcondra, who had been a mistress of the Prince of Wales.[6] Since she had already been attacked on that same road, known for its violent assaults and hold-ups, Peg was not being particularly prudent. Walking home at dusk with Collins, five ruffians jumped on them, stripped them to their shifts and raped them. Collins managed to stab one of them with a pair of scissors, but the gang persisted. When they had finished, they ran off, carrying the women's shoes and stockings. In this miserable condition the women returned to Mrs H, who found some clothes for them. They finally reached their own lodgings at two o'clock in the morning, their landlady bursting into tears on hearing what had happened. A few days later they both showed signs of the pox. Peg would normally use the services of blind William Lionel Jenkins, the apothecary on 45 Dame Street, and surgeon Charles Bolger of 13 Suffolk Street, who was connected to the Lock Hospital, but both were unavailable. Instead she turned to her good friend, the apothecary Mr Brady. Appalled at their misfortune, he rushed to their aid. However he felt there was no alternative but to put them on a course of salivation.

Mercury was considered to be the only effective 'cure' for venereal disease. It could be administered in the form of an ointment, a steam bath or a pill. As late as 1816, Sir Everard Home was reporting to the Royal Society in London on the efficacy of mercury as a cure:

> The most truly specific medicine that we have been hitherto acquainted with is mercury for the venereal disease, and it is completely established that this remedy, when in the circulation, is equally efficient in the cure of a recent chancre produced by innoculation, and a venereal sore throat, in consequence of the disease having been carried into the circulation.[7]

Salivation occurred when the mercury in the body literally poisoned it, making the person sweat profusely, the toxins supposedly being brought out of the body. Unfortunately, the side effects could be as painful and terrifying as the disease itself. Many patients who underwent mercury treatments suffered from extensive tooth loss, ulcerations, hair dropping out by the handful and brain damage. In many cases, people died from significant mercury poisoning.

Both the women were reduced to skin and bones within three months. Their money had run out once again, their clothes were in pawn and they were in debt to their landlady for £10. On top of this their landlady asked them to quit the house, but kindly said she would not ask for the money owing. Mr Brady again came to the rescue and found lodgings for Peg and Peggy in Temple Bar. While the younger woman grew stronger, Peg fell foul of a fever and grew weaker by the day. She recounted, 'as poor Brady who has just left me, on feeling my pulse and inspecting my tongue declared I was not in a condition to sit up. Though I found my head light, I had recollection enough to know my situation; and I candidly confess I had forebodings of my speedy decease.' Dr James's Fever Powders seemed to rid her of her affliction. This medicine had been patented by the English physician Robert James, with claims that it cured high temperatures and various other maladies. Indeed, it purported to cure everything from gout and scurvy to distemper in cattle. Though its efficacy was often questioned, the powder had a history of being used for fevers since it was introduced in 1746.

Although her fever broke, Peg's strength deteriorated. 'While I write I feel a gradual decline from a broken heart and a destroyed constitution! Destroyed alas! Near the last moments of my life! My fingers refuse to do their office. Oh! I am sick at heart – my very brain wonders – I fear it is dooms day with me!' Peg knew she was dying. While salivation would certainly not have cured her, it may even have hastened her demise. Although the syphilis had weakened her considerably, it may actually have been Dr James's Fever Powder which finally killed her.[8]

On 18 March 1797, as Peg's death approached, Peggy Collins sombrely addressed a letter to their 'dear, dear friend', Edward J____ Esq:[9] 'I am now to inform you, that poor dear companion Mrs Leeson, is in the last stage of decline.' She was not expected to live. Two or three eminent doctors attended her at the end, but 'they said her strength was entirely exhausted, and she was in that state from the decay of nature, that all human art could not recover her, and desired I would prepare for a speedy dissolution.' Revd Dr Leonard, her spiritual advisor, was with her often, and a great comfort to her at her death. At this stage the women were eking out a poverty-strapped existence in the same poor lodging house in Fownes Street, Temple Bar.

According to the next letter from Peggy (possibly written to the apothecary Edward Jones of nearby Fleet Street), dated 22 March 1797, 'This morning at about four o'clock, my poor friend paid the great debt of nature, she died without the smallest evident pain, nature being completely exhausted.' On her deathbed, Peg's last words echoed Rochester's 'Elegy': 'All Nature's work, now from before me fly / Live not like Leeson, but like Leeson die.'

Peg left a will detailing about £3,000 in bonds and IOUs, but none of them were worth the paper they were written on. Her erstwhile companion disparagingly declared, 'a parcel of Blacklegs, Whores, Swindlers, and unprincipled men [had] shamefully borrowed money with an intention of never paying'. After paying off all her debts, there was not enough to pay for her funeral. Their grocer, Mr Peter Henegan of St James's Street, who had given them huge credit on sugar, tea, wines and various consumables, proved himself a true friend and footed the bill for Peg's burial. Others also assisted, including Mr Tinkler of Great George's Street; Bernard Murray, cheesemonger of 3 South Great George's Street; Billy Watson, printer from 7 Capel Street; and Miss Love, Peg's former protégé.

Years later Peg would still be talked about. *Fraser's Magazine for Town and Country* in 1830 under the title 'The Illustrious House of Plunkett' reported, 'Peg Plunkett, in my father's time, was the most famous person of the family. She, as the story goes, very particularly patronised the Irish bishops of her day.'[10] The reporter here suggests that she sexually serviced the bishops, and indicates that they were clients of her establishment. This was not a fact which Peg had high-lighted in her memoirs. Her obituary in the *Dublin Evening Post* for 17 May 1797 reported:

She figured for a long time in the *bon ton* – and absolutely made the fashion. It was her practice to confine her favours to *one*, or in other words to select a temporary husband. In this state she lived with several gentlemen in a style of fashionable elegance – but before her death her circumstances were so narrow, as to leave her but little above indigence.

The *Gentleman's Magazine* for April 1797 briefly mentioned her death, 'In Fownes-Street, Dublin, Margaret Leeson, alias the famous Peg Plunkett'. The *Oral and Public Advertiser* for 25 March 1797 stated, 'Mrs Margaret Leeson, alias the famous Peg Plunket, died in Fownes Street, Dublin yesterday night. This Lady was one of the most celebrated Courtezans in Europe. If report speaks the truth, she had a pension of three or five hundred a year upon the Irish Establishment.' Alas, Peg died with nothing to her name. Whether the Duke of Rutland had kept his promise to add her to the Pension List or not, Peg had spent it all. A life oscillating between extravagance and penury had taken its final toll. Peg Plunkett, otherwise known as the courtesan Mrs Leeson, was interred in St James's churchyard.

Epilogue

In the marriage, birth and death reels in the National Library of Ireland, there is a reference to a Margaret Plunkett from Angelsea Street, Dublin, who died on 9 December 1796, and was buried in St James's Church graveyard, St James's Street, Dublin. In the past, the deceased's age and time of death were often recorded incorrectly, so this may have been our Peg, as Angelsea Street runs perpendicular to Fownes Street and she may well have lived on the corner of both. Her final, posthumously published, memoirs state at the end, 'On the death of Mrs Margaret Leeson, who departed this mortal Life on 22nd Day of March 1797, in the 70th year of her Age.' Maybe her companion who was with her at the end, Peggy Collins, believed her to be that old. However, one thing we can say with some certainty is that she was not seventy in the year of her death, as reported.

I visited the graveyard in an attempt to establish the real date of Peg's death. I found the Catholic St James's Church built in 1724 easily enough, but there was no graveyard attached. I went next door to the church hall and a gentleman who ran a charity within informed me that St James's Church of Ireland (Protestant) churchyard was over the road; they 'allowed' Catholics to be buried there too. I walked over the road and retraced my steps back to the Protestant graveyard, which I had dismissed when passing it earlier. I looked forlornly at the double padlock, and contemplated the spiked railings. I could not come this far and then not get in. I saw a chap having a cigarette on the doorstep of a block of flats a few doors down so went over to him.

'Hello there, I am wondering if you can help me. I am trying to try to find someone who I believe is in this graveyard. Is there any way I can get in through the flats, round the back and through a hedge or a bit of wall somewhere?'

The man could not have been happier to help. 'There is a huge wall and fencing all the way round – no shrubs – you can't get in this way.' He saw my face drop and added, 'But I think the man down there in the pub has the keys. Ask for Mick behind the bar.'

When I walked into the bar, everyone looked up. I repeated my speech: 'Hello there, I am wondering if you can help me. I am trying to find someone who I believe is in this graveyard. I was told that you might hold some keys. Is there any way you could let me in?'

Mick looked at me, looked back at his pint, and decided which to go for. 'Well we can go and try,' he said.

So off we went back to the padlocked railings, and lo and behold! The mighty gates fell open. As this happened, an older gentlemen in a bobble cap suddenly appeared behind us and said, 'I am supposed to be meeting with the council . . .' At which I took off through the gates towards the cemetery before anyone stopped me. I left the barman talking to the bobble-capped man. Then I turned to see the bobble-capped man following me. I hastened on, but he caught up with me.

'I hope you don't mind me piggybacking on your entrance there. I have been waiting ten years to get into this graveyard.'

Good grief, I thought, someone more determined than me.

He turned out to be a kind, informative gentleman, dedicated to recording information on the crumbling gravestones. He was part of the St James's Graveyard Project, which had started some years before. 'It's disgusting, isn't it, how they have let the graveyard go to seed. You wouldn't find this in England, would you?'

'Well, yes, sometimes they are even vandalised.'

I told him who I was searching for.

'Was she Catholic?' he asked. I nodded. He showed me how the Catholic gravestones differed from the Protestant ones. The Catholic ones had a cross with a circle etched around them in Celtic style.

'It might make it easier to find her, but to be honest, you won't find much left from the eighteenth century, I'm afraid. The weather has worn away the stone engravings.'

As I walked round, I found this to be true. Many of the grave-stones had simply sunk into the earth and were no longer visible. While I was in the library, I had gone through the graveyard inscriptions he and his colleagues had admirably tried to save, but there was no mention of Peg.

'It doesn't mean she wasn't here,' he said in a bid to cheer me up. 'It's just that the grave will have sunk now, nothing left except her bones. Anyhow, whoever leaves first, let the other know so we don't lock each other in.'

The last thing I wanted was to spend the night locked in a graveyard on what was becoming an impossible mission. But at least I had got a look at the graveyard where Peg lay. I headed back to my hotel, which, in a strange coincidence, I later found out adjoined the street she had died in, Fownes Street.

As I sauntered back across the road, I saw, in the middle of the road, the 'Fountain', an obelisk with four sundials with a drinking fountain at its base, built in 1790 by the Duke of Rutland, the Lord Lieutenant. It was an old custom that funeral processions passing the fountain would circle it three times before carrying on to the cemetery. Peg would have been able to say goodbye at last to one of her best-known and best-loved paramours . . .

In Peg's Image

When I visited Russborough House in County Kildare, home to the Earls of Milltown, there was a photograph on the mantelpiece which was the same as that used on the cover of Mary Lyons's edition of *The Memoirs of Mrs Leeson* (1995) with the caption '*Portrait of a Lady as Diana* (Margaret Leeson by Pompeo Batoni (1708–87))'. Batoni was an Italian painter in high demand for portraits from young men travelling through Rome. Both the 2nd Earl of Milltown ('Mr Leeson') and his father had their portraits painted by him while on their grand tour between 1750 and 1752. The female portrait comes from the Milltown Collection (currently in the National Gallery of Ireland) so there is certainly a connection between this portrait and the Earls of Milltown. It is thought to be either the wife[1] or daughter of the 1st Earl. Peg would have been too young to be the sitter at this time, given my new datings of her life. Also, as Francis Leeson points out, the lady in the portrait is not very pretty.

The painting at the National Gallery in Dublin (NGI.703) is catalogued as 'The Presumed Portrait of the Marchesa Caterina Gabrielli

as Diana, 1751'. The curator of British art at the NGI, Adrian Le
Harivel, wrote to me:

> The actual identity of this and the pendant picture of a shepherdess
> with a lamb (Mahon bequest to the NGI) is still a puzzle. The present
> identity [as the Marchesa] is due to the former Head Curator, Sergio
> Benedetti (*NGI Essential Guide*, 2002, p. 72), who did not put a note
> in the dossier as to why and probably discussed it with Sir Denis
> Mahon (now deceased). There is no comparative photo of the
> Marchesa on file either. In 1997 when Benedetti curated *The
> Milltowns, a Family Reunion* (NGI) he followed the traditional
> suggestions that this was the second wife or daughter of the 1st Earl,
> neither of whom could have sat to Batoni in the flesh. It was then
> called 'A Lady of the Leeson Family as Diana' (Cat. 12), exhibited
> with the Mahon painting (Cat. 11). Although Batoni did paint the
> 2nd Earl in the same year, it is of different size and not pendant to
> either of the above: 99 x 73cm versus 50 x 39.5cm for each of the two
> women. There was a third picture *Portrait of a Lady with a Peacock*
> [i.e., Juno] by Batoni in the Dowager Countess of Milltown's hand-
> written list, at the end of the nineteenth century, that did not come to
> the Gallery in the Milltown Gift. It turned up at an Adam's auction in
> Dublin (24 February 1999) and was acquired by the Gallery
> (NGI.4661) for historic interest. It is rather crude and at present cata-
> logued as English c.1750. For a time NGI.703 was indeed thought to
> be the notorious Margaret Leeson, prostitute and Madame, who
> adopted the 1st Earl's surname, becoming his best client and seem-
> ingly mother of various illegitimate children [but not by him]. It was
> used on the modern edition of her memoirs, and though there is a
> slight resemblance to the young Peg Plunkett engraved by James
> Watson after William Hoare, this was wishful thinking and makes no
> sense datally or socially, as you will understand.[2]

In any case, according to my calculations, Peg would only have been
about nine or ten when the painting was undertaken in around 1751.

The other images said to be of Peg are probably not her either. J.T.
Gilbert in *A History of the City of Dublin* refers to a portrait of Peg
undertaken by John Brooks, who died about 1760. He left Dublin for

London in about 1746, while Peg was still a child. As Francis Leeson points out, 'She herself did not visit London until about 1780 so it is hardly likely that a portrait of her by this artist ever existed.' Another portrait of Peg is attributed to William Hoare (1707–92), who was associated with Batoni. He settled in Bath, which Peg visited at least once 'for an importation of impures' (a union meeting of prostitutes). Francis Leeson states, 'However, no trace of the original painting exists, and it is evident that some engravings supposedly made from it have been passed off as being Peg.'[3] Another engraving made by James Watson is given as being Peg Plunkett, but J. Chaloner Smith in his *British Mezzotinto Portraits Described* gives the opinion that the picture is 'not of Miss Plunkett but of the printer's daughter'.[4] How he ascertained this is unclear, but someone put her name to the print circulated by John Bewles and sold it from the Blackhorse in Cornhill. I like to think this may be of her, but we cannot be certain. It seems we may be left without any knowledge of what Peg actually looked like, and perhaps the only real picture we have left to us is the one she gave to us through her memoirs.

Notes

Preface: *The Memoirs of Mrs Leeson*

1   *Oxford Dictionary of National Biography* (*ODNB*).
2   See Norma Clarke, *Queen of Wits. A Life of Laetitia Pilkington* (London, Faber and Faber, 2008).
3   Lydia M. Thompson, *The Scandalous Memoirists. Constantia Phillips, Laetitia Pilkington and the Shame of 'Publick Fame'* (Manchester, MUP, 2000), p. 22.
4   See Julie Peakman, 'Memoirs of Women of Pleasure', *Women's Writing*, vol. 11, no. 2, 2004, pp. 163–84; *Whore Biographies 1700–1825* (London, Pickering & Chatto, 2007–8), 8 volumes.

Chapter 1: *Violence and Family Affairs*

1   All quotes not referenced in this book can be found in Peg's memoirs.
2   I have chosen to footnote all my sources except for the quotes from Peg herself as they are simply too numerous. All these can be found in either the original publications *The Memoirs of Mrs Margaret Leeson* or the reprints. (see Select Bibliography)
3   Peg spells it Killough, but it is now known as Killagh, a hamlet about ten miles north-east of Mullingar. Spellings were known to change over time, but I have chosen to stick with the eighteenth-century version. The *Irish Directory* shows the place as the property of the Rectory of the Diocese of Meath. Old maps show Corbetstown about three miles south of Killough. Killagh House, County Westmeath, may be connected to her.
4   Two recent editions of Peg's memoirs exist, as far as I am aware. Mary Lyons (ed.), *The Memoirs of Mrs Leeson* (Dublin, Lilliput Press, 1995), and Francis Leo Leeson, 'The Memoirs of Peg Plunket. A modern and condensed edition', typewritten MS, 1965, British Library (shelfmark: Cup.701.c.5). I have found both extremely useful. Mary Lyons accepts Peg's birth date as 1727; Francis Leeson has questioned this dating, as I do.
5   Francis Leo Leeson, op. cit.
6   Frank Geary and Tom Stark, 'Trends in Real Wages during the Industrial Revolution: A View from across the Irish Sea', *Economic History Review*, vol. 57, no. 2, May, 2004, pp. 362–95.

7   J.G. Simms, 'The Protestant Ascendancy, 1691–1714', in T.W. Moody & W.E. Vaughan (eds.), *A New History of Ireland Volume IV: Eighteenth-Century Ireland 1691–1800* (Oxford, OUP, 2009), pp. 12–13.

8   For a fuller background to Irish history, see William Edward Hartpole Lecky, *A History of Ireland in the Eighteenth Century* (London, Longmans Green & Co, 1913; reprint Elibron Classics, 2006), vols. I and II; Moody and Vaughan; and Sarah Foster, 'Buying Irish: Consumer Nationalism in 18th-century Dublin', *History Today*, vol. 47, no. 6, 1997.

9   J.L. McCracken, 'Social Structure and Social Life, 1714–60', T.W. Moody and W.E. Vaughan, *A New History of Ireland* IV (Oxford, OUP, 2009), pp. 31–122, p. 31. No census was taken until 1821, so we only have the estimates of historians to guide us.

10   Jonathan Swift, *A Modest Proposal for preventing the children of poor people in Ireland, from being a burden on their parents or country, and for making them beneficial to the publick* (Dublin, 1729).

11   Michael Drake, 'The Irish Demographic Crisis of 1740–41', *Historical Studies*, vol. VI, T.W. Moody (ed.) (London, Routledge & Kegan Paul, 1968); David Dickson, *Arctic Ireland: The Extraordinary Story of the Great Frost and Forgotten Famine of 1740–41* (Belfast, White Row Press Ltd., 1997); Felicity Nussbaum (ed.), *The Global Eighteenth Century* (Baltimore, John Hopkins University Press, 2003), p 275.

12   Wilkes, *Misc. Observations on Ireland*, quoted in J.L. McCraken, Moody and Vaughan, p. 42–3.

13   See Patricia M. Bennis, *St John's Fever and Lock Hospital Limerick, 1780–1890* (Cambridge Scholars Publishing, Newcastle upon Tyne, 2009), p. 6.

14   William Robert Fitzgerald (1749–1804) became Earl of Offaly on the death of his elder brother George in 1765, and the following year, when his father was created Duke of Leinster, he assumed the title Marquess of Kildare. In 1768, he made the grand tour for a year. On his father's death in 1773, Kildare became the 2nd Duke of Leinster and assumed the role of Ireland's premier peer. Financial pressures on the family were temporarily eased two years later when, on 7 November 1775, he married Emilia Olivia St George (1759–98).

15   Dardistown, sometimes called Durdistown. The *Irish Directory* of 1814 shows Corbetstown, where Peg's father owned property, as the residence of Francis D'Arcy Esq. The Fetherstons, also known as the Fetherstonhaughs, settled at Durdistown in 1726 and were neighbours of Peg's family. See *Burke's Landed Gentry*, where both families appear; Francis Leeson MS, BL, p. 29.

Chapter 2 – *The First Indiscretion*

1   The barracks stood on the piece of ground where the garda station now stands.

2   D. Dickson, *Ireland 1600–1800: New Foundations* (Dublin, Helicon, 1987), pp. 147–51.

3   Richard Twiss, *Tour Of Ireland 1775* (London, 1776), p. 54.

4   James Kelly, *The Liberty and Ormond Boys: Factional Riots in Eighteenth-Century Dublin* (Dublin, Four Courts Press, 2005).

5   Rebecca Probert, *Marriage Law & Practice in the Long Eighteenth Century: A Reassessment* (Cambridge, CUP, 2009); S. Parker, *Informal Marriage, Cohabitation and the Law, 1750–1989* (Basingstoke, Macmillan Press, 1990).

6   A.P.W. Malcomson, *The Pursuit of the Heiress. Aristocratic Marriage in Ireland 1740–1840* (Belfast, Ulster Historical Foundation, 2006), p. 156.

7   Of 10,781 foundlings admitted in the decade from 1750, about 3,800 died (about 49 per cent); Fred Powell, 'Dean Swift and the Dublin Foundling Hospital', *Irish Quarterly Review*, vol. 70, no. 278/279 (Summer/Autumn, 1981), pp. 162–70; Gary A. Boyd, *Dublin 1745–1922, Hospitals, Spectacles and Vice* (Dublin, Four Courts Press, 2006), p. 26; J. Robins, *The Lost Children: A Study of the Charity Child in Ireland, 1700–1900* (Dublin, LPA, 1980), p. 25; W.D. Wodsworth, *A Brief History of the Ancient Foundling Hospital of Dublin* (Dublin, A. Thomas, 1876).

8   Sister Mary Genevieve, 'Mrs Bellew's Family in Channel Row', *Dublin Historical Record*, vol. 22, no. 3 (Old Dublin Society, 1968), pp. 230–41.

Chapter 3: *The Crossroads*

1   In a later edition she confirms, 'I complied and that very night removed to the house of one Kelly in Clarendon Street whose wife was a *knowing lady* and a woman of some address.' Leeson, *Memoirs*, 1798 edition, p. 4.

     The house belonged to Mr Kelly, his 'wife' using the name Mrs Butler as her working name. His son, Michael Kelly, Peg called 'the Crupper-Making Squire of Whitehall'.

2   Róisín Healy, 'Suicide in Early Modern and Modern Europe', *Historical Journal*, vol. 49, no. 3, (Sept. 2006), pp. 916, 919. As she points out, there is no academic written examination of suicide in Ireland, although Mark Finnane discusses it briefly in a section on 'mania and melancholia' in his book *Insanity and the Insane in Post-Famine Ireland* (London, Croom Helm, 1981), pp. 150–61; as does Georgina Laragy, 'Suicide and Insanity in Post-Famine Ireland', in Catherine Cox, Maria Luddy (eds.), *Cultures of Care in Irish Medical History, 1750–1970* (London, Palgrave, 2010), pp. 79–91.

3   In the latter stages of her life when she contemplates the immoral deeds she has committed throughout her life, she fears hell as her retribution.

4   Peg never mentioned her sisters by their first names.

5   In a report entitled, *State of the Hospital published in November 1750*, Mosse's colleague, Benjamin Higgins, suggests Mosse's reasons for establishing the hospital. Higgins quoted in Boyd, p. 25.

6   Ibid, p. 63.

7 Capt. R.T. Claridge, *Hydropathy; or The Cold Water Cure, as practiced by Vincent Priessnitz, at Graefenberg, Silesia, Austria*, 8th edn. (London, James Madden and Co., 1843) p. 27. Full text at https://archive.org/details/39002086176733.med.yale.edu. Accessed 18.09.2014.

8 Colm Scudds, 'Old Coach Roads from Dublin 1745–1821', *Dublin Historical Record*, vol. 54, no. 1 (Spring, 2001), pp. 4–15.

9 'In 1741 the journey to Belfast cost four English crowns from Dublin and took three days, stopping at Drogheda on the first night and at Newry on the second. A year or two later, it was specified that the coach would always run with six able horses. Based on a 5 a.m. start, the journey could be done in two days in summer, three in winter.' 'The Famine', *History Ireland*, vol. 15, no. 5 (Sept./Oct 2007), http://www.historyireland.com/18th-19th-century-history/irelands-time-space-revolution-improvements-to-pre-famine-travel/. Accessed 18.09.2014. Also see J.H. Andrews, 'Road Planning in Ireland before the Railway Age', *Irish Geography*, 5 (1) (1964); D. Broderick, *The First Toll Roads: Ireland's Turnpike Roads, 1729–1858* (Cork, Collins Press, 2002).

10 Colm Scudds, 'Old Coach Roads'.

11 Richard Twiss, *Tour of Ireland* (London, 1776), p. 73.

12 William Cadogan, *An Essay upon Nursing and the Management of Children from their Birth to Three Years of Age* (London, Committee of the Foundling Hospital, 1748).

13 In her memoirs, Peg give him as 'another relation Mr H___P___, in High Street'; this must have been Henry Plunkett, woollen-draper, operating from 20 High Street; see *Merchants and Traders Dublin, Watson's Almanack*, 1783, p. 65.

Chapter 4: *The Downward Spiral*

1 Leeson, *Memoirs*, 1798 edition, p. 7. Thomas Caulfeild was the first cousin of Revd Charles Caulfeild (1686–1768) and his brother James (1682–1734), 3rd Viscount Charlemont, father of James (1728–99), 1st Earl. See Francis Leeson, p. 35; William Caulfeild (1665–1737), his father, married Lettice, daughter of Sir Arthur Gore, 1st Baronet by his wife Eleanor, daughter of Sir George St George, and was father of (among others) Thomas Caulfeild, Toby Caulfeild and St George Caulfeild, all of whom were also MPs for Tulsk. William's residence was Donamon Castle, County Roscommon, which he inherited from his father, another Thomas, in 1691.

2 M.J. Tutty, 'Clontarf', *Dublin Historical Record*, vol. 21, no. 1 (Mar.–May, 1966), pp. 2–13.

3 Thomas is described in Playfair's *British Family Antiquity 1810 Vol. IV* as 'formerly an eminent wine merchant'. Francis Leeson, p. 35.

4 Raymond Gillespie & R.F. Foster (eds.), *Irish Provincial Cultures in the Long Eighteenth Century.*(Dublin, Four Courts Press, 2012)

5 C.C. Maxwell, *Dublin Under the Georges, 1714–1830* (London, Faber and Faber,

1946), p. 101; L.A. Clarkson, 'Hospitality, housekeeping and high living in eighteenth-century Ireland', in J. Hill and C. Lennon (eds.), *Luxury and Austerity* (Dublin, University College Dublin Press, 1999), pp. 84–105.

6 J. Robins, *Champagne and Silver Buckles: The Viceregal Court at Dublin Castle, 1700–1922* (Dublin: Lilliput Press, 2001), p. 72.

7 A Thomas Caulfeild appears on a list of insolvent debtors in Dublin in 1772, so he may well have gone bust in his later years: http://www.igp-web.com/igparchives/ire/countrywide/xmisc/debtors-1772.txt. Accessed 26 May 2014.

8 Emma Hamilton was lucky enough to find a young keeper, Charles Greville, nephew of Sir William Hamilton, to pay to look after her daughter. She rarely had a chance to visit her though, and when she did, she wrote about it affectionately but tinged with sadness. When Charles passed Emma on to his older uncle, Sir William Hamilton, he took on the obligation of paying for the child. Neither of the men allowed the child to live in the same residence with them. See Julie Peakman, *Emma Hamilton* (London, Haus, 2005).

9 J.T. Gilbert, *A History of the City of Dublin*, vol. II (Dublin, McGlashan and Gill, 1859) p. 112.

Chapter 5: *An Honourable Man*

1 Her age here is an estimate based on her memoirs and the turn of events. We know she was around fifteen years old when she first went to Dublin, as she states this in her memoirs. She then hovered back and forth between her family home in Killough and Dublin, with a stay in Tullamore in between. During this period she had managed a brief elopement with Mrs Shannon's lover. We know that she was with Dardis in 1760 for about a year, and Caulfeild for about a year after that. This would have made her somewhere in her early twenties.

2 The 1st Earl was an Irish Peer and politician, and held a seat in the Irish House of Commons, representing Rathcormack in County Cork, between 1743 and 1756. He was created Baron Russborough in 1756, then Viscount Russborough of Russellstown in County Wicklow in 1760, finally becoming earl on 10 May 1763. See the second edition of Peg's memoirs in NLI. Peg rewrote a shortened introduction with information on the people she had mentioned in the first edition. In it, she mentioned that her Mr Leeson was related to the earls of Milltown. See: http://www.heritagecouncil.ie/fileadmin/user_upload/conservationplans/Russborough_Conserv_Plan.pdf. Accessed 13/10/2014.

3 Cynthia O'Connor, *The Pleasing Hours. The Grand Tour of James Caulfeild, 1st Earl of Charlemont* (Cork, Collins Press, 1999), pp. 101–2.

4 Joseph Leeson III (1730–1801) was the first son of the 1st Earl of Milltown, and was to become the 2nd Earl of Milltown; the Hon. Brice Leeson was the second son and later 3rd Earl of Milltown (1735–1807) (they also had a sister, Mary). Francis Leeson believes Peg's Mr Leeson to be the 2nd Earl of Milltown, but Mary Lyons

does not mention this connection. If Peg's Mr Leeson was not the 2nd Earl, then it was most likely one of his brothers or step-brothers. His father had three wives: Joseph III's mother, Celia Leigh (d. 1737), whom he married in 1729; a second wife, Anne Preston (d. 1766), whom he married in 1738, and by whom he had several children, about whom little is known; a third wife, Elizabeth French (d. 1768), whom he married in 1768, with whom he had children: Cecilia, William, Florence, Arabella and Robert. My only question mark around this is Peg's assertion that he offered to marry her and wanted to introduce her to his family. This would have been unlikely, but not unheard of for a woman in Peg's position, as other mistresses had gone on to marry titled men. The other query lies around Peg's own nature – if she was the mistress of a man who was to become an earl, she would have been the first one to mention it in her memoirs. Perhaps it was her respect for him (she called him an 'honorable man' and is one of the few lovers she seems to have thought decent) which kept her from bringing shame on him and his family by exposing their affair. Information from Francis Leeson MS and Russborough House.

5   David A. Fleming, 'Diversions of the People: Sociability among the Orders of Early Eighteenth-Century Ireland', *Eighteenth Century Ireland*, no. 17, pp. 99–111.

6   L.M. Cullen, 'Economic Development, 1750–1800', in Moody and Vaughan, p. 180.

7   Moody and Vaughan, pp. 44, 244, 383.

8   The Lennox family were a notable British family. The fourth sister, known as Georgiana Carolina Fox, became 1st Baroness Holland (1723–74), having eloped with and married Charles Fox the politician. The fifth youngest sister Cecilia died of a wasting disease, probably tuberculosis. See Stella Tillyard, *Aristocrats: Caroline, Emily, Louisa, and Sarah Lennox 1740–1832* (London, Chatto & Windus, 1994) for an informative read on the sisters.

9   An example is seen of the structure of housekeeping at the houses of the Lennox sisters, Louisa and Emily, who lived in Carton House and Castletown House respectively; Tillyard, *Aristocrats*, pp. 211–12.

10 A Mrs Delaney describing meals to her sister; http://www.historyireland.com/ 18th-19th-century-history/breakfast-dinner-and-supper-in-georgian-dublin-2. Accessed 19 June 2014.

11 See Francis Leeson, MS, introduction.

12 Bernard Mandeville, *A Modest Defence of Chastity* (London, A. Bettesworth, 1726).

13 For example, Harriette Wilson's sister, Sophia Dubochet, was first mistress, then wife to Lord Berwick; and the Earl of Berkely married his fifteen-year-old mistress Mary Cole.

14 James Livesey, 'The Dublin Society in Eighteenth-Century Irish Political Thought', *Historical Journal*, vol. 47, no. 3 (Sept. 2004), pp. 615–40; Henry F. Berry, *A History of the Royal Dublin Society*. http://archive.org/stream/historyofroyalduooberr/ historyofroyalduooberr_djvu.txt. Accessed 22/10/2013.

15 Irish Architectural Archives. A Directory of Irish Architects 1720–1940. http:// www.dia.ie/architects/view/5423 Viewed 22/10/2013.

Chapter 6: *Love of a Lifetime*

1   The 1798 edition of Peg's memoirs gives his full name as Robert Lawless (see
     Memoirs, p. 7). Mary Lyons refers to him as John Lawless. It is unlikely Peg would
     get this wrong but her editor might have done.

2   On 23 June 1779, Margaret Lawless (1763–1829) married John Scott (8 June
     1739–98), who became 1st Baron Earlsfort, between 1784 and 1789, then 1st
     Viscount Clonmell between 1789 and 1793, and was finally created Earl of Clonmel
     in 1779. Also referred to as 'Copperfaced Jack', he became Lord Chief Justice of the
     King's Bench for Ireland between 1784 and 1789.

     Margaret Lawless was the daughter and eventual heiress of Patrick Lawless of
     Dublin by his wife Mary Lawless (sister to Nicholas Lawless, 1st Baron Cloncurry),
     and grand-daughter of Robert Lawless and Mary Hadsor; http://www.cracrofts-
     peerage.co.uk/online/content/clonmell1793.htm. Accessed 26 May 2014.

3   Rivalries between Smock Alley and Crow Street (the latter run by Barry Springer)
     had meant that both theatres had been in financial difficulty. Henry Mossop had
     taken over the Theatre Royal in 1760, but by 1762 was deeply in debt and was plan-
     ning his escape to join Garrick in London. Mossop complained to Garrick, 'The
     theatrical business, for the latter part of the season, has been extremely indifferent,
     and has turned out much inferior to what I expected from the novelty of the
     performers from England . . . the plays hardly answered the expenses.' *Theatre in
     Dublin, 1745–1820 Calendar of Performances*, pp. 816–17.

4   Chris Morash, *A History of Irish Theatre 1601–2000* (Cambridge, CUP, 2002), p. 49.

5   Chris Morash and Shaun Richards, *Mapping Irish Theatre: Theories of Space and
     Place* (Cambridge, CUP, 2013), p. 30.

6   Morash, *History of Irish Theatre*, p. 35.

7   Gilbert, *History of the City of Dublin*, vol. II, pp. 305–6.

8   *Tait's Edinburgh Magazine*, vol. 8 (1841), p. 31.

9   David Kelley, 'The Conditions of Debtors and Insolvents in Eighteenth-Century
     Dublin', in David Dickson (ed.), *The Gorgeous Mask: Dublin 1700–1850* (Dublin,
     Trinity History Workshop, 1987), pp. 98–120; p. 107.

10   From an 1841 report by Dr Francis White MRCSI, one of the Inspectors General of
     Gaols in Ireland. http://freepages.genealogy.rootsweb.ancestry.com/~mturner/
     cork/jane_prison.htm. Accessed 10/10/2014.

11   Philip Luckombe, *A Tour Through Ireland* (Dublin, T. Lowndes, 1780), p. 51.

12   David A. Fleming, 'Diversions of the People: Sociability among the Orders of Early
     Eighteenth-Century Ireland', *Eighteenth Century Ireland*, no. 17, pp. 99–111.

13   Peg's reference was to *An Heroic Epistle from Kitty Cut-a-Dash to Oroonoko*, a polit-
     ical verse satire on the situation in Ireland, published in Dublin in 1778. Peg's
     nickname was obviously applied retrospectively, as at the time Kitty was with
     Cavendish (he died in 1776), and the epistle had not been published.

14   Gilbert, *History of the City of Dublin*, vol. III, p. 221; A.P.W. Malcomson, *The Pursuit*

of the Heiress: Aristocratic Marriage in Ireland 1740–1840 (Belfast, Ulster Historical Foundation, 2006).

[15] There is some discrepancy here. Francis Leeson (in his MS) believes Lord Boyne to be Richard Hamilton, 4th Viscount Boyne (1724–89), while Mary Lyons believes it to be Frederick Hamilton, 3rd Viscount Boyne (1718–72). Since the latter was the elder of the two brothers, and didn't he die until 1772, Richard would not have become Lord Boyne until that date – that is, unless Peg has accorded him a title anachronistically in her memoirs, which she sometimes did. I am apt to believe it was Frederick because of his racy lifestyle. Boyne's peerage had been created in 1717 for his grandfather, Gustavus Hamilton, a Scottish military commander who had been made 1st Baron Hamilton of Stackallan in County of Meath two years previously.

[16] Robert R. Bataille, *The Writing Life of Hugh Kelly: Politics, Journalism and Theatre in Late Eighteenth-Century London* (Carbondale, Southern Illinois University Press, 2000), p. 120.

[17] Arnold Horner, 'Ireland's Time-Space Revolution. Improvements to Pre-Famine Travel', *History Ireland*, vol. 15, no. 5 (Sept–Oct, 2007), pp. 22–7.

[18] There is evidence of a Smith Ramadge company registered as dry goods importers in the membership list of the New York Chamber of Commerce, 1768–75. Taken from J.A. Stevens, *Colonial Records of the New York Chamber of Commerce 1768–1784* (New York, John Trow, 1867), 2 vols.; J.B. Bishop, *A Chronicle of One Hundred and Fifty Years: The Chamber of Commerce of the State of New York* (New York, Charles Scribner, 1918). http://www.geog.cam.ac.uk/research/projects/chambersofcommerce/newyork.pdf. Accessed 6 July 2014.

[19] Cleghorn had excelled academically at an early age and had been sent to Edinburgh at fifteen to study physics and surgery. At only nineteen years of age, he was appointed surgeon to the 22nd Regiment of Foot stationed in Minorca, where he spent the next thirteen years. He left the island and followed his regiment to Ireland in 1749, although he moved to London the following year. He must have liked what he saw of Ireland as he returned to Dublin in 1751 and chose to settle there until his death in 1789.

[20] *The Book of the Rotunda Hospital: An Illustrated History of the Dublin Lying-In Hospital from its Foundation in 1745 to the Present Time*, Appendix II, p. 26.

Chapter 7: *A Young Clergyman*

[1] This a conservative estimate based on the information she provides (one child with Dardis, one with Caulfeild and five with Lawless), but she may have had more who died stillborn.

[2] John Meade (1744–1800) briefly represented Banagher in the Irish House of Commons. In 1766, in anticipation of his marriage to rich heiress Theodosia,

daughter of Robert Hawkins-Magill, Meade had been created Viscount Clanwilliam of County Tipperary and Baron Gilford of the Manor of Gilford in County Down. He would become the 1st Earl of Clanwilliam in 1776. Through his marriage, the Gill Hall estate in Gilford in County Down had come into the Meade family, but their riches were not to last. Around 1783, it was reported that 'the possessors of such an affluent income were so immersed in debt as to have their personal property seized and sold by a public auction'.

3 http://www.proni.gov.uk/introduction__clanwilliam_meade_d3044.pdfwww. proni.cov. (Public Record Office of Northern Ireland, T3465/M/3/3); (T3465/M/3/3). Accessed 6 July 2014.

4 Hugh Boulter, *Letters written by his excellency, Hugh Boulter, DD, Lord Primate of all Ireland etc* (Dublin, 1770), vol. I, pp. 208–10, 224.

5 See Kevin Whelan, *Endurance and Emergence Catholics in Ireland* (Dublin, Irish Academic Press, 1990). Kirby Miller has estimated that 30 per cent of those leaving Ulster for colonial America were Protestant but not Presbyterian; see Kirby A. Miller, 'Emigrants and Exiles: Ireland and the Irish Exodus to North America', *History Ireland*, vol. 7, no. 3 (Autumn 1999).

6 Richard J. Purcell, 'Irish Contribution to Colonial New York', *Irish Quarterly Review*, vol. 30, no. 117 (Mar. 1941), pp. 107–20.

7 *Alumni Dublineses* online, p. ix. http://digitalcollections.tcd.ie/home/index. php?DRIS_ID=LCN10378529_0003. Accessed 10 July 2014.

8 According to the peerage site he graduated with a BA in 1767, which fits with his alumni records; http://www.thepeerage.com/p26850.htm#i268493. Accessed 6 July 2014.

9 MS 378.41SC *Alumni Dublineses*, p. 479, MS Room, Trinity College, Dublin.

10 *Fraser's Magazine for Town and Country*, vol. 5 (1832), p. 504.

11 Leeson, *Memoirs*, 1798 edition, p. 10.

12 James Kelly's 'Infanticide in Eighteenth-Century Ireland', *Irish Economic and Social History*, vol. 19, no. 5 (1992), pp. 5–26.

13 Maria Luddy, *Prostitution and Irish Society, 1800–1940* (Cambridge, CUP, 2007), p. 124.

14 Leeson, *Memoirs*, 1798 edition, p. 11.

15 Brian Boydell, 'Music, 1700–1850', in Moody and Vaughan, pp. 568–618; p. 582.

16 Arthur Young, *A Tour of Ireland 1776–9*, (Dublin S. Powell, 1770), p. 17.

17 For discussion about images of Peg see the Epilogue. Francis Leeson believes no image of her exists, but these mezzotints would have at least given an idea of hairstyles worn at the time by women of similar status.

18 Sean Donnelley, 'A German Dulcimer Player in Eighteenth Century Dublin', *Dublin Historical Record*, vol. 53, no. 1 (Spring, 2000); his obituary was in the *Evening Post*, 5 May 1791.

Chapter 8: *Violence and Brothel-keeping*

1 The date must have been 1778. Peg mentions the child she had with her at the time of the Pinking Dandies incident in November 1779 was a two-year-old child she had with Lambert, who must have been born in 1777 and conceived in 1776. Since Lawless left eighteen months before she took up with Lambert, this puts his leaving for America around 1774 and his return in 1778 (Peg says four years later). Peg was eight months pregnant with Lawless's child at the time of the Pinking Dandies incident so Lawless must have been back in Ireland by 1778, and she mentions that the Pinking Dandies were looking for Lawless when they broke into her house. Lawless's excuse for the lack of communication was the American War of Independence. Peg also mentions that his father and brother had received his letters soon after his departure, despite his assertions about communication difficulties during the war.

2 It has been estimated at both three days in a stagecoach in the mid-eighteenth century, and thirty-one hours in a mail coach at the beginning of the nineteenth century. Keenan states, 'In the year 1800 the Dublin to Cork coach was still making two overnight stops, one in Kilkenny and one in Fermoy'; E.M. Johnston-Liik, *MPs in Dublin: Companion to History of the Irish Parliament, 1692–1800*, p. 44; William Williams, *Creating Irish Tourism: The First Century, 1750–1850* (London, Anthem Press, 2011), p. 9.

3 McConnell's *Cork Directory* for 1755.

4 Arthur Young, *A Tour in Ireland* (Dublin, S. Powell, 1780; reprint 1809), p. 80.

5 O'Grada, pp. 54-60.

6 J.D. Herbert, *Irish Varieties for the last fifty years: written from recollections 1836* (London, William Joy, 1836).

7 Ibid.

8 Bryan MacMahon, '"A most ingenious mechanic": Ireland's First Airman', *History Ireland*, vol. 18, no. 6 (November/December 2010), pp. 22–4. Crosbie had been at Trinity College, entering in 1773 at seventeen years old; *Alumni Dublinenses*.

9 Jonah Barrington, *Personal Sketches of His Own Time* (London, Kessinger, 1830–32), p. 282.

10 Richard Moncrieff and William Worthington were both Sheriffs of the County of the City of Dublin during 1779–80, and both later held the posts of alderman and mayor.

11 Dr Vance apparently had no training as an obstetrician, yet was attending surgeon at the Hospital for the Incurables in 1771 and at the Meath Hospital in 1781. See *Watson's Almanack*, 1771 and 1781.

12 Although Peg mentions a daughter who Lambert kept until she was four years old, she must have her age wrong as Lawless was only away for four years and she met Lambert eighteen months after he left.

13 Kevin P. O'Rouke, 'Dublin Police', *Dublin Historical Record*, vol. 29, No 4 (Sept 1976), pp. 138–47.

14 Ibid.
15 Herbert, *Irish Varieties*.

Chapter 9: *Spats and Trips*

1 John O'Keeffe, *Recollections of the Life of John O'Keeffe, Written by Himself* (London, 1826), vol. 2, p. 22.
2 James Boaden, *Memoirs of Mrs Siddons*, vol. 1 (London, Henry Colburn, 1827), p. 115.
3 The fact that she was a 'rival' to Peg would place them as a similar age, thus reinforcing my date of Peg's birth as around 1742. It is unlikely she would have been comparing herself with a woman nearly twenty years younger if she had been born in 1727.
4 Kathleen S. Murphy, 'Judge, Jury, Magistrate and Soldier: Rethinking Law and Authority in Late Eighteenth-Century Ireland', *American Journal of Legal History*, vol. 44, no. 3 (July 2000), p. 231. http://digitalcommons.calpoly.edu/cgi/viewcontent.cgi?article=1054&context=hist_fac; Accessed 25 July 2014.
5 Sparked by resistance to the Catholic Relief Act of 1778, the Gordon Riots, as they became known, erupted onto the streets of London in June 1780 and escalated into a sustained assault on government properties and institutions. They were fuelled by popular resentment against the American War of Independence, which resulted in the mob setting fire to many private houses of members of Parliament, central London prisons and the tollbooths on bridges, as well as attacks on the Bank of England.
6 M.J. Tutty, 'The City of Dublin Steam Packet Company', *Dublin Historical Record*, vol. 18, no. 3 (June, 1963), pp. 80–90.
7 Cormac F. Lowth, 'Shipwrecks Around Dublin Bay', *Dublin Historical Record*, vol. 55, no. 1 (Spring, 2002), pp. 50–63.
8 http://corkshipwrecks.net/ssshipwrecklist18thcent.html. Accessed 24/09/2014.
9 From 'Pall Mall', *Survey of London*, vols. 29 and 30: St James Westminster, Part 1 (1960), pp. 322–24. URL: http://www.british-history.ac.uk/report.aspx?compid=40579 Date accessed: 20 November 2013.
10 Saul David, *Prince of Pleasure. The Prince of Wales and the Making of the Regency* (London, Abacus, 1999), pp. 15, 31.
11 Leeson, *Memoirs*, 1798 edition, p. 15.

Chapter 10: *Returning Home*

1 James Gandon (1743–1823) was one of Ireland's leading architects and also designed the Four Courts and the King's Inns in Dublin.
2 Previous estimates had been set much lower – at about two and three-quarter

million, based on returns of hearth-money, but these were revised in K.H. Connell, 'Land and Population in Ireland c. 1780–1845', *Economic History Review*, 1950, p. 278; J.H. Andrews, 'Land and People, c. 1780', in Moody and Vaughan.

3 Barry Yelverton, sen. (1736–1805), 1st Viscount Avonmore, was an Irish judge and politician, who gave his name to Yelverton's Act, passed in 1782, 'settling and assuring the forfeited and other estates in this kingdom, and for the regulation of trade, and other purposes: and whereas it is at all times expedient to give every assurance, and to remove every apprehension concerning the title of lands'. http://www.irishstatutebook.ie/1781/en/act/pub/0011/print.html. Accessed 13 July 2014.

4 Kimberly Chrisman, 'Unhoop the Fair Sex: The Campaign Against the Hoop Petticoat in Eighteenth-Century England, *Eighteenth-Century Studies*, vol. 30, no. 1 (Fall, 1996), pp. 5–23.

5 *London Magazine*, vol. 10, no. 2 (1741), p. 75.

6 Quoted in Phillis Cunnington, *Costumes of the Seventeenth and Eighteenth Century* (Boston, Plays Inc., 1970), p. 93.

7 Brian Boydell, 'Venues for Music in 18th century Dublin', *Dublin Historical Record*, vol. 29, no. 1 (Dec. 1975), pp. 28–34.

8 http://smockalley.com/wp-content/uploads/2013/05/Research-Guide-for-Archival-Sources-of-Smock-Alley-Theatre.pdfaccessed 21/11/2013.

9 The bailiffs were identified by Peg as Sheridan, Maloney, Mooney and Broome in her introduction to the 1798 edition of her memoirs.

10 B. Doorley, 'Newgate Prison', in David Dickson (ed.), *The Gorgeous Mask* (Dublin, Trinity History Workshop, 1987), pp. 122–3.

11 This was to become a common trope in eighteenth-century whores' memoirs; Julie Peakman, 'Memoirs of Women of Pleasure: The Whore Biography, 1795–1825', in *Women's Writing Journal*, 'Sex, Gender and the Female Body' special issue, 2004, pp. 163–84.

Chapter 11: *The Two Bobs*

1 William H. Grattan Flood, *A History of Irish Music* (Dublin, Browne and Nolan, 1906).

2 *Lady's Magazine*, March 1776; *Lady's Magazine*, March 1791.

3 James Kelly, '"Drinking the Waters": Balneotherapeutic Medicine in Ireland, 1660–1850', *Studia Hibernica*, no. 35 (2008–9), pp. 99–146.

4 Wilbur Lucius Cross, *The Life and Times of Laurence Sterne* (New York, Macmillan, 1909), p 398.

5 Francis Elrington Ball, 'The Antiquities from Blackrock to Dublin', *Journal of the Royal Society of Antiquaries of Ireland*, fifth series, vol. 10, no. 4 (Dec. 31, 1900), pp. 307–18.

6   Nigel Surry, 'James Northcote at Portsmouth', *Burlington Magazine*, vol. 136, no. 1093 (Apr. 1994), pp. 234–7.

7   Jennifer Gall, *In Bligh's Hand: Surviving the Mutiny on the Bounty* (Canberra, National Library of Australia, 2010), p. 38.

8   Brigadier General Richard Mathews's will is in the National Archives, Kew, PROB 11/1134/336: Will of Richard Mathews, late Brigadier General and Commander in Chief of the Land Forces in the Honorable United East India Company's Service of Bombay, East Indies, dated 24 October 1785; *Town and Country Magazine*, vol. 20 (1788), p. 165. Eustace P. Beryl, 'Index of Will Abstracts in the Genealogical Office, Dublin', *Analecta Hibernica*, no. 17 (1949), pp. 145, 147–348.

9   The army list shows he obtained an ensign's commission in February 1784, in the 67th Foot, and was promoted to lieutenant in March 1785, but he then disappears from the army lists.

10   John C. Greene, *Theatres in Dublin, A Calendar of Performances*, vol. 6, 1745–1820.

11   In the first half of the 1750s there were about eight fully developed banking houses in Dublin, with a few others scattered in major towns such as Galway, Athlone and Belfast. The existing banks were drastically reduced in number between 1754 and 1760, with the collapse of eight of them. L.M. Cullen, 'Economic Development, 1691–1750', in Moody and Vaughan, pp. 154–8.

12   Newcomen's bank, built in 1781, is an example of the shift in architecture from the Palladian school to the preference for neoclassical design. Anne Cruickshank, 'The Visual Arts, 1740–1850', in Moody and Vaughan, p. 506. The Bank of Ireland first operated from a house previously owned by Charles Blakeney, moving to College Green in 1803.

Chapter 12: *The Army Men and Some Disagreeable Adventures*

1   Thomas Bartlett, *Ireland: A History* (Cambridge, CUP, 2010), p. 179.

2   G.I. Brown, *Count Rumford: The Extraordinary Life of a Scientific Genius* (Stroud, Sutton Publishing, 1999).

3   http://www.militaryarchives.ie/collections/online-collections/maps-plans-drawings. Accessed 16/10/2014.

4   Christine Casey, *The Buildings of Ireland* (New Haven, Yale University Press, 2005), pp. 26–7.

5   Kenneth P. Ferguson, 'The Army in Ireland from the Restoration to the Act of Union' (unpublished Ph.D. thesis, Trinity College, Dublin, 1983), pp. 90–91; James Kelly and M.J. Powell (eds.), *Clubs and Societies in Eighteenth-Century Ireland* (Dublin, Four Courts Press, 2010).

6   Ferguson, 'The Army in Ireland', p. 85; *Volunteers Journal*, 18 Aug. 1784.

7   Martyn J. Powell, 'Mathew Carey and Anti-Military Sentiment in the *Volunteers*

Journal and the *Pennsylvania Evening Herald*' (unpublished, dissertation, Aberystwyth University, 2011); S.J. Connolly, 'The defence of Protestant Ireland, 1660–1760', in Bartlett and Jeffery (eds.), *A Military History of Ireland* (Cambridge, CUP, 1996), pp. 242–3.

8   Hanger and McGuire are untraceable, but Lieutenant Boyle, Captain Stephen Freemantle, Major Henry Mock and Captain Francis Craddock were all aide-de-camps. Peg's connection to Freemantle is directed in a squib in the headline notice in the *Dublin Evening Post*, 3 May 1783, p. 3A. Freemantle is referred to as 'Major Domo Friezemantle', and Mrs Leeson and Moll Hall are named as themselves. See Lyons, p. 256.

9   Leeson, *Memoirs*, 1798 edition, p. 22.

10   *History*, vol. 36, no. 126–7, pp. 57–72 (February 1951).

11   *Dublin Evening Post*, 26 June 1786; *Volunteers Journal*, 9 June 1784.

12   The 67th Regiment of Foot had landed in Ireland in 1775, and in 1782 were directed to assume the county title of the South Hampshire Regiment. They were to embark for the West Indies in early 1785 from Ireland to relieve the 55th Regiment. They proceeded from Barbados to Antigua in the autumn of 1785. Richard Cannon, *Historical Record of the Sixty-seventh, Or the South Hampshire Regiment* (London, 1849), p. xxvi.

13   Lyons gives this beau as the Honorable Richard St Leger, captain and aide-de-camp to the Lord Lieutenant, p. 256, but I think it more likely to have been John St Ledger.

14   *The Correspondence of George, Prince of Wales, 1770–1812*, ed. A. Aspinall, 8 vols. (1963–71), vol. 1, p. 57.

15   *ODNB*.

16   In the preface to her *Memoirs*, 1798, p. 24, she identified him as John Wh__ly; see *Buck Whaley's Memoirs*, p. xxix.

17   In her memoirs Peg refers to him only as Counsellor B____y; Lyons suggests possibly barrister J.E. Batty of 1 Chatham Street, or Peter Bayley of College Green or Richard Bayley of South King St. Lyons (ed.) p. 256.

18   Joseph Hamilton, *The Only Approved Guide Through All the Stages of a Quarrel* (Dublin, 1829), pp. viii–ix.

19   The initiators of these rules appear to have been a gentlemen's club known as the Knights of Tara had been formed in Dublin, and held a monthly meeting at the theatre in Capel Street where fencing practice was encouraged, and prizes handed out to the best opponent at quarterly exhibitions. The ladies came to watch in full morning dress, each handing over a foil to whoever she chose as her champion for the day, and their presence animated the contestants. The combatants dressed in jackets festooned with ribbons, each wearing the favourite colour of his female supporter who wrote up codes of honour, initially for fencing. Jonah Barrington tells of them in his sketches: 'The association did not last above two or three years. I cannot tell why it broke up. I rather think, however, the original fire-eaters thought it frivolous, or did not like their own ascendency to be rivalled . . . a comprehensive

code of the laws and points of honour was issued from the southern fire-eaters, with directions that it should be strictly observed by all gentlemen throughout the kingdom, and kept in their pistol cases, that ignorance might never be pleaded. This code was not circulated in print, but very numerous written copies were sent to the different country clubs, &c. . . . These rules brought the whole business of duelling into a focus, and have been acted upon down to the present day. They called them in Galway the Thirty-six Commandments' (Barrington, *Personal Sketches*, pp. 292–3). See also Hamilton, 1829, pp. 210–12.

[20] For example, of 225 duels fought between 1776 and 1790, only 2 per cent were without seconds; James Kelly, *That Damn'd Thing Called Honour: Duelling in Ireland, 1570–1860* (Cork, Cork University Press), p. 173.

[21] Hamilton, 1829, pp. 109–10.

[22] *Volunteers Journal*, 5 March 1784; *Belfast News-Letter*, 20–24 Aug. 1784.

[23] Sir Edward Newenham MP was another anti-militarist campaigner. Anti-military sentiment was also used by Mathew Carey in Dublin in the *Volunteers Journal*. Carey also had a connection with the *Freeman's Journal* at the end of 1780. The newspaper's anti-military sentiment was obvious in October 1780 when it attacked the military after soldiers had rioted following the acquittal of a man accused of ham-stringing. M.J. Powell, 'Ireland's Urban Houghers: Moral Economy and Popular Protest in the Late Eighteenth Century', in Michael Brown and Sean Donlan (eds.), *Boundaries of the State: The Laws and Other Legalities of Ireland* (Farnham, Ashgate, 2011), pp. 231–53.

[24] *Hibernian Journal*, 2–4 Feb. 1784; *Hibernian Journal*, 16–19 Jan. 1784.

[25] *Volunteers Journal*, 19 March 1784.

Chapter 13: *Lords, Ladies and Gentlemen*

[1] Leeson, *Memoirs*, vol. III, 1797, p. 2.

[2] Although the British government purchased a former ranger's house in Phoenix Park in 1781 to act as a personal residence for the Lord Lieutenant, it was not until major renovations in the 1820s that the Viceregal Lodge came to be used regularly for this purpose.

[3] J.L. McCracken, 'The Social Structure and Social life 1714–60', in Moody and Vaughan, p. 49.

[4] Barrington, *Historic Memoirs of Ireland*, vol. II, p. 225.

[5] This tale was also related about the actress Peg Woffington and John Manners, 3rd Duke of Rutland, so may well have been appropriated by Peg. Janet Camden Lucey, *Lovely Peggy. The Life and Times of Margaret Woffington* (London, Hurst & Blackett, 1952), p. 69. Years later, the incident was reported in the Arts and Entertainment section of the *Telegraph* for 2 June 1796 under the title 'The Princess at the Opera and the conduct of the People there'.

6 F. Erlington Ball, *A History of County Dublin*, p. 19; https://archive.org/details/
   historyofcountydo1ball.

7 Richard Meade, 2nd Earl of Clanwilliam (1766–1805) is identified in the introduction to the 1798 edition of volume III of Peg's memoirs, p. 22.

8 He was born in 1770, and Sally was still alive when the incident happened. She died
   in 1784, so it must have happened no later than the year of her death.

9 Walter Butler (1770–1820) became Viscount Thurles in 1791 when his father John
   succeeded to the earldom.

10 A.M. Fraser, 'David Digues La Touche, Banker, and a Few of His Descendants',
    Dublin Historical Record, vol. 5, no. 2 (Dec. 1942–Feb. 1943), pp. 55–68.

11 Peg refers to him only as Surgeon A____r.

12 B. Rolston and M. Shannon, *Encounters: How Racism Came To Ireland* (Dublin,
    Colour Books Ltd., 2002).

13 Thomas M. Truxes, 'Ireland, New York, and the Eighteenth-Century Atlantic
    World', *American Journal of Irish Studies*, vol. 8, 2011, pp. 9–40.

14 Public Records Office of Northern Ireland, T 765/2/2/249; W.H. Crawford, review
    of *Letterbook of Greg & Cunningham, 1756–57*, in *Irish Economic and Social History*,
    vol. 30 (2003), pp. 144–5; Thomas M. Truxes (ed.), *Letterbook of Greg &
    Cunningham, 1756–57* (Oxford, OUP for the British Academy, Records of Social
    and Economic History, new series, 28, 2001), pp. xxxii, 430.

Chapter 14: *The 'Impures', or Ladies on the Town*

1 The letter was dated 'Wednesday 10th', 'the day after the Lord Mayor's great day
   here', which was 9 November 1784.

2 This was not the first or the last case Peg would sue, and she was notoriously litigious. See *Daily Evening Post*, 18 October 1788, for Peg's debtor's action.

3 According to the *Dublin Post* of that year, Beau Myrtle was a Mr Scott, MA student
   at Trinity College Dublin; 'A Gallery of Illustrious Irishmen', *Dublin University
   Magazine: A Literary and Political Journal* (July–December 1836), p. 107. E-book
   found at http://books.google.co.uk/books?id=W1pRAAAAYAAJ&pg=PA107&lpg
   =PA107&dq=beau+myrtle+1784+dublin&source=bl&ots=HnemkoQY9l&sig=RIj
   UbWV55R_6b1FK-SL6_7JvDxQ&hl=en&sa=X&ei=Sh_VU--6IIr17Abar4
   DAAw&ved=0CCAQ6AEwAA#v=onepage&q=beau%20myrtle%201784%20
   dublin&f=false. Accessed 27 July 2014. According to the *Alumni Dublineses*, only
   one student named Scott received an MA for the appropriate date (1788): Richard
   Scott, who was a sizar.

4 Sir Edward Sullivan (ed.), *Buck Whaley's Memoirs* (1906, reprint 2009), p. 30. In his
   introduction to the memoirs, Sullivan quotes a ditty: 'Peg Plunkett on her horse /
   was surely there of course'.

5 James McCrane had run it from 1773 up to 1785, but James Sheridan took over

ownership in 1785, rebuilding it and renaming it the Donegall Arms. Raymond O'Regan, *Hidden Belfast: Benevolence, Blackguards and Balloon Heads* (Cork, Mercier Press, 2010), p. 81.

6 Lyons states this was Mrs Ann Pottinger, his sister-in-law, p. 263.

7 Arabella Denny, second daughter of Thomas Fitzmaurice (d. 1741), 21st Lord of Kerry, and his wife, Anne (d. 1737) was a keen philanthropist. After her husband's death in 1742, with no children of her own, she made a continental tour, returned to Dublin and started to visit the Dublin Foundling Hospital in 1759. Denny arranged for the employment of a wet nurse from her own funds and spent money on expanding and improving the building. Her work moved one contemporary to write that she 'had put a stop to barbarity and murder and saved the lives of thousands'. J.A. Robins, *The Lost Children: A Study of the Charity Child in Ireland, 1700–1900* (Dublin, LPA, 1980), p. 25; Mona Hearn, *Thomas Edmondson and the Dublin Laundry: A Quaker Businessman, 1837–1908* (Dublin, Irish Academic Press, 2004), p. 7.

8 J. Warburton, J. Whitelaw and R. Walsh, *The History of the City of Dublin; from the Earliest Accounts to the Present Time*, 2 vols. (London, 1818), p. 771.

9 At first, the female penitents were banned from taking part in the services, but in 1770 a new larger chapel was built and they were allowed to participate if kept hidden, according to Dean Bayley, 'so that the worship of God might be celebrated with propriety and order'. A. Peter, *A Brief Account of the Magdalen Chapel, Lower Leeson Street, Dublin* (Dublin, 1907) p. 18.; Boyd, p. 137.

10 R.B. McDowell in Moody and Vaughan, p. 709.

11 Captains Carleton and Atkinson were both, according to Lyons, officers of the watch of St Anne's Parish, Dublin.

12 R.B. McDowell in Moody and Vaughan, p. 709.

13 The veracity of these whores' clubs is reinforced by Fanny Murray's memoirs, in which a similar one is mentioned in London. See Julie Peakman, *Whore Biographies 1700–1825* (London, Pickering and Chatto, 2006), vol. 3, p. 2.

14 *Dublin Evening Post*, 24 December 1779.

15 The former is mentioned in *Dublin Evening Post*, September 1788, under 'Dalky's Excursion'; the latter in both her own memoirs and those of Jonas Barrington, vol. 1, pp. 405–6.

16 *General Advertiser*, 13 October 1786.

Chapter 15: *Masquerade and Marriage*

1 Also at the masquerade were Mrs Sturgeon, Mrs Digges and Mrs Rowe (formerly Ashmore). Mrs Brookes came accompanied by one of her girls, Mary Russell from Limerick (who also happened to be an arsonist).

2 Identified by the annotation of the 1797 edition of Peg's *Memoirs* in NLI.

3 Ebeneezer Radford Roe or Rowe is identified through the annotations of the 1797

edition of Peg's *Memoirs*. His obituary was carried by the *Dublin Evening Post*, 6 June 1793, p. 3.

4 Mary Lyons identifies him as George Phillips, born in Killeen, County Tyrone, in 1708/9, who took his BA at TCD in 1734 and his MA in 1738. 'This appears to be the only G____ P____ in orders from the right part of Ireland'. Lyons, p. 258.

5 The *Gentleman's Magazine* mentions his obituary in 1796: vol. 80, p. 618; Freemen of Cork 20/6/1792 (Ref. U.11), 'Index/Digest to Council Books of the Corporation of Cork with alphabetical list of Freemen'.

6 Buck's mother had been married to 'a common unlettered *hind* near Tipperary', who according to Peg, had the good fortune to uncover a crock of money while digging a trench for potatoes. His father had bought himself a farm and built his way up so as to enable him to leave his son over £5,000 a year. His obituary is in the *Dublin Evening Post*, 8 May 1794. p. 3.

7 According to Lyons, there are various references to Lewellen in satires directed at Francis Higgins in the *Dublin Evening Post* in summer 1789. See Lyons, p. 260, footnote p. 160; also see Rowan Archibald Hamilton, *A Brief Investigation of the Sufferings of John, Anne, and Mary Neal* (Dublin, P. Cooney, 1788).

8 Hon. Barry Yelverton (1763–1824). For a full description of Yelverton, see Barrington, *Personal Sketches*, vol. II, pp. 37–9.

9 His father, Barry Yelverton, sen. (1736–1805), became 1st Viscount Avonmore, who gave his name to Yelverton's Act of 1782, which effectively repealed Poynings's Law.

10 William Blackstone, *Commentaries on the Laws of England* (Oxford, 1765–9), vol. 1, p. 442.

11 Barrington, *Personal Sketches of his Own Time*, p. 290.

12 Op. cit.

13 For more information on the Scottish Beggars Benison, see Peakman, *Lascivious Bodies, A Sexual History of the Eighteenth Century*, pp. 129–47.

14 Possibly Mrs Robert Hill of Drumcondra, who died in 1796. Lyons. p. 261.

15 The *Cabinet of Love* was a collection of pornographic poems printed under their own title page, and first appeared at the close of the fourth edition of *The Works of the Earls of Rochester and Roscommon* in 1714, or his *Poems*, as Peg refers to them. Little is known about *Kitty and Amynter*.

Chapter 16: *Summer Trip to Killarney*

1 See Janet E. Mullin, '"We Had Carding": Hospitable Card Play and Polite Domestic Sociability among the Middling Sort in Eighteenth-Century England', *Journal of Social History*, vol. 42, no. 4 (Summer 2009), pp. 989–1008.

2 Maria Fitzherbert was born in 1756.

3 Lindsay Falvey, *Falvey Family History* (Melbourne, 2003).

4 Denny had been created a baronet in 1782, but twelve years later was killed in a duel by Colonel John Gustavus Crosbie. At the time, Crosbie was a candidate in a parliamentary by-election for County Kerry, and took offence at some supposed breach of neutrality on the part of Denny, the sitting MP. A duel followed on 20 October 1794, with Denny shot fatally through the head on the first shot. According to the newspapers, this was effected 'by the haphazard aim of a man who had never before discharged a pistol in his life'. *Irish News*, 1794/7; also http://www.geocities. com/layedwyer/oconnor.htm. Accessed 10/2/14. Denny's father-in-law, Crosbie Morgell, MP for Tralee, was also to die in an untimely fashion. He filled his pockets with stones and drowned himself in Dublin. His hat and umbrella were found 'purposely placed together on the wharf, in such a manner as to preserve them from the incurrent tide'. Morgell is said to have modelled his suicide on that of Richard Power. Political disagreements ensured men lived precariously.

5 Miss Chute, although she was married to a captain in the army, was on this occasion attended by an admirer in Mr Fitzgerald. O'Brien had invited his friends Mr Walter Eager and his wife; and another couple, within which the woman was bigamously married to John Cavendish Maudsley. According to Peg, she was the daughter of 'Attwood', a blind brogue maker of Tralee. However, the woman in question was not Atwood but Miss Alton, who, as a girl, had gone to stay with an uncle of hers in Cork, a Mr Anthony Gumble Croneen. While she was there, he gave her hand to an already married man, John Cavendish Maudsley. Maudsley had claimed his first wife was dead, but about a month later, friends of his first wife found out he had in fact remarried. Mandsley was prosecuted for bigamy and sentenced to transportation for life. The March Assizes for 1774 indicated that Mandsley was convicted in City Court for marrying Miss Alton when his former wife Miss Griffith was still alive. Bigamy was a serious crime in the eighteenth century, but was easily fallen into by those who were too poor to get a divorce. Miss Alton had afterwards married a Mr C., who, according to Peg, ruined Maudsley.

6 Thomas Crofton Crocker (ed.), *Killarney Legends* (London, 1831), p. 45.

7 William Shaw Mason, *A Statistical Account, or Parochial Survey of Ireland*, vol. 1 (Dublin, Graisberry & Campbell, 1814).

8 The second son of an Irish gentleman in County Galway, Daly had turned to acting when his father had given up on him. He had been taught by the actor-manager Charles Macklin, returning to Ireland after he had made his first entrance on the London stage. Daly's popularity had increased on his marriage to one of Ireland's favourite actresses, Mrs Lister. He had eventually acquired the lease of Smock Alley Theatre, Dublin, which he opened in 1781, and some of the most eminent actors of the time performed there under his management, among them John Philip Kemble, Macklin, Mrs Jordan, Mrs Inchbald, Mrs Billington, and Mrs Siddons. Daly then became proprietor of Crow Street Theatre, as well as of Smock Alley and of some Irish provincial theatres.

9 Given as Miss Elizabeth F___m___g, probably Fleming, this being a common name in Cork city.

Chapter 17: *Problems and Pleasures in Pitt Street*

1   Robert Fannin operated his shop at 15 Bride's Alley; *Wilson's Directory.*

2   *Wonders and Mysteries of Animal Magnetism Displayed; Or The History, Art, Practice, And Progress of that Useful Science, From Its First Rise In The City Of Paris, To The Present Time. With Several Curious Cases and New Anecdotes Of The Principal Professors.* Eighteenth Century Collections Online (London, 1791), pp. 11–12.

3   John Pearson, *A Plain and Rational Account Of The Nature And Effects Of Animal Magnetism: In A Series Of Letters. With notes and an appendix. By the editor.* Eighteenth Century Collections Online, (London, 1790), pp. 13–15; John Bell, 'Professor of Animal Magnetism', *The General and Particular Principles Of Animal Electricity And Magnetism, &c.,* Eighteenth Century Collections Online (London, 1792), p. 2.

4   Pearson, *A Plain and Rational Account,* p. 37.

5   Those gentlemen of Cork who were among his disciples included Drs Longfield, Callanan and Gibbings; Sir Henry Mannix; Mr Bousfield; Mr M.R. Westrop; Sir Robert Warren; Mr Leslie; Mr Morrison; Mr Hearvey and Mr Deaves; Edmond R. Kinselagh; Mr Hickman; Mr Grey; Sir R. Kellett; Mr Bonwell and Father Synan, also Mr White; Mr J. Franklin; Mr Snowe; Mr Bastable and Mr Dan Connell; Mr Pope; Mr George Jack; Tommy Howard; Mr St Leger; Mr Travers; Mr T. Jones; Mr Wassy; Mr Durden; Mr Haly and Mr Knapp.

6   *The Journal of Elizabeth Lady Holland: (1791–1811),* vol. 2, p. 14. http://www.questia.com/read/26159876/the-journal-of-elizabeth-lady-holland-1791–1811. Accessed 20/10/2014.

7   His disguise was exposed when he fell in love with Catherine Ann Egan, daughter of a Kilkenny surgeon, who was unimpressed with his beard. Egan was the toast of Dublin, even before her first appearance on stage at the Smock Alley Theatre where she had played six consecutive nights in November 1784. She did however consent to leave the stage and marry him, the pair living a happy, somewhat less prosperous life together. Barrington, *Personal Sketches,* vol. 1, pp. 230–41.

8   Henry, *Dublin Hanged.*

9   Peg must have her dates confused or is misremembering as she had already dismissed Miss Grove from her house on her return form Killarney in 1789.

10 Probably Clare, son of John, wire-drawer and copyist, mentioned before by Peg.

11 A baptism is registered for 'Bartle Corcoran of N/R' on 13 August 1765: http://churchrecords.irishgenealogy.ie/churchrecords/details/f1bc1a0224683. Accessed 16/2/14. Bartholomew Corcoran's sign stood at the Inns Quay in the 1770s; see Mary Pollard, *A Dictionary of Members of the Dublin Book Trade 1550-1800* (London, Bibliography Society, 2000), p. 383; Thomas Wall, *The Sign of Doctor Hay's Head* (Dublin, M.H. Gill and Son Ltd., 1958).

12 Only given as Jack S____e and P___ W___.

Chapter 18: *Retirement and Debtors' Prison*

1 See Brian Inglis, *Freedom of the Press in Ireland* (London, Faber and Faber, 1954), p. 58.

2 J.F. Fuller, 'Amyas Griffith: A Chequered Career', *Kerry Archaeological Magazine*, vol. 3, no. 15 (Oct., 1915), pp. 162–75.

3 Moll Hall was Peg's close friend, another reason I think Peg was of similar age.

4 Joseph Wilson (d. 1793), Belfast portrait and landscape painter, flourished from around 1770 onwards.

5 Identified by a contemporary annotator in her edition of vol. III, *Memoirs of Mrs Leeson* (1798), as Marquis of Abercorn, John James Hamilton, died in 1818.

6 What we would now call a foot fetishist, but then there was no term for such sexual obsessions.

7 Betsy's husband had already died fighting in the American War of Independence. She was the illegitimate daughter of William Crosbie, 1st Earl of Glandore (known as 'Billy the Beau'). He had died in 1781. Her mother, a beautiful well-educated young lady, had been debauched by the earl when she was only fifteen years old and had died in childbirth. Wracked with guilt, the earl had sent his daughter to the best school he could find in Cork. Here she met a man called Edmonds, the illegitimate son of a gentlemen of great fortune of the same name, whom she married. Her father never forgave Betsy for marrying him.

8 F. Erlington Ball, *A History of County Dublin*, p. 23; https://archive.org/details/historyofcountydo1ball.

9 John Kennedy, glass merchant in Stephen Street, George Tinker the paper stainer, and William Corbet the printer and bookseller of Great Britain Street all provided some assistance. Her old friends, bricklayer Thomas Swords; Mr Courtney; Frank Higgins, proprietor of the *Freeman's Journal*; master builder David Weir; ironmonger James March of 28 Kennedy's Lane's; Patrick Marsh the auctioneer at Brides Alley; Peter Le Favre; merchants Hans and Prices Blackwood; Arthur Stanley, a merchant in Bride Street; and the Beresfords (possibly Fanny Beresford's family) all helped. The list continued with Mr Henegan of Mount Brown; Richard Manders of James's Street; Captain William Ormsby, governor of the Four Courts Marshalsea; Revd Mr Keagh and Dr McDowell of the Meeting House Chapel; Dr Tuke; Councillor Vavaser and Councillor Leo McNally of Dominick Street; law councillor John Egan of 13 Ely Place and Councillor John Philpot Curran; Mr John Magee of Swift's Hospital; and the men in the printing and bookselling trade who encouraged the sale of her memoirs.

10 Lyons, pp. 238–9.

11 Some Catholic priests had taken the oath of abjuration and converted to Protestantism in order to be able to continue their religious work, which may account for his title.

Chapter 19: *Final Days*

1 Donald D. Eddy and J.D. Fleeman, *A Preliminary Handlist of Books to which Dr. Johnson Subscribed* (Charlottesville, Bibliographical Society of the University of Virginia, 1993).

2 Archibald Hamilton Rowan, *A Brief Investigation of the Sufferings of John, Anne, and Mary Neal* (Dublin, P. Byrne, 1788).

3 B.H. Blacker, *Brief Sketches of the Parishes of Booterstown and Donnybrook* (Dublin, George Herbert, 1860), pp. 92, 175.

4 Peg quotes the newspaper clipping in her memoirs. See Lyons, p. 245.

5 The Insolvency Acts ran from 1791, 1793, 1794, 1795, 1797 and 1800.

6 Possibly Mrs Robert Hill. See Lyons, p. 261.

7 Sir Everard Home, 'Experiments and Observations to Prove That the Beneficial Effects of Many Medicines are Produced through the Medium of the Circulating Blood, More Particularly That of the Colchicum Autumnale upon the Gout', *Philosophical Transactions of the Royal Society of London*, vol. 106 (1816), pp. 257–61.

8 Dr James's Fever Powder had been examined in 1791 by a respected doctor and chemist of the time, Dr George Pearson. He determined that the powder was made of a mix of antimony and calcium phosphate. Because antimony is a toxic substance, the powder was deemed a contributing factor to the death of author Oliver Goldsmith in 1774. Its use was characterised by severe vomiting, sweating and a metallic taste in the mouth, and resembled arsenic poisoning, but Peg would have already had similar side effects with the salivation.

9 Probably Edward Jones, an apothecary in Fleet Street. Lyons, p. 267.

10 *Fraser's Magazine for Town and Country*, vol. 5, 1830, p. 105.

Epilogue

1 This source points to the female portrait as being a picture of his second wife; M. Wynne, 'The Milltowns as Patrons', in *Apollo*, XCIX (February 1974), pp. 104–11.

2 Additionally, according to the introduction by director Homan Potterton in the *National Gallery of Ireland Illustrated Summary Catalogue of Paintings* (Dublin, Gill & Macmillan, 1981), p. 7, the portrait no. 703 is given the title of 'Lady Leeson as Diana'.

3 F. Leeson, MS, p. 13.

4 Ibid., p. 14.

List of illustrations (in order of appearance)

Peg Plunkett, *National Portrait Gallery*
William Robert Fitzgerald, 2nd Duke Leinster, *National Portrait Gallery*
Benjamin Thompson, Count Rumford, *Harvard Art Museums*
Charles Manners, 4th Duke Rutland, *Belvoir Castle, Leicestershire/Bridgeman Images*
Sarah Isabella Somerset, Duchess of Rutland, *Belvoir Castle, Leicestershire/Bridgeman Images*
John Fane, 10th Earl of Westmorland, *National Portrait Gallery*
Sarah Anne Child, *Wikipedia*
Anne Catley, *National Portrait Gallery*
Captain John Hayes St Leger, *Getty Images/The Print Collector*
Joseph Leeson, 2nd Earl of Milltown, *National Gallery of Ireland*
Portrait of a Lady as Diana, *National Gallery of Ireland*
Dublin map, *Getty Images/Historical Map Works LLC*
The Custom House, Dublin, *Private Collection/The Stapleton Collection/Bridgeman Images*
Trinity College, Dublin, *Private Collection/The Stapleton Collection/Bridgeman Images*
Dublin's foundling hospital, *antiqueprints.com*
Russborough House, *Julie Peakman*
Satire of 'bell hoop' dresses, *Wikipedia*
Detail from *Progress of a Woman of Pleasure, Wikipedia*
'Beer Street', *London Metropolitan Archives, City of London/Bridgeman Images*
'The Fountain', James St, Dublin, *National Gallery of Ireland*
The title page of Peg's memoirs, *Julie Peakman*
The parish record of Peg's death, *Julie Peakman*
St James' graveyard, Dublin, *Julie Peakman*

Select Bibliography

THE MEMOIRS

Leeson, Margaret, *Memoirs*, vols. I and II, 1795 (printed for the Authoress, Dublin)

Leeson, Margaret, *Memoirs*, vol. III, 1797 (printed for the Authoress, Dublin)

Leeson, Margaret, *Memoirs of Mrs Leeson*, 1798 edition (printed for the Authoress, Dublin)

Leeson, Francis Leo, 'The Memoirs of Peg Plunket. A modern and condensed edition', typewritten MS, 1965, British Library (shelfmark: Cup.701.c.5)

Lyons, Mary (ed.), *The Memoirs of Mrs Leeson* (Dublin, Lilliput Press, 1995)

PRIMARY SOURCES

Ambross, Miss, *The Life and Memoirs of the Late Miss Anne Catley* (London, J. Bird, 1790)

Anon., *An Heroic Epistle from Kitty Cut-a-Dash to Oroonoko* (Dublin, 1778)

Anon., *Wonders and Mysteries of Animal Magnetism Displayed; or the History, Art, Practice, and Progress of That Useful Science, From Its First Rise in the City of Paris, to the Present Time. With several Curious Cases and New Anecdotes of the Principal Professors* (London, 1791)

Barrington, Jonah, *Historic Memoirs of Ireland* (London, R. Bentley, for H. Colburn, 1833)

Barrington, Jonah, *Personal Sketches of His Own Times* (London, Kessinger, 1832)

Bell, John, 'Professor of Animal Magnetism' in *The General and Particular Principles of Animal Electricity and Magnetism* (London, 1792)

Blacker, B.H, *Brief Sketches of the Parishes of Booterstown and Donnybrook* (Dublin, George Herbert, 1860)

Boaden, James, *Memoirs of Mrs Siddons* (London, Henry Colburn, 1827)

Boulter, Hugh, *Letters Written by His Excellency, Hugh Boulter, DD, Lord Primate of all Ireland etc* (Dublin, 1770)

Cadogan, William, *An Essay upon Nursing and the Management of Children from their Birth to Three Years of Age* (London, Committee of the Foundling Hospital, 1748)

Crocker, Thomas Crofton, (ed.), *Killarney Legends* (London, Fisher, Son & Jackson, 1831)

Fitzgerald, John, *The Cork Remembrancer, an Historical Register* (Cork, J. Sullivan, 1783)

Hamilton, Joseph, *The Only Approved Guide Through All The Stages of a Quarrel* (Dublin, 1829)

Herbert, J.D., *Irish Varieties for the Last Fifty Years: Written from Recollections* (London, William Joy, 1836)

Leeson, Francis Leo, 'The Milltown Leesons', MS, 1967

Luckombe, Philip, *A Tour Through Ireland* (Dublin, T. Lowndes, 1780)

Mandeville, Bernard, *A Modest Defence of Chastity* (London, A. Bettesworth, 1726)

Mason, William Shaw, *A Statistical Account, Or Parochial Survey of Ireland* (Dublin, Graisberry & Campbell, 1814)

O'Keeffe, John, *Recollections of the Life of John O'Keefe* (London, 1826)

Pearson, John, *A Plain and Rational Account of the Nature and Effects of Animal Magnetism: in a Series of Letters* (London, W & J Stratford, 1790)

Playfair, William, *British Family Antiquity* (London, 1810)

Rowan, Archibald Hamilton, *A Brief Investigation of the Sufferings of John, Anne, and Mary Neal* (Dublin, P. Byrne, 1788)

Swift, Jonathan, *A Modest Proposal for Preventing the Children of Poor People in Ireland, from Being a Burden on Their Parents or Country, and For Making Them Beneficial to the Publick* (Dublin, 1729)

Twiss, Richard, *Tour of Ireland* (London, 1776)

Whaley, Thomas, *Buck Whaley's Memoirs. Written by Himself in 1797* (London, Alexander Moring, 1906)

Young, Arthur, *A Tour of Ireland 1776–9* (Dublin, S. Powell, 1780)

Newspapers

Belfast News-Letter
Dublin Evening Post
Dublin Gazette
Dublin University Magazine: A Literary and Political Journal
Faulkner's Journal
Gentleman's Magazine
Hibernian Journal
Hibernian Magazine
Lady's Magazine
London Magazine
Pue's Occurrences
Town and Country Magazine
Volunteer's Journal

Directories

Alumni Dublineses
Burke's Landed Gentry
Irish Directory of 1814

McConnell's *Cork Directory for 1755*
Watson's Almanack
Wilson's Directory

SECONDARY SOURCES

Andrews, J. H., 'Road Planning in Ireland before the Railway Age', *Irish Geography*, 5 (1) (1964)

Aspinall A. (ed.), *The Correspondence of George, Prince of Wales, 1770–1812*, 8 vols. (London, Cassell, 1963–71)

Ball, F. Elrington, *The Judges in Ireland 1221–1921* (London, John Murray, 1926)

—*A History of County Dublin* (Dublin, Greene's Bookshop, 1995)

—'The Antiquities from Blackrock to Dublin', *Journal of the Royal Society of Antiquaries of Ireland*, fifth series, vol. 10, no. 4 (Dec. 31, 1900), pp. 307–18

Barnard, T.C., 'Farewell to Old Ireland', *Historical Journal*, vol. 36, no. 4 (Dec. 1993), p. 912

Bartlett, Thomas, *Ireland: A History* (Cambridge, CUP, 2010)

Bataille, Robert R., *The Writing Life of Hugh Kelly: Politics, Journalism and Theatre in Late Eighteenth-Century London* (Carbondale, Southern Illinois University Press, 2000)

Bennis, Patricia, M. *St John's Fever and Lock Hospital Limerick, 1780–1890* (Newcastle upon Tyne, Cambridge Scholars Publishing, 2009)

Bishop, J.B., *A Chronicle of One Hundred and Fifty Years: The Chamber of Commerce of the State of New York* (New York, Charles Scribner, 1918)

Boyd, Gary A., *Dublin 1745–1922: Hospitals, Spectacles and Vice* (Dublin, Four Courts Press, 2006)

Brian Boydell, 'Venues for Music in 18th century Dublin', *Dublin Historical Record*, vol. 29, no. 1 (Dec. 1975), pp. 28–34

Broderick, D., *The First Toll Roads: Ireland's Turnpike Roads, 1729–1858* (Cork, Collins Press, 2002)

Brown, G.I., *Count Rumford: The Extraordinary Life of a Scientific Genius* (Stroud, Sutton Publishing, 1999)

Burke, Helen M., 'The Revolutionary Prelude: The Dublin Stage in the Late 1770s and Early 1780s', *Eighteenth-Century Life*, vol. 22, no. 3 (November 1998)

Cannon, Richard, *Historical Record of the Sixty-seventh, Or the South Hampshire Regiment* (London, Parker, Furnivall & Parker, 1849)

Casey, Christine, *The Buildings of Ireland* (New Haven, Yale University Press, 2005)

Chrisman, Kimberly, 'Unhoop the Fair Sex: The Campaign Against the Hoop Petticoat in Eighteenth-Century England', *Eighteenth-Century Studies*, vol. 30, no. 1 (Fall 1996), pp. 5–23

Claridge, Capt. R.T., *Hydropathy; or The Cold Water Cure, as practiced by Vincent Priessnitz at Graefenberg, Silesia, Austria*, 8th ed. (London, James Madden and Co., 1843)

Clarkson, L.A. (1999) 'Hospitality, housekeeping and high living in eighteenth-century Ireland' in J. Hill and C. Lennon (eds.), *Luxury and Austerity* (Dublin, University College Dublin Press, 1999)

Connell, K.H., 'Land and Population in Ireland c. 1780–1845', *Economic History Review*, new series 2, no. 3, 1950

Connolly, S.J., 'The defence of Protestant Ireland, 1660–1760', in Thomas Bartlett and Keith Jeffery (eds.), *A Military History of Ireland* (Cambridge, CUP, 1996)

Cross, Wilbur Lucius, *The Life and Times of Laurence Sterne* (New York, Macmillan, 1909)

Cullen, L.M. (1981) *The Emergence of Modern Ireland, 1600–1900* (London, Batsford Academic Educational, 1986)

Cunnington, Phillis, *Costumes of the Seventeenth and Eighteenth Century* (Boston, Plays Inc., 1970)

David, Saul, *Prince of Pleasure. The Prince of Wales and the Making of the Regency* (London, Abacus, 1999)

Dickson, David, *Arctic Ireland: The Extraordinary Story of the Great Frost and Forgotten Famine of 1740–41* (Belfast, White Row Press Ltd, 1997)

Dickson, David, *Ireland 1600–1800: New Foundations* (Dublin, Helicon, 1987)

Donnelley, Sean, 'A German Dulcimer Player in Eighteenth Century Dublin', *Dublin Historical Record*, vol. 53, no. 1 (Spring 2000)

Doorley, B., 'Newgate Prison' in David Dickson (ed.), *The Gorgeous Mask* (Dublin, Trinity History Workshop, 1987), pp. 122–3

Drake, Michael, 'The Irish Demographic Crisis of 1740–41', *Historical Studies* VI, T.W. Moody (ed.), (London, Routledge & Kegan Paul, 1968)

Eager, F.J., *The Eager Family in County Kerry* (Dublin, privately printed, 1860)

—*Genealogical History of the Eager Family* (Dublin, privately printed, 1861)

Eddy, Donald D. and Fleeman, J.D., *A Preliminary Handlist of Books to which Dr. Johnson Subscribed* (Charlottesville, Bibliographical Society of the University of Virginia, 1993)

Eustace, P. Beryl, 'Index of Will Abstracts in the Genealogical Office, Dublin', *Analecta Hibernica*, no. 17 (1949)

Falvey, Lindsay, *Falvey Family History* (Melbourne, 2003)

Ferguson, Kenneth P., 'The Army in Ireland from the Restoration to the Act of Union' (unpublished Ph.D. thesis, Trinity College, Dublin, 1983)

Finnane, Mark, *Insanity and the Insane in Post-Famine Ireland* (London, Croom Helm,1981)

Fitzgerald, Brian, *Lady Louisa Connolly* (London, Staples, 1950)

Fitzgerald, Brian (ed.), *Correspondence of Duchess of Leinster* (Dublin, Irish Manuscripts Commission, 1949)

Fleming, David A., 'Diversions of the People: Sociability among the Orders of Early Eighteenth-Century Ireland', *Eighteenth-Century Ireland*, no. 17, pp. 99–111

Flood, W.H. Grattan, 'Eighteenth Century Italians in Dublin', *Music & Letters*, vol. 3, no. 3 (Jul. 1922), pp. 274–8

—*A History of Irish Music* (Dublin, Browne and Nolan, 1906)

Foster, Sarah, 'Buying Irish: Consumer Nationalism in 18th-century Dublin', *History Today*, vol. 47, no. 6, 1997

Fraser, A.M., 'David Digues La Touche, Banker, and a Few of His Descendants', *Dublin Historical Record*, vol. 5, no. 2 (Dec. 1942–Feb. 1943), pp. 55–68

Frazer, William, 'On the Dublin Stocks and Pillory', *Proceedings of the Royal Irish Academy. Polite Literature and Antiquities*, vol. 2 (1879–88), pp. 456–60

Fuller, J.F, 'Amyas Griffith: A Chequered Career', *Kerry Archaeological Magazine*, vol. 3, no. 15 (Oct. 1915), pp. 162–75

Gall, Jennifer, *In Bligh's Hand: Surviving the Mutiny on the Bounty* (Canberra, National Library of Australia, 2010)

Geary, Frank and Stark, Tom, 'Trends in Real Wages during the Industrial Revolution: A View from across the Irish Sea', *Economic History Review*, vol. 57, no. 2 (May 2004), pp. 362–95

Genevieve, Sister Mary, 'Mrs Bellew's Family in Channel Row', *Dublin Historical Record*, vol. 22, no. 3 (Old Dublin Society, 1968), pp. 230–41

Gilbert, J.T., *A History of the City of Dublin*, vol. I (Dublin, James McGlashan, 1854)

Gilbert, J.T., *A History of the City of Dublin*, vols. II & III (Dublin, McGlashan & Gill, 1859)

Gillespie, Raymond and Foster, R.F., (eds.) *Irish Provincial Cultures in the Long Eighteenth Century* (Dublin, Four Courts Press, 2012)

Greene, John C., *Theatre in Dublin, 1745–1820. A Calendar of Performances*, vols. six (Bethlehem, Lehigh University Press, 1993)

Hammond, Joseph W., 'George's Quay and Rogerson's Quay in the Eighteenth Century', *Dublin Historical Record*, vol. 5, no. 2 (Dec. 1942–Feb. 1943)

Healy, Róisín, 'Suicide in Early Modern and Modern Europe', *Historical Journal*, vol. 49, no. 3 (Sept. 2006)

Hearn, Mona, *Thomas Edmondson and the Dublin Laundry: a Quaker Businessman, 1837–1908* (Dublin, Irish Academic Press, 2004)

Henry, Brian, *Dublin Hanged* (Dublin, Irish Academic Press, 1994)

Hill, J., and Lennon, C. (eds.), *Luxury and Austerity* (Dublin, University College Dublin Press, 1999)

Horner, Andrew, 'The Famine', *History Ireland*, vol. 15, no. 5 (Sept./Oct 2007)

Horner, Arnold, 'Ireland's Time-Space Revolution. Improvements to Pre-Famine Travel', *History Ireland*, vol. 15, no. 5 (Sept./Oct 2007), pp. 22–7

Inglis, Brian, *Freedom of the Press in Ireland* (London, Faber and Faber, 1954)

Johnston-Liik, E.M., *MPs in Dublin: Companion to History of the Irish Parliament, 1692–1800* (Belfast, Ulster Historical Foundation, 2006)

Kelley, David, 'The Conditions of Debtors and Insolvents in Eighteenth-Century Dublin' in David Dickson (ed.), *The Gorgeous Mask: Dublin 1700–1850* (Dublin, Trinity History Workshop, 1987), pp. 98–120

Kelly, James and Powell, M.J., (eds.), *Clubs and Societies in Eighteenth-Century Ireland* (Dublin, Four Courts Press, 2010)

Kelly, James, '"Drinking The Waters": Balneotherapeutic Medicine In Ireland, 1660–1850', *Studia Hibernica*, no. 35 (2008–9), pp. 99–146

— *That Damn'd Thing Called Honour: Duelling in Ireland, 1570–1860* (Cork, Cork University Press, 1995)

— *The Liberty and Ormond Boys, Factional Riots in Eighteenth-century Dublin* (Dublin, Four Courts Press, 2005)

Laragy, Georgina, 'Suicide and Insanity in Post-Famine Ireland' in Catherine Cox, Maria Luddy (eds.), *Cultures of Care in Irish Medical History, 1750–1970* (London, Palgrave, 2010)

Laragy, Georgina, 'Wolfe Tone and the Culture of Suicide in Eighteenth-Century Ireland', *History Ireland*, vol. 21, no. 6 (November/December 2013), pp. 20–22

Lecky, William Edward Hartpole, *A History of Ireland in the Eighteenth Century* (London, Longmans, Green & Co, 1913; reprint Elibron Classics, 2006), vol. I and II

Livesey, James, 'The Dublin Society in Eighteenth-Century Irish Political Thought', *Historical Journal*, vol. 47, no. 3 (Sept. 2004), pp. 615–40

Lowth, Cormac F., 'Shipwrecks Around Dublin Bay', *Dublin Historical Record*, vol. 55, no. 1 (Spring 2002)

Lucey, Janet Camden, *Lovely Peggy. The Life and Times of Margaret Woffington* (London, Hurst & Blackett, 1952)

Luddy, Maria, *Prostitution and Irish Society, 1800–1940* (Cambridge, CUP, 2007)

McAsey, Carmel, 'Peg Woffington', *Dublin Historical Record*, vol. 23, no. 1 (June 1969), pp. 23–35

MacMahon, Bryan, '"A most ingenious mechanic": Ireland's First Airman', *History Ireland*, vol. 18, no. 6 (November/December 2010), pp. 22–4

Malcomson, A.P.W., *The Pursuit of the Heiress: Aristocratic Marriage in Ireland 1740–1840* (Belfast, Ulster Historical Foundation, 2006)

Maxwell, C.C., *Dublin Under the Georges, 1714–1830* (London, Faber and Faber, 1946)

Moody, T.W. and Vaughan, W.E. (eds.), *A New History of Ireland Volume VI: Eighteenth-Century Ireland 1691–1800* (Oxford, OUP, 2009)

Morash, Chris and Richards, Shaun, *Mapping Irish Theatre: Theories of Space and Place* (Cambridge, CUP, 2013), p. 30

Morash, Chris, *A History of Irish Theatre 1601–2000* (Cambridge, CUP, 2002)

Mullin, Janet E., '"We Had Carding": Hospitable Card Play and Polite Domestic Sociability among the Middling Sort in Eighteenth-Century England', *Journal of Social History*, vol. 42, no. 4 (Summer 2009), pp. 989–1008

Murphy, Kathleen S., 'Judge, Jury, Magistrate and Soldier: Rethinking Law and Authority in Late Eighteenth-Century Ireland', *American Journal of Legal History*, vol. 44, no. 3 (Jul. 2000)

National Gallery of Ireland Illustrated Summary Catalogue of Paintings (Dublin, Gill & Macmillan, 1981)

Nussbaum, Felicity (ed.), *The Global Eighteenth-Century* (Baltimore, John Hopkins University Press, 2003)

O'Connor, Cynthia, *The Pleasing Hours. The Grand Tour of James Caulfeild, 1st Earl of Charlemont* (Cork, Collins Press, 1999)

O'Rouke, Kevin P., 'Dublin Police', *Dublin Historical Record*, vol. 29, no. 4 (Sept. 1976), pp 138–47

O'Regan, Raymond, *Hidden Belfast: Benevolence, Blackguards and Balloon Heads* (Cork, Mercier Press, 2010)

Parker, S., *Informal Marriage, Cohabitation and the Law, 1750–1989* (Basingstoke, Macmillan Press, 1990)

Peakman, Julie, 'Memoirs of Women of Pleasure: The Whore Biography, 1795–1825' in *Women's Writing Journal*, 'Sex, Gender and the Female Body' special issue, 2004, pp. 163–84

—*Emma Hamilton* (London, Haus, 2005)

—*Lascivious Bodies: A Sexual History of the Eighteenth Century* (London, Atlantic, 2004)

—*Mighty Lewd Books, The Development of Pornography in Eighteenth-Century England* (London, Palgrave, 2002)

—*Whore Biographies, 1700–1825* (London, Pickering and Chatto, 2006)

Peter, A., *A Brief Account of the Magdalen Chapel, Lower Leeson Street, Dublin* (Dublin, Hodges, Figgis & Co., 1907)

Pollard, Mary, *A Dictionary of Members of the Dublin Book Trade 1550–1800* (London, Bibliography Society, 2000)

Powell, Martyn J., 'Mathew Carey and Anti-Military Sentiment in the *Volunteers Journal* and the *Pennsylvania Evening Herald*' (unpublished dissertation, Aberystwyth University, 2011)

Powell, Fred, 'Dean Swift and the Dublin Foundling Hospital', *Irish Quarterly Review*, vol. 70, no. 278/279 (Summer/Autumn 1981), pp. 162–70

Powell, M.J., 'Ireland's Urban Houghers: Moral Economy and Popular Protest in the Late Eighteenth Century' in Michael Brown and Sean Donlan (eds.), *Boundaries of the State: The Laws and Other Legalities of Ireland* (Farnham, Ashgate, 2011)

Probert, Rebecca, *Marriage Law & Practice in the Long Eighteenth Century: A Reassessment* (Cambridge, CUP, 2009)

Purcell, Richard, J. 'Irish Contribution to Colonial New York', *Irish Quarterly Review*, vol. 30, no. 117 (Mar. 1941), pp. 107–20

Robins J., 'The Lost Children: A Study of the Charity Child in Ireland: 1700–1900' (Dublin, LPA, 1980)

Robins, J., *Champagne and Silver Buckles: The Viceregal Court at Dublin Castle, 1700–1922* (Dublin, Lilliput Press, 2001)

Rolston, B. and Shannon, M., *Encounters: How Racism Came To Ireland* (Dublin, Colour Books Ltd., 2002)

Scudds, Colm, 'Old Coach Roads from Dublin, 1745–1821', *Dublin Historical Record*, vol. 54, no. 1 (Spring 2001), pp. 4–15

Stevens, J.A., *Colonial Records of the New York Chamber of Commerce 1768–1784* (New York, John Trow, 1867)

Strickland, Walter, *Dictionary of Irish Artists* (Dublin, Maunsel & Co., 1913)

Surry, Nigel, 'James Northcote at Portsmouth', *Burlington Magazine*, vol. 136, no. 1093 (Apr. 1994), pp. 234-237

Tillyard, Stella, *Aristocrats: Caroline, Emily, Louisa, and Sarah Lennox 1740–1832* (London, Chatto & Windus, 1994)

Truxes, Thomas M., 'Ireland, New York, and the Eighteenth-Century Atlantic World', *American Journal of Irish Studies*, vol. 8, 2011, pp. 9–40

Truxes, Thomas M. (ed.), *Letterbook of Greg & Cunningham, 1756–57* (Oxford, OUP, 2001)

Tutty, M.J., 'The City of Dublin Steam Packet Company', *Dublin Historical Record*, vol. 18, no. 3 (June 1963), pp. 80–90

—'Clontarf', *Dublin Historical Record*, vol. 21, no. 1 (Mar.–May 1966), pp. 2–13

Wall, Thomas, *The Sign of Doctor Hay's Head* (Dublin, M.H. Gill and Son Ltd., 1958)

Warburton, J., Whitelaw, J. and Walsh, R., *The History of the City of Dublin; from the Earliest Accounts to the present time*, 2 vols. (London, 1818)

Whelan, Kevin, *Endurance and Emergence: Catholics in Ireland* (Dublin, Irish Academic Press, 1990)

Williams, William, *Creating Irish Tourism: The First Century, 1750–1850* (London, Anthem Press, 2011)

Wodsworth, W.D., *A Brief History of the Ancient Foundling Hospital of Dublin* (Dublin, A. Thomas, 1876)

Wynne, M., 'The Milltowns as Patrons', *Apollo* XCIX, February 1974, pp. 104–11

Index